D1611656

BEING,

MAN,

&

DEATH

James M. Demske

BEING,

MAN,

&

DEATH

A Key to Heidegger

The UNIVERSITY PRESS
of KENTUCKY : 1970

Standard Book Number 8131–1194–3
Library of Congress Catalog Card Number 70–94065

COPYRIGHT © 1970 BY THE UNIVERSITY PRESS OF KENTUCKY

A statewide cooperative scholarly publishing agency serving Berea College, Centre College of Kentucky, Eastern Kentucky University, Kentucky State College, Morehead State University, Murray State University, University of Kentucky, University of Louisville, and Western Kentucky University.

Editorial and Sales Offices: Lexington, Kentucky 40506

Contents

Abbreviations for Heidegger's Works

AP Vom Wesen und Begriff der *physis*, Aristoteles Physik B I (On the Nature and Concept of *physis* in Aristotle's Physics, B I)

DS Die Kategorien- und Bedeutungslehre des Duns Scotus (Duns Scotus' Theory of Categories and Meaning)

ED Aus der Erfahrung des Denkens (From the Experience of Thought)

EM Einführung in die Metaphysik (Introduction to Metaphysics)

FD Die Frage nach dem Ding (The Question of the Thing)

FW Der Feldweg (The Country Lane)

GL Gelassenheit (Serenity)

HB Brief über den "Humanismus" (Letter on "Humanism")

HD Erläuterungen zu Hölderlins Dichtung (Explanations of Hölderlin's Poetry)

HG Hegel und die Griechen (Hegel and the Greeks)

HH Hebel—der Hausfreund (Hebel, the Family Friend)

HW Holzwege (Woodland Trails)

ID Identität und Differenz (Identity and Difference)

KM Kant und das Problem der Metaphysik (Kant and the Problem of Metaphysics)

KS Kants These über das Sein (Kant's Thesis on Being)

N I Nietzsche, Band I (Nietzsche, Volume I)

N II Nietzsche, Band II (Nietzsche, Volume II)

PW Platons Lehre von der Wahrheit (Plato's Doctrine of Truth)

SF Zur Seinsfrage (On the Question of Being)

SG Der Satz vom Grund (The Principle of Ground)

SZ Sein und Zeit (Being and Time)

US Unterwegs zur Sprache (On the Way to Language)

VA Vorträge und Aufsätze (Lectures and Essays)

WD Was Heisst Denken? (What Summons Thought?)

WG Vom Wesen des Grundes (On the Essence of Ground)

WM Was Ist Metaphysik? (What Is Metaphysics?)

WP Was Ist das—die Philosophie? (What Is Philosophy?)

WW Vom Wesen der Wahrheit (On the Essence of Truth)

1

Introduction:
Perspectives on
Death

"All men are mortal." For formal logic this is the classic example of a certain type of proposition, a universal affirmative or "A" proposition. But besides being a logical entity, it is also a statement, a judgment, an affirmation. Considered in its content, the phrase is the expression of an insight which has been decisive for man's understanding of himself since the dawn of western thought: the awareness of his own mortality, the consciousness of death.

This insight makes its presence felt in the thought of the earliest Greek philosophers. It is there by implication in the musings of Thales and Anaximander on the rise and decline, the coming-to-be and passing-away of all things. It finds more definite expression in Parmenides' frequent characterization of human beings as "the mortals" (*brotoi*), and becomes still more explicit in some of the sayings of Heraclitus, such as Fragment 21: "All that we seek while awake, is death," and Fragment 48: "Now the name of the bow is life, but its work is death."

Traditional metaphysics has understood the judgment "All men are mortal" as a statement about the nature of man, expressible in the universal abstract proposition, "All men are essentially, i.e., according to their nature, mortal." The philosophers of existence of the nineteenth and twentieth centuries have added a new accent to the proposition by their stress on the concrete circumstances of individual men's lives. For them the sentence would read: *"Each and every* man is mortal," or, even more accurately, "I am mortal." With characteristic irony Kierkegaard reminds us of the highly personal character of death: "Before I pass over to universal history . . . it seems to me that I had better think about this, lest existence mock me because I had become so learned and highfalutin that I had forgotten to understand what will some time happen to me as to every human being—sometime, nay, what am I saying: suppose death were so treacherous as to come tomorrow!"[1]

Among those who have pondered long and deeply on the concrete features of human existence in the twentieth century is Martin Heidegger. Because of his unique emphasis on the problem of being as intricately interwoven with the problem of man, his version of the statement about human mortality would read: "Each and every man *is* mortal," i.e., "I *am* mortal." Mortality, for Heidegger, is not a mode of ceasing-to-be, but a mode of being, indeed *the* mode of being characteristic of existing man. Every man exists as mortal; his mortality is so intimately connected with his existence that he is concretely this mortal being, or still more concretely and precisely, he exists as this being-mortal, as being-unto-death.

Death thus becomes for Heidegger one of the key problems, if not *the* key problem, in the philosophical attempt to understand human existence. Not only does he pose the problem with a previously unheard-of force and sharpness, but he confers upon it a new ontological depth, since it is a problem touching being itself.

I. *Death in Heidegger*

The following pages attempt to document and analyze the connection in Heidegger's thought between the problem of death and the problems of being and man. Death plays a subsidiary, yet necessary, role in the work of Heidegger. It is only subsidiary, because the central theme is always man and being: in the earlier works human existence is explored in all its facets, while in the later writings the focus is on being itself. Nonetheless, death is by no means an accidental topic, for without it the problems of man and being could not unfold in the way they do. While death is not

2

the protagonist of the Heideggerian drama, it is still the indispensable antagonist, without which the actions of the protagonist would be unthinkable.

It follows that the concept of death is especially well suited to serve as a guide through the labyrinth of Heidegger's thought. It belongs to the area of his central concern, which is the problem of being as appearing to man, or, seen from the other end of the relation, the problem of human existence in the world of being. Thus, Heidegger's philosophy of death can be understood only against the background of his philosophy of man and of being, and, conversely, his philosophy of man and of being will be appreciated in its full significance and rigorous continuity only insofar as his thoughts on death receive adequate consideration. The problems of death on the one hand, and being and man on the other, mutually illumine and clarify one another.

These two problem complexes are intimately related to each other. In the succeeding study, death will be seen to play a decisive role in the gradual turning which represents the innermost dynamic of Heidegger's thought. In the beginning stage, i.e., in the analysis of human existence contained in *Sein und Zeit* (*Being and Time*), death is the "existential of totality" (*das Ganzheitsexistenzial*) in the structure of Dasein; death determines and embraces the totality of human existence. This all-enveloping quality is expressed by the designation of Dasein as "being-unto-death": Dasein in its uttermost potentiality exists as nothing more and nothing less than being-unto-death.

As Dasein's existential of totality, death belongs to the ontology of man, to the intelligibility of human existence. But it is not just one existential structure alongside several others; it is rather the totality of the structure: everything about man is enveloped in the term "being-unto-death." Because of this feature of completeness, death is the one aspect in which man is powerless over his own structure, even over his own intelligibility. Death refuses to fit neatly into the list of existential structures, because it is broader than all these combined. It remains the one unknown factor, the indissoluble remainder in every equation of human existence. Because of death, man cannot be a neatly solved puzzle or a tidy package of intelligibility closed within himself. Death leaves man "open," or necessarily pointing to something beyond himself, ultimately to being itself. Death is the "open wound" in Dasein, which leaves the problematic

3

of existence susceptible to, even clamoring for, further development. In Heidegger's thought this development is the turning from Dasein to being, and death makes this turning not only possible, but necessary.

In the writings composed after the turning, death is still important, although, in contrast to its prominence in *Sein und Zeit*, it remains for the most part in the background. In the later Heidegger, death is the "privileged place" in which being is illuminated in a special way. Death is the point of the definitive breakthrough, the breach through which being and Dasein can come in contact. It is the point in man's self-understanding at which being flashes with its greatest brilliance and deepest obscurity, in the full splendor of its mystery. It is called the "redoubt of being" (*das Gebirg des Seins*), the secret fastness in which being at the same time conceals and reveals itself most profoundly. As death in the analysis of Dasein is the existential of totality and thus the "measure" of man's being, so in later writings death is the foremost place of the revelation of being, the measure of being-showing-itself-to-man, the "measure of the immeasurable" (*die Massgabe des Unermesslichen*).

The distinctive role of death in Heidegger's thought shows up markedly against the background of the age-old philosophical problem of *finitude*. In Heidegger's initial phase, death is the existential-ontological basis of the finitude of man: Dasein is finite, because it exists as being-unto-death. In the latter phase, being shows itself as finite by a strange combination of self-revelation and self-concealment in death. Death is the preeminent mode of being's coming-to-presence and fading-into-withdrawal, the high point of the mysterious coupling of these two moments, positive and negative, which constitute all of being's manifestations. Death is the hiding place, the mountain fastness where being dwells in its brightest openness and darkest hiddenness. Thus, Heidegger sees death as the reason for the finitude of both man and being: man is finite because he exists *unto* death; being is finite because it comes to presence in its most privileged way *in* death.

At this point we must attempt to forestall two fairly common misconceptions. First of all, Heidegger's philosophical views on death do not spring from or support a pessimistic view of reality. In fact, Heidegger insists that his thought is neutral with regard to such ontic attitudes as optimism or pessimism, since he is dealing only with the transcendental area of ontological conditions of possibility and trying to uncover the structures of experience which render optimism and pessimism possible.

Still less is the notion of the finitude of being a proclamation of atheism. Heidegger's concern is always with being as experienced by man in daily existence, and thus with being as manifesting itself within definite limitations. He remains scrupulously aloof from the question of infinite being. The ground of being which he seeks is not in the realm of the transcendent, but of the transcendental.[2]

II. *Death as Seen by Socrates*

To throw into sharper relief the originality of Heidegger's conception, it will be helpful to contrast it with the traditional view of death in western philosophy. For the sake of brevity, this view can be distilled from Plato's famous dialogue *Phaedo,* an essay which has exercised a definitive influence on western man's philosophizing about death and the prospects of a life beyond.

The *Phaedo* is the last of the four Platonic dialogues which tell the story of the trial, imprisonment and death of Socrates (*Euthyphro, Apology, Crito, Phaedo*). A record of Socrates' farewell speech in prison as he awaits the hour of execution, *Phaedo* has an air of immediacy regarding the problems of death and immortality which has few parallels in western literature. Far from regarding death as a terror to be shunned or glossed over, Socrates, before drinking the hemlock, speaks of it as the fulfillment of his greatest yearning. He has always claimed to be nothing more than a "philosopher," a lover of wisdom, and maintained, "the fact is, those who tackle philosophy aright are simply and solely practicing dying, practicing death all the time, but nobody sees it. If this is true, then it would surely be unreasonable that they should earnestly do this and nothing else all their lives, yet when death comes they should object to do what they had been so long earnestly practicing" (64a, Rouse 467).[3]

The reason for this amazing view, so contrary to all that men instinctively feel in the face of death, is Socrates' conviction that death is nothing but "a freeing and separation of soul from body" (67d, Rouse 470; cf. 64c, Rouse 467). Such a separation is highly desirable to the philosopher, since what he loves most is truth, and truth is attained only by the soul, the body being merely a hindrance in its search: "[the soul] reasons best when none of these senses disturbs it, hearing or sight, or pain, or pleasure indeed, but when it is completely by itself and says good-bye to the body, and so far as possible has no dealings with it, when it reaches out and

5

grasps that which really is" (65c, Rouse 468). Only in death is the soul "pure and rid of the body's foolishness" (67a, Rouse 470), and thus able to grasp "that which really is." Accordingly, "one who is really in love with wisdom . . . holds firm to this same hope, that he will find it in the grave, and nowhere else worth speaking of" (68b, Rouse 471).

True to his lifelong calling, Socrates thus looks with composure, even with desire, upon the lethal potion. His last recorded words exhibit not despair or resentment, but a spirit of reverence: "but at least, I suppose, it is allowed to offer a prayer to the gods and that must be done, for good luck in the migration from here to there. Then that is my prayer, and so may it be!" (117b–c, Rouse 520–21) "With these words," Phaedo continues, "he put the cup to his lips and, quite easy and contented, drank it up" (ibid.).

The Greek view of death may thus be summarized as follows:

1. Death is the separation of the soul from the body, the dissolution of man as a composite being into his component parts.

2. It is a particular case of the general phenomenon of passing-away observable in any changeable being, an example of *phthora, corruptio,* ceasing-to-be, as opposed to *genesis, generatio,* coming-to-be. Thus in the *Phaedo* Socrates speaks of death as follows: "don't consider it as regards men only . . . ; if you wish to understand more easily, think of all animals and vegetables, and, in a word, everything that has birth" (70d, Rouse 473).

3. Death is an event marking the end of a man's life; it is the final limit of the time line spanning his life's history.

4. Death lies in the future. Since it is something we have to look forward to, the question naturally arises: what will come after death?

In each of these points, Heidegger's conception appears to be the exact opposite of the classical view:

1. As Heidegger considers man not in his substantial compositeness, but in the immediately experienced structural unity of his acts, death does not separate man, but binds him together, completing the totality of his existence.

2. Death is the uttermost of man's potentialities, embracing and uniting all his other potentialities. Thus it is not considered metaphysically as a generally observable objective fact of nature, but phenomenologically, as something manifesting itself in human understanding. As

6

being-unto-death, man is not regarded in that which he has in common with animals and plants, but in that which is uniquely distinctive in him.

3. Death is not an event which puts an end to life, but an existential-ontological determination of existence; as such, it is a part of life itself. It is not something occurring just at the end of a man's life, but something always present, from the very beginning of life, as a constitutive element of existence.

4. Death does not, then, lie in the future, but in the here and now, affecting every act in which existence is realized. It is seen not by looking ahead, but by reflecting, by looking back upon existence. Accordingly, the question of what will come after death does not arise.

At first sight, Heidegger's view may seem strange or even preposterous. It can be properly evaluated, however, only when one has due regard for his phenomenological starting-point and method, which are in many ways the direct opposite of metaphysical thinking. This study will attempt to investigate Heidegger's philosophy of death in the context of his total thought and method, in order to provide some basis for understanding his conclusions. A peripheral value of the study should be a certain illumination of the phenomenological method itself, or, at least, of Heidegger's version of it.[4]

III. Other Studies of Death in Heidegger

Despite the importance of death in Heidegger's thought, relatively few studies have been devoted explicitly to this theme. The first and only thorough discussion to appear to date is the book of Adolf Sternberger, *Der verstandene Tod* (Leipzig, 1934). Often quoted by other commentators, this has become something of a standard work on the subject of Heidegger's view of the problem of death. Shorter treatments by European writers include two brief essays published in Holland by M. A. H. Stomps (1938) and S. U. Zuidema (1948), a competent but noncritical exposition in German by Janis Cedrins (1949), and an article in German by Wolfgang Kroug analyzing death as a "possibility-to-be" (1953).[5]

Further light is shed by certain studies comparing Heidegger's ideas of death with those of other modern thinkers: Joachim Wach's book on death according to Schopenhauer, Feuerbach, Simmel, and Heidegger; the dissertation by Karl Lehmann on death in Heidegger and Jaspers; the book by the Dutch critic R. F. Beerling, comparing the views of Simmel, Heidegger, and Jaspers, and following rather closely Sternberger's judgment of Heidegger; the study of death in Heidegger and Sartre by Régis Jolivet; and finally, in English, the article by J. Glenn Gray on death in the philosophy of Jaspers and Heidegger.[6]

The most conspicuous fact about all these studies is that they are restricted exclusively to Heidegger's earlier works. All base their analyses on Heidegger's utterances about death in *Sein und Zeit* (1927), with an occasional citation from Heidegger's *Kant und das Problem der Metaphysik* (*Kant and the Problem of Metaphysics*, 1929), from *Vom Wesen des Grundes* (*On the Essence of Ground*, 1929), or from *Was Ist Metaphysik?* (*What Is Metaphysics?* 1930). No study of death in Heidegger has as yet considered the treatment of this theme in his later works. To fill this gap, we propose to trace this aspect of Heidegger's thought through the whole of his published work.

IV. *Outline and Methodology*

In order to highlight the differences and the similarities between the earlier and later treatments of death in Heidegger's writings, the approach of the present study will be chronological: Heidegger's works will be discussed in the order in which they were composed, which in many cases differs significantly from the order of their publication.[7] For the purposes of this study, Heidegger's writings can conveniently be divided into five stages: (1) the analysis of existence (*Daseinsanalyse*) carried out in the pages of *Sein und Zeit*, to be discussed in chapter two; (2) the development of the horizon or background of the death-thematic through a gradual turning (*die Kehre*) in the direction of Heidegger's thought, observable in the first compositions after *Sein und Zeit* (chapter three); (3) the consolidation of the position won by the turning in *Einführung in die Metaphysik* (*Introduction to Metaphysics*), which was first given as a university lecture course in 1935, but was not published until 1953 (chapter four); (4) the poetry interpretations and essays on the problem of language, written from the standpoint of the new position (chapter five); (5) the discussion of the essence of *thing* and the dwelling of man upon the earth, in connection with the problems of technology and the novel conception of the "quadrate" (chapter six).

8

It must be borne in mind that the following study is designedly confined to the subject of death in Heidegger. The boundaries of investigation are thus clearly marked out: first, no attempt will be made to discuss all the themes of Heidegger's thought, but only those necessary for the complete treatment of the theme of death; second, not every individual work of Heidegger will be analyzed, but only those in which death and/or other topics intimately connected with it appear; third, there will be no explicit comparisons drawn with the thought of other philosophers on this point. Our concern is to work out thoroughly the philosophy of death of this one contemporary thinker, with the hope of providing a key to the understanding of his thought, and of constructing a solid basis for evaluating his contribution to western philosophy.

2

Death in the
Analysis of Dasein

Heidegger's most detailed treatment of the problem of death is found in his first great work, *Sein und Zeit*. The book demands extensive treatment, even at the risk of creating a one-sided view of Heidegger's thought by laying a heavy stress on its initial "existentialist" phase. The risk must be taken, however, since *Sein und Zeit* lays the foundations upon which all future development of Heideggerian themes is built. The danger will be minimized by paying careful attention to the overriding intention of Heidegger's whole philosophical effort, the problem of being, which forms the context in which the problem of death arises.

I. *The Context of the Treatment of Death*

The analysis of death forms an inner moment of the analysis of existence, which in turn is part of the attempt to work out a suitable approach to the question of being. These three themes—being, Dasein or human existence, and death—are related to each other in the manner of three concentric circles. Working inward from the outermost circle, we shall first discuss the question of being as the all-embracing horizon and ultimate goal of Heidegger's investigation, then pass on to the analysis of Dasein as the means of working out an approach to this question, and finally treat the problem of death as a moment in the analysis of Dasein.

A. *The Question of Being*

Since the age of Plato and Aristotle, the question of being, of the real, of the apparent real and the "really real," has been the central concern of western philosophical thought. Nonetheless, between Aristotle and us there has been, in Heidegger's view, a great hiatus, a period of forgottenness during which the question of being has been taken for granted and never again thematically explored. Instead, the philosophic tradition has been content to regard the problem as solved, by calling being a transcendental notion—the most universal concept possible, not properly definable but self-evident, about which no further questions can or need be asked.[1]

But, says Heidegger, it is precisely these characteristics of the notion of being that should goad philosophers on to further inquiry. That being is the most universal of all notions means that it is the most abstract and, therefore, the most devoid of positive content; thus it is the concept most in need of being "filled" by means of a radically basic kind of questioning. Likewise, indefinability is a totally negative determination, which fairly cries out for a more positive type of searching. Finally, the philosopher should be deeply disturbed by the seemingly self-explanatory character of being, since it is precisely his task to probe more deeply into all that presents itself as initially self-evident in ordinary experience. Thus it is not only fitting but urgent that philosophy focus once again on the long neglected but uniquely vital question of being (SZ 2–4).[2]

The opening up of the overgrown path to the question of being is the task of *Sein und Zeit*. The fact that this is Heidegger's chief interest is abundantly clear from his statement of purpose at the beginning of the book: "Our aim in the following treatise is to work out concretely the question of the meaning of 'being' " (SZ 1). But it is even more decisively evident from the fact that he calls attention to this goal at each step along the way and explicitly reiterates it at the end: "One must seek a way of casting light on the fundamental question of ontology . . . toward this alone the foregoing investigation is *on the way*" (SZ 437).[3] In the light of this evidence, it is somewhat difficult to understand why so many commentators have classified Heidegger as an existentialist, as if his sole, or at least primary concern were the philosophy of man.

For a proper evaluation of Heidegger's thought, it is essential to achieve a clear understanding of the question of being as he initially approaches it. First, the question is not about being itself, but about the *meaning* of being. What do we really mean when we say "being" or "is"? What do men have in mind, what do they intend when they speak of being? Upon what are they focusing when they use this notion which so strangely permeates and controls their entire speech and thought? The question is not: "What *is* being?" but rather: "What do we *mean* by 'being'?"

Thus Heidegger's question about being is readily recognizable as a phenomenological one. Phenomenology inquires about things as they appear to us, about the content and significance of our concepts, about the contents of consciousness. To this extent, Heidegger's posing of the question of being follows the method of his early master, Edmund Husserl. But Heidegger's originality is evident. Where Husserl's phenomenological method endeavored to reduce a phenomenon to its content in consciousness, prescinding from ("bracketing") its reality or nonreality, that is, its real or merely fictitious being, Heidegger applies the phenomenological question to being itself. Not only does he not pass over or bracket being; he explicitly focuses on it by asking: What do we really mean by the verb "to be"? What are we saying, what are we thinking about, when we say or think that something "is" or "is real"? What are we intending, what do we see, when we use the terms "being," "is," "real"?[4]

A further caution is required. When we use the term "being," we invariably tend to think of it as a thing; we speak of a being or of several beings. This is to use the term substantively, as a noun. While this usage is certainly legitimate, it can obscure the important fact that "being" is primarily a verbal form, a participle, and only in a derivative and somewhat artificial sense a noun. Just as "running" indicates the continuing of the action expressed by the verb "to run," so "being" indicates the continuing of the "action" expressed by the verb "to be." Only secondarily, and somewhat misleadingly, does it designate a substantive state or condition or thing. In attempting to pose his fundamental question, Heidegger uses the term "being" primarily in the active, dynamic, verbal sense, even though language and grammar force him to write it as a noun (*das Sein*). Being is not a thing, a substance, an object, but an act, an event, a process, and indeed the most primordial of all acts, events, or processes, the act of be-ing underlying all other possible acts. Lest this be lost sight of, it would be well to supply the corrective phrase, "to be understood verbally," whenever one encounters the term "being" in the context of Heidegger's thought.[5]

B. *The Function of the Analysis of Dasein*

The problem of the proper approach to the question of the meaning of being must be settled before we can even begin to think of an answer. Thus, Heidegger raises the preliminary question of methodology. Before asking: How should the question of being be answered?, he asks: How should the question be posed? What resources are at our command for attacking such a fundamental and all-embracing question? If being includes absolutely all that is, and even all that can be, where does one start?

What has already been said about the character of the question of being provides us with a hint: if the question of being aims at discovering what we really mean when we say "being," then the point of departure must be an investigation of our meaning. We must ask: How does man come to speak of "being" at all, and to pose the question of being? What is the mode of being of *man*, who understands being in such a way that he can inquire about its meaning? If man of all beings has the unique prerogative of saying "being," then a study of man should tell us something about his question of the meaning of being, and possibly about the answer to the question. Our investigation must thus begin with an analysis of man, precisely under the aspect of his posing the question and of his preliminary understanding of being which makes this question possible.

The problem of a correct point of departure is also approachable from another side. If we wish to investigate the notion of being, then we must investigate some individual being (some thing-which-is), for only in beings does being come to light. But which individual can qualify as capable of representing all other beings? Is there any one being which is an exemplar, in which being manifests itself in a special way? For the modern philosophers of existence, as well as for those of the classical tradition, this being is man. Man not only has being; he knows that he has it, and assumes a definite stance with regard to it. He is most fundamentally distinguished by the fact that his essential mode of existence includes a certain preontological understanding of being: man "*is* in the manner of an understanding of being" (SZ 12). In man being is not only implicitly but explicitly manifest. He is the "lighting-up place" of being, the one spot in the entire realm of beings where being "is there" as itself. As the bearer of this unique privilege and burden, man is the "there" of being, or more simply the there-being. Heidegger's working-out of the question of being will therefore begin with a preparatory analysis of man as Dasein (SZ 11–15).[6]

The problem and methodology of Sein und Zeit have now become more concrete. An analysis of Dasein must be carried out in order to prepare the way for the posing of the question of being and for an eventual phenomenological ontology.[7] Heidegger is aiming at an ontic foundation of ontology, a foundation through the analysis of that being in which ontology takes its origin and remains rooted as an existential possibility. The elaboration of the being of this particular being should help us to arrive at a proper statement of the question of being in general. Sein und Zeit will therefore undertake an analysis of Dasein in the service of the broader project of working out the question of the meaning of being itself.[8]

C. *The Method of the Analysis*

There can be no question here of attempting to reproduce Heidegger's entire analysis of Dasein; its range is too broad and its penetration too deep. We shall rather restrict the discussion to those aspects of the analysis which have an essential connection with the theme of death.

First, a word must be said about method. The analysis of Dasein in *Sein und Zeit* is phenomenological, existential and ontological. We shall treat of Heidegger's special understanding and adaptation of phenomenology, the meaning he assigns to the terms existential and ontological as opposed to the terms existentiell and ontic, and finally the apparent problem posed by the hermeneutic circle which is intrinsic to his methodology.

Heidegger's method in investigating Dasein is phenomenological; he attempts to bring the phenomena to light. Here it is important to note that Heidegger does not understand phenomenon in the Kantian sense of appearance as contrasted with the thing in itself, but rather in the original Greek sense of something coming into view, showing itself, making itself manifest, emerging into the light.[9]

In Heidegger's view, the becoming-manifest of the phenomenon does not take place through the agency or mediation of some other being, but through the activity, indeed through the being of the phenomenon itself; it shows itself by itself and through itself. Heidegger is not thinking of merely surface aspects of beings, such as those which impose themselves immediately upon the senses; his phenomenology is not a new empiricism. That which shows itself is rather something which, at first glance, seems to be peripheral or even concealed; to be seen adequately, it must first be brought into focus, led out to center stage. It is that which shows itself "antecedently and concomitantly, but unthematically," in such a way that it can be "brought to self-manifestation in a thematic way" (SZ 31). In other words, the phenomenon for Heidegger is something which comes to light as having been already present from the very beginning of a particular experience, which shows itself simultaneously with the perception of more obvious aspects of a being, and which can be brought into explicit focus by man's reflection. Controlled and systematic reflection of this kind is precisely the task of phenomenology.

To summarize: *phenomenon*, in Heidegger's sense of the term, may be defined as that which shows itself by itself and through itself, in an unthematic but thematizable way; phenomenology is the reflective process of letting that be seen which shows itself by and through itself, in the manner in which it shows itself (SZ 27–31).[10]

According to the above description, the phenomenon par excellence, which phenomenology should let be seen, must be something implicit in experience, showing itself at the very heart of experience but in an unthematic way. It must be something which, at first sight, does not seem to show itself, but rather seems to remain hidden beneath the surface of experience, and yet pertains essentially to it, even constituting its ground and inner meaning. The most universally implicit feature of all experience, says Heidegger, cannot be this or that being, or any particular being; it can only be the being of beings, or being itself. The phenomenon par excellence, then, which is accordingly the fundamental theme of phenomenology, is the being of beings (SZ 34–35).

But the being of beings, according to a tradition going all the way back to Aristotle, is the theme of ontology. This is the "meta-physical" science introduced by the Stagirite in Book 4 (Gamma) of the *Metaphysics*: "There is a science which studies Being *qua* Being, and the properties inherent in it in virtue of its own nature."[11] Is Heidegger reverting to one of the earliest forms of western philosophy, the study of being as being? Is he doing nothing more than introducing an ancient science under a new disguise? Or, if he is introducing something new, is he preempting the domain formerly ruled by ontology in the name of phenomenology?

The latter is indeed the case. Due to Heidegger's concept of the phenomenon, phenomenology evolves into ontology, and conversely, ontology has only one approach to reality: the method of phenomenology. As Heidegger summarily puts it: "Phenomenology is our way of access to what is to be the theme of ontology, and it is our way of giving it demonstrative precision. *Ontology is possible only as phenomenology*" (SZ 35). Thus Heidegger's analysis of Dasein will be phenomenological, and, by that very fact, ontological. It will let the phenomenon par excellence, namely, being, be seen in and by itself, in the way in which it shows itself in the Dasein which is its exemplar and lighting-up place.

Since the search for the meaning of being must begin with an investigation of man, Dasein, we must first seek out the particular mode in which being manifests itself in man. The mode of being of Dasein is "existence." The analysis of Dasein, in its specific mode of being, will accordingly be an investigation of existence, an "existential analysis."

To understand what is involved in the existential analysis, one must first grasp the basic significance of existence in Heidegger's thought. Existence is the specifically human mode of being, the distinguishing characteristic of Dasein. All other beings merely are; Dasein alone exists. This means that Dasein differs essentially from all other beings by the fact that it does not merely have being, but it has to be. It is not merely something there, not a pure object like a rock on a beach. Rather it has a responsibility for its own being and an obligation to be significant. Dasein recognizes its own being as a task to be fulfilled; it must do something about its being.

Dasein is thus confronted with itself; it has a divided being. Insofar as it steps out of and stands over against itself, it assumes an attitude toward its own being. Too, Dasein understands itself as a being which has to be; it comprehends itself, to some extent, in its own being. And because it knows itself in its own being, it possesses an understanding of the being of other beings, in fact the being of all beings, and even, to some degree, being itself (SZ 12–13, 41–42).

Dasein's understanding of being is by no means a fully developed knowledge or an explicit comprehension. It is merely a dim, implicit awareness of being which infallibly accompanies every human act. Understanding in this connection is more a knowing how to: Dasein knows how to be. Thus it has a primordial understanding of its own being and, thereby, of being itself (cf. SZ 123–24, 143, also KM 205).

The notion of existence as the specifically human mode of being thus includes the notes of having to be, having concern about and an attitude toward one's being, and having an understanding of being itself. These qualities may be said to comprise the peculiar being of Dasein. The investigation of Dasein will accordingly be an existential-ontological analysis.

The terms *existential* and *ontological* are to be distinguished respectively from *existentiell* and *ontic*. The first pair applies to the deeper level of intelligibility, the realm of the underlying structures, while the second pair refers to the more immediate surface level of the concrete acts of existence. Thus, the adjective *existential* describes the basic structures of existence, the underlying elements which render various aspects of man's concrete existence intelligible and subject to theoretical penetration. *Existentiell,* on the other hand, pertains to the actual concrete actions of man's experience, actions which flow from his existential structure. The existentiell level is the actual realization of the potencies inherent in the existential structure. The distinction between *ontological* and *ontic* should be similarly understood. *Ontological* refers to the internal structures which underlie and constitute the being of a being as its conditions of possibility. *Ontic* means those actions which are externally observable, which are made possible by the ontological structures.[12]

Before plunging into the details of the existential-ontological analysis, we must first face what seems an insurmountable difficulty. The analysis aims at the working-out of the being-structures of Dasein in order to prepare for the proper posing of the question of the meaning of being. But doesn't this presuppose that I already know what I am trying to find out? How can I investigate the being of Dasein unless I already know what being is? And if I already know what being is, why study Dasein as a step toward asking the question of being? Isn't there a logical fallacy, a vicious circle here? (SZ 7, 152, 314)

Heidegger replies by denying the presupposition of this objection—that Dasein can be adequately studied according to the rules of formal logic. These rules are drawn from man's experience with mere entities, beings which are ontic, for which being is a "given" but not a matter of concern. But Dasein is radically different. It not only has being; it understands its being, relates to it, is concerned about it. Dasein is not merely ontic; it is essentially ontological, endowed with the glory and the burden of understanding being. Because of this completely unique structure, the rules of formal logic cannot explain man, but can only confine him in a straightjacket which kills off what is most specifically his own—that he is the "there" of being, and therefore essentially not closed in, but opened out. Dasein must be investigated by a different kind of logic, corresponding to its own unique structure.

The vicious circle, then, is a fallacy of formal logic, and does not disturb the existential analysis since it moves on an entirely different plane. However, there is a kind of circularity in Dasein's being, "an ontological circle-structure" (SZ 153). This consists in the fact that Dasein has a preontological understanding of being, a dim awareness, even prior to all reflection, of what being means. It is precisely this preunderstanding which makes possible Dasein's subsequent, more highly developed and nuanced understanding of the meaning of being. The circle of understanding is not a vicious circle, then, but an aspect of the structure of meaning rooted in Dasein's existential constitution; it is "the expression of the existential *prestructure* of Dasein itself" (SZ 153).

Since Dasein is constituted by the fact that it has a dim understanding of being prior to all explicit reflection upon its own existence, the existential analysis must take place from within the ontological circle; Dasein cannot possibly step outside this structure, any more than a man can step outside his own skin. The investigative procedure proper to Dasein, then, cannot be the adducing of new evidence gathered from without, but it must proceed along the lines of an explanation of what is "within," of what is already given and in some way already known. It will be a careful explicitation of what is implicit in the realization of existence, a discovery of something which has always been there, but has never been thematically grasped.

Heidegger calls this method "hermeneutic," a term which is more commonly applied to the interpretation of the Bible. In Heidegger's phenomenology the hermeneutic method is the explicitation, the unfolding and laying out to plain view, of something prereflectively understood. It is a "kind of interpreting . . . described as the working-out and appropriation of an understanding" (SZ 231). What we have said about the radically distinctive mode of being of Dasein should suffice to show that this hermeneutic method is by no means arbitrarily imposed, but is a necessary consequence of Dasein's ontological circularity. Thus, "what is decisive is not to get out of the circle, but to enter into it in the proper way" (SZ 153), "to leap into the 'circle,' primordially and wholly" (SZ 315) in order to bring into the clear light of explicit knowledge what is already hazily known, and dimly, but really, understood.[13]

D. *The Preparatory Analysis of Dasein as Concern*

For Heidegger the basic state and fundamental constitution of Dasein is "being-in-the-world." We shall first attempt to understand the wide-ranging implications of this term, and then sketch briefly the structures of being-in-the-world, which will finally find their unity in the comprehensive tripartite structure of concern.

Dasein is certainly not in the world in a purely spatial sense, as wine is in a glass or a coat is in a closet. The relationship is much more profound, corresponding to the greater complexity of the structure of Dasein as existence. As the being which understands being, Dasein exists in the world as being consciously present to beings other than itself, as well as to itself and to the task of its own existence. It must relate to all the things, persons, events, and ideas which it encounters in experience as coming from the outside, as being somehow other than itself, in the constant context of its own responsibility to be. Dasein is accordingly in the world as the unique being which is concerned about its own being, whose own existence is somehow at stake in everything it experiences and encounters.

Thus Dasein, even though existing as being-in-the-world, still has its own life to live, its own being to be. Existence is always exclusively one's own, and is thus characterized by an inevitable and undeniable "mineness": the being which concerns Dasein is always primarily "mine." Moreover, since my being is totally unique and specific to me alone, it imposes an ontological obligation. It is not a pure gratuity, but an assigned task (not a *Gabe*, but an *Aufgabe*, says Heidegger), and one which I alone am called upon to fulfill. This immediately gives rise to two possibilities: I can either succeed or fail at the task of my own existence; I can exist "authentically" or "inauthentically" (SZ 53, 42–43, 12).

The notion of existence as Dasein's specific mode of being involves another important consequence. Since Dasein not merely has being, but

19

has to be, its being is not a static endowment, but something to be fulfilled or achieved. This means that Dasein is always stretched forward toward its own still-to-be-realized being; it is always beyond or out in front of itself. Its being is never complete actuality, but always includes possibility; for Dasein, "to be" means "can-be." When I say "Dasein *is* such and such," I am also saying "Dasein *can be* such and such."

Heidegger's notion of possibility is difficult to grasp, especially since it seems to be identified with human existence itself, or to constitute the *actuality* of Dasein. What is clear, however, is that he is not using the term *possibility* in its traditional sense. He does not understand it metaphysically, as synonymous with contingency or as potentiality in contrast to actuality, nor does he mean it logically, as the noncontradictoriness of constitutive notes, nor psychologically, in the sense of freedom of choice (*libertas indifferentiae*). Rather, in Heidegger's existential phenomenology, possibility indicates what Dasein can be or do or become, insofar as this is constitutive of what he is.

A man's actuality is defined by his potentialities; his state of being is determined by the fact that he is never purely static but necessarily changing, dynamic, being born, living, growing, aging, declining, dying. Dasein, so long as it exists, always has unrealized possibilities, and these constitute it as who and what it actually is at any moment of its life's history. Put briefly, Dasein *is* what it *can be*. In this sense, possibility, or power-to-be, or potentiality, is "the most primordial and ultimate positive way of ontologically characterizing Dasein" (SZ 143–44).

The potentialities of Dasein thus exist not in the distant future, separated from the present; rather they are the modes of being in which Dasein presently exists. And since Dasein knows itself, is consciously confronted by its own existence, these potentialities constitute the means by which Dasein understands itself. They form the background of its self-knowledge, the horizon in which it sees itself, the screen on which it projects its own self-image. Dasein understands what it is by knowing what it can be.

This primordial understanding, which reveals the being of Dasein as an anticipatory drive toward being, a power-to-be stretched out ahead of itself, is not an explicitly recognized act of knowledge, but rather a basic structure of existence, a transcendental concomitant of existence, which lies beneath all ontic acts of knowledge as their ground or condition of possibility. This type of understanding is not existentiell and ontic, but existential-ontological. It is a ground structure of Dasein's existence, what Heidegger calls an "existential." It constitutes the first of the basic structures of Dasein as being-in-the-world (SZ 142–45).

But this existential understanding always has a certain tone or attunement. Just as Dasein recognizes itself on the ontic level as always "having moods," so its ontological self-understanding is embedded in a kind of precognitive temper or disposition. Dasein does not know itself in a vacuum or in a neutral way, free from all affective reactions, but finds itself always in a particular situation in which it is joyful or sad, exuberant, contented, depressed, quiet, excited. This continual being-in-a-mood on the ontic level is grounded in the ontological structure which Heidegger calls "Befindlichkeit," which we may translate as "ontological disposition."

Constant being-in-a-mood brings Dasein back to itself, makes it aware of itself as being already there. In this way the ontological disposition reveals the primordial fact that Dasein is, thus revealing the pure fact of existence. Heidegger calls this basic fact "thrownness" or "facticity." Just as Dasein's ontological understanding reveals being-in-the-world as a capacity to be, or as being-ahead-of-itself, so the ontological disposition of Dasein manifests being-in-the-world as thrownness or facticity, as already-being-in-the-world (SZ 142–43, 134–40).

But Dasein as facticious existence or existing facticity does not exist in an empty universe, isolated and solipsistic, but rather "in the world," among other beings. As we have seen, this being-in is not to be understood spatially or materially, as water is in a glass, but rather existentially. Dasein is in the world in the sense that it exists with beings, in the presence of other things. Moreover, Dasein is "with" the beings of its environment in the mode of "presence," that is, it knows them and has some understanding and familiarity with which it approaches them. It is precisely this antecedent mode of implicit understanding which makes it possible for Dasein to encounter the beings around it. Furthermore, Dasein's "being-with" other beings occurs in the manner of being concerned with other beings. With regard to nonhuman beings this concern takes the form of a "taking care of" (Besorgen); with regard to other men, it occurs as "caring for" (Fürsorge). These are the two modes of concern which characterize Dasein's relation to the other beings of its world (SZ 53–57, 121–22).

Heidegger also calls "being-with" by another name: "fallenness" among beings. The term is not meant in a derogatory sense, but simply points to the fact that Dasein, by virtue of its intrinsic structure of being-with, finds itself as already caught up by other beings, and thus necessarily runs the risk of losing itself to these.

As being-with, Dasein has the tendency to understand itself not from itself and through its own distinctive mode of being, but from its understanding of the other beings it encounters. A further complication arises from the fact that Dasein tends to understand itself and the other beings of its world not by means of an original interpretation, but by an uncritical acceptance of "public opinion," of the judgment of the anonymous crowd, of what "people" (das Man) say. By doing this, Dasein itself becomes anonymous, faceless, one of the crowd. It loses its own real self and becomes a "people-self" (Man-selbst) (SZ 126–30, 175–76). Thus the existential structure of fallenness reveals being-in-the-world as a being-with the beings one encounters within one's world, together with the tendency to lose one's own authentic self to these beings.

These three existential-ontological structures constitute the being of Dasein. They make up the concrete, unified totality of being-in-the-world. This totality is involved in every actualization of existence; Dasein always understands itself existentially as existence, thrownness, and fallenness: as being-ahead-of-itself, as already-being-in-the-world, and as being-with. Heidegger sums up this three-membered unity in the following formula: "the being of Dasein means being-ahead-of-itself-already-in-(the-world-) as being-with (beings encountered within the world)" (SZ 192).

This structural totality is called "care" or "concern" (Sorge). The term has a purely existential-ontological meaning. It signifies that Dasein, as being-in-the-world, is that being (1) which is confronted with its being as a task to be fulfilled, whose own being is a being which "can be," (2) which finds itself as already thrown into existence, and (3) which exists in the midst of other beings, taking care of and caring for them. In this highly articulated sense, the being of Dasein is "concern" (SZ 191–96).

E. Death in the Analysis

This brief account of the preliminary analysis of Dasein raises the question of originality and completeness. Is the characterization of Dasein as concern an original, sufficiently profound, and fundamental interpretation? Does it do justice to the being of Dasein in its authenticity and completeness? Despite a certain profundity, the foregoing analysis, as Heidegger points out, cannot lay claim to such characteristics, for it has shown only how Dasein can exist *inauthentically* (through fallenness, as an anonymous "people-self") and *incompletely* (in its various possibilities-to-be, all of which are open to further possibilities, and none of which is total and definitive). There arises, then, the task of focusing on Dasein in its possible authenticity and completeness of existence (SZ 231–33).

It is precisely the attempt to grasp Dasein in its completeness that leads to the treatment of death. Even speaking ontically, the totality of human existence must embrace all aspects of life, from beginning to end, from birth to death. And if we consider Dasein ontologically, we immediately recognize a certain incompleteness in its basic structure: as long as Dasein lives, there always remains something which it can be, but is not yet. Dasein is like a painting which is never completed; it always has further possibilities not yet realized, aspects, events, accomplishments which are not yet a part of its actuality. In fact, the picture will never be completed until death. This is the final arc of the circle of existence, the missing piece needed to complete the picture. Thus the end of Dasein is its completion. Death belongs to the totality; in fact it completes the totality of Dasein. Death must accordingly become the explicit theme of investigation if the analysis of Dasein is to be complete (SZ 233–34, 372–73).

The following treatment of the theme of death in *Sein und Zeit* will proceed in four steps. We shall work out the existential concept of death, study death in relation to the authenticity and inauthenticity of existence, establish the ontological meaning of death, and evaluate the analysis of death in the total context of the picture of man and the understanding of being contained in *Sein und Zeit*.

II. *The Existential Concept of Death*

We have seen that the being of Dasein, grasped as concern, necessarily includes the element of being-ahead-of-itself. Because of this aspect Dasein is never closed, never finished: "This element in the structure of concern tells us unambiguously that in Dasein there is always something *still outstanding*, which, as a potentiality-to-be for Dasein itself, has not yet become 'actual' " (SZ 236).

Moreover, the last outstanding potentiality of Dasein is death, which remains outstanding so long as Dasein exists. It seems that the element of being-ahead-of-itself thus makes it impossible ever to catch up with death and bring it into the structure of Dasein. As the ancient witticism of Epicurus indicates, so long as Dasein is, its death is still outstanding, and vice versa, when death becomes a reality, Dasein is no more.[14] How, then, can death possibly be included in the analysis of Dasein? To state the problem in this way is to consider death in its purely ontic dimension, as an event which has not yet happened, but will one day occur to put an end to the life of a human being. As such, death is admittedly something not yet real, existing only as a possible future biological state or event. Considered in this way, death cannot be included in the structure of Dasein, for its role consists precisely in the suppression of this structure.

Heidegger's investigation, however, does not consider Dasein ontically, on the level of the existentiell realization of existence, but ontologically, in the structural elements of its existence. Thus the question must be asked in another way: what can be said about death when it is seen existentially-ontologically? What is death in relation to man, when man is considered not merely as an entity, but as *existing*, in the fullness of meaning which Heidegger gives to this term? In other words, what is death in the existential sense?

A. *Death as an Existential*

What kind of a "not-yet" is death, existentially considered? Is it proper to designate the not-yet of death as something "outstanding"? Heidegger's answer is negative, for something outstanding is always something not yet present-at-hand (*vorhanden*) in the manner of a mere entity. This could be the outstanding amount of a debt, or the invisible final quarter of a three-quarter moon, or the future full maturity of unripe fruit. Death, however, cannot be considered merely as an entity which is not yet present-at-hand, for man himself is no mere entity, but an existent (SZ 242–44). Death too must be considered existentially, in its relation to man's existence as concern and as the there of being. In this perspective, the not-yet of death is not something outstanding, but something "beforestanding," i.e., something standing before Dasein as it exists in the manner of being always ahead-of-itself, something confronting Dasein in the totality of its existence.

Death is thus a possibility of the being of Dasein, a potentiality

always before and with him, right from the very beginning of his existence. As an old bit of folk wisdom expresses it, "As soon as a man is born,
he is old enough to die." In the existential-ontological sense, this means
that death belongs to the very constitution of man; it is an essential
element of the being of Dasein. In this sense, "death is a way to be, which
Dasein takes over as soon as it is" (SZ 245). In this way of thinking death
is considered not as the brute fact of cessation, or the point-like event of
coming to an end, for this would be an ontic mode of expression. Death is
an ever-present element in the ontological structure of Dasein, a determination of existence, which Heidegger calls an "existential." The particular
name of this existential is "being-unto-end" or "being-unto-death" (*Sein
zum Tode*, SZ 245).

Death in the existential sense must therefore be distinguished from
ontic death, i.e., death as the terminal point of the lifeline, as a facticious
event breaking into a man's life-history and producing the condition of
"no-longer-being-in-the-world," and from the perishing of nonhuman or-
ganisms (animals and plants), which factually come to an end, but assume
no attitude or relation to their cessation, and thus have no "being-unto-
end" (SZ 247). In contrast with these meanings of the term, the existential view shows death to be an ever-impending potentiality which belongs
necessarily to the being of Dasein, determining it not just at the moment
of dying, but always and already, even prior to our noticing it: "Dasein is
dying as long as it exists" (SZ 251). In this sense, death is the structure by
which Dasein exists as being-unto-death, the structure of being-mortal.
Death as an existential is thus a mode of being, a way to be, in fact *the*
way in which Dasein exists. It is an essential part, if not, indeed, the
culmination and crown of human life.[15]

Can the analysis of death be approached as an existential through the
death of other men? Certainly this is a common part of everyday experience; what family has not known the loss of a loved one? But, on closer
inspection, this avenue offers no real approach to the existential analysis,
since strictly speaking we do not experience the death of another. We can
be present at the moment of another's death, but we do not live the
experience ourselves, we do not know death "from within." In such an
experience, death does not reveal itself in its own proper being, as a
determination of *my own* existence. The only death which I can ever
experience from within will be my own, and then, unfortunately, it will
be too late for an existential analysis.

Accordingly, neither the death of another nor one's own death is a phenomenon which offers material for an ontological analysis of existence. Since there is thus no ontic-existentiell access, the only way that remains open is that of existential analysis. Heidegger accordingly returns to the line of reasoning which led to the elaboration of the being of Dasein as concern. Following this pattern, he attempts to uncover the existential structures of death, in order to formulate a purely existential-ontological concept and definition (SZ 237–40). We shall accompany him in this pursuit, sketching first the existential structure of death according to the three constitutive elements of concern, and then completing the sketch by considering death as it manifests itself in life.

B. *The Analysis of Concern*

As we have seen, the being of Dasein comprises three elements or moments: existence or being-ahead-of-itself; facticity or thrownness, by which Dasein finds itself as already-being-in-the-world; and finally fallenness, or being-with the things encountered in the world.

The moment of existence or being-ahead-of-itself means that Dasein understands itself by projecting itself against the horizon of its possibilities. Death is one of these; in fact, it is the possibility of all possibilities, because it stands ahead of Dasein in a unique way, forming the most ultimate possibility of its being. Put crudely, the last thing that Dasein can be, is dead. But death is the extreme possibility of existence in a much more profound and less ontic way, in the sense that it has an aspect of totality which no other possibility has. It enfolds and engulfs all other possibilities, just as it enwraps Dasein's total being-in-the-world, wholly and entirely. In this possibility, "the issue is nothing less than Dasein's being-in-the-world. Its death is the possibility of no-longer-being-able-to-be-there" (SZ 250). As Heidegger provocatively expresses it: "death is the possibility of the complete impossibility of Dasein" (SZ 250), "the possibility of the impossibility of any existence at all" (SZ 262). Death, then, involves the totality of Dasein's own irreplaceable and incommunicable being, all that is most distinctive, proper, and personal to Dasein. Death is the most its own (*eigenste*) of all the possibilities of Dasein. Moreover, death throws Dasein completely on its own, causing it to stand alone, and dissolving all of its relations to other beings; it is thus a nonrelational (*unbezügliche*) possibility. And since this is the extreme and total possibility, Dasein has no resources to avoid,

26

overtake, or recover from it; death is thus an insuperable or unsurpassable (*unüberholbare*) possibility (SZ 250).[16]

The element of facticity in concern reveals the thrownness of Dasein; through its ontological disposition Dasein finds itself already-in-the-world. Insofar as death belongs to being-in-the-world, Dasein is also thrown into death, which it finds as its ultimate possibility-to-be. Thus Dasein exists as thrown being-unto-death; thrown unto its own most distinctive possibility, which is nonrelational and unsurpassable (SZ 251).

The third moment of concern, fallenness, reveals Dasein as being-with other beings confronting it in the world, among which it generally exists inauthentically by accepting from them external norms for its activity. Inauthenticity is especially noticeable in the matter of death, for here Dasein tends to follow the crowd most abjectly, accepting the evasive and pacifying general attitude that death is really not relevant to life, indeed not even to be mentioned in polite, enlightened conversation. If at times one becomes aware that he too must face death, one sidesteps the problem with the comforting cliché: "Of course everybody must die some day, but . . . not just yet." In this way Dasein effectively blinds itself to the existential reality of death as something written ineradicably into its basic ontological structure, and therefore as an ever-present possibility of its own being. Dasein flees from its own death; it exists in a mode of inauthentic flight which conceals death as an existential (SZ 252).

This brief analysis according to the three moments of concern thus reveals death as the possibility-to-be of Dasein (1) which is most distinctively its own, nonrelational, and unsurpassable, (2) into which it is thrown, and (3) from which it usually inauthentically flees by concealing its true nature.

C. *The Analysis of Our Everyday Certainty*

Our everyday inauthentic being-unto-death knows about death, even with certainty. But the certainty is beclouded by a falsely pacifying equivocation, which reveals itself in the thought: "One must die some day, but not just yet." More accurately this means: "But *I* am not going to die just yet." The anonymous "one," which initially includes the speaker, is unthinkingly turned into a completely nonpersonal "one," who is really "no one." This "no one" dies, but "certainly not I."

Can such an equivocal and evasive attitude contribute anything toward a genuine existential concept of death? The everyday certainty of death is based on the undeniable empirical fact that men die. But since this certitude comes from the outside rather than from within oneself, and is always related to other men and not oneself, it does not strike Dasein in its own uniqueness but only as a vague "someone," who also has to die some day like the others. The death of which Dasein is certain is thus strictly speaking not its own, but that of a vague "someone." There is accordingly the possibility of evading and ignoring death in its existential minoness, as something which is individually and exclusively one's own.

But precisely this phenomenon of evading death shows that man is certain of death on a level of existence much deeper than that of external sensible experience. For if he had merely an empirical certainty of death, a conviction coming only from without and referring not to his own death but only to that of others, why then would he feel it necessary to protect *himself* from death? Why must *he* flee, why must *he* equivocate in order to be comforted in the face of death?

These questions indicate that man's fear of death comes rather from within, from a primordial self-knowledge involving the awareness of one's own existential fragility. The death from which man flees because of his everyday certainty is not death rendered harmless by being relegated to the realm of the misfortunes of others, but death insofar as it constitutes a threat to one's own being, or, ontologically speaking, insofar as it pertains to the basic structure of one's own existence; otherwise flight would be pointless. Man is sure of death from within. He knows death insofar as it touches his own being. In fact, he is just as certain of death as he is of his own being-in-the-world, for death is merely the reverse side of this same coin.

The phenomenon of flight from death reveals what it was trying to conceal: that Dasein has a certainty about death which is not purely external and empirical, but rather interior and existential, because rooted in Dasein's very existence as one of its constitutive structures. This type of certainty differs also from the purely theoretical certainty of scientific knowledge. In fact, "it does not belong at all to the gradations of evidence we can have about the present-at-hand . . . [but] is more primordial than any certainty that relates to entities encountered within-the-world or to formal objects; for it is certain of being-in-the-world [itself]" (SZ 265).

Thus the vain attempt to rest satisfied with a merely empirical certainty about death, which would leave open the possibility of evading the question of one's own death, shows rather that death is a possibility which is so profoundly a part of Dasein's structure that it is existentially certain, as certain as existence itself (SZ 257–58, 265).[17]

There is a further point. By the innocent sounding phrase, "but not just yet," Dasein is furtively trying to deny to death its ever-present possibility, to postpone death to some indeterminate future, to a "sometime." Paradoxical though it may seem, Dasein is endeavoring to attach a temporal definiteness to its certainty about death, by assigning it a place in the distant future. But this further attempt at subterfuge only reveals another essential structure of the existential concept of death, namely, that it is completely indefinite and undetermined with regard to its "when." The desire to put off death into an indefinite future is inauthentic, precisely because the possibility of death cannot be put off; death is possible at each and every instant. The certainty of the fact of death is thus coupled inextricably with the uncertainty or indeterminacy of its "when." The everyday flight from the ever-present existential possibility of death thus reveals that death is an indeterminately certain possibility of Dasein (SZ 258).

On the basis of the analysis just completed, first of the three moments of concern and then of the everyday certainty of death, we can now formulate the full existential concept of death. Death in the existential sense is the thrown being of Dasein unto its own most proper and distinctive possibility, which is nonrelational, unsurpassable, certain, and indeterminate with respect to its "when," from which Dasein generally flees in an inauthentic attempt to conceal its true nature.

III. *Inauthentic Being-unto-Death*

How does the phenomenon of inauthenticity present itself in the matter of being-unto-death? The anonymous "someone-self" knows death from its experience of the death of others. It sees death merely as a "case of death," an everyday event that one reads about in the papers and sometimes experiences among one's own friends and relatives. Death is not at all conspicuous, but is simply taken for granted as part of everyday life. Thus death sinks to the status of a completely normal occurrence, something that crosses the ken of one's existence fleetingly, without leaving any traces, without exciting any special notice or raising any special questions; it is reduced to a condition of bland inconspicuousness.

This inconspicuousness makes it possible to talk about death impersonally and without involvement, to let death disappear into the equivocation of the phrase, "everybody has to die some day, but it's not my turn yet." Dasein succumbs to the temptation to ignore death as a structure of its own existence, to cover up the fact that death is the most distinctive possibility of its own being. Thus an inauthentic being-unto-death is further marked by the structures of equivocation and temptation.

Moreover the inauthentic someone-self tries to console itself and others regarding death. It speaks words of sympathy, it tries to distract the sorrowing and even the dying themselves from thoughts of death. It tries to tranquilize, to calm and pacify itself and others in the face of death.

This equivocal, tranquilizing attitude does not even allow genuine anxiety to arise in the face of death as Dasein's possibility of totality, but generates an ontic fear of an ordinary impending occurrence. While genuine anxiety would bring Dasein to confront itself in its totality, and would thus open the way to authenticity, fear is regarded by public opinion merely as cowardly insecurity, as weakness which is to be conquered or at least hidden from view. Ontic fear of death, rather than leading to authenticity, can do no more than estrange Dasein from its own most proper possibility and thus from its own authentic self (SZ 252–55; cf. 177–78).

These structures—inconspicuousness, equivocation, temptation, tranquilizing, and estrangement—are all characteristics of everyday inauthentic being-in-the-world. They reveal inauthentic being-unto-death as continual evasive flight from death, by which Dasein distorts, misunderstands, and conceals death as its own most intimate, proper, and distinctive possibility-to-be (SZ 254).

The result of these considerations is not merely negative. The inauthentic flight from death witnesses to something positive, namely, that Dasein is subject to the law of death even in its most unthinking everydayness. Even in inauthenticity, death is a critical issue. Dimly, but really, Dasein knows about death as its own most proper and most distinctive, nonrelational and unsurpassable potentiality-to-be, even if this is merely in the deficient manner of an untroubled indifference. Thus the discussion of Dasein's inauthentic attitude opens the way to a study of its proper comportment, of authentic being-unto-death.

IV. *Authentic Being-unto-Death: The Existential Project*

How should Dasein properly understand and comport itself toward death? Heidegger answers this question in two stages. First he projects an outline of authentic being-unto-death in its underlying existential-ontological structures. Second, he tries to show that this existential projection is also existentielly and ontically realistic—capable of being realized in actual existence. Looking at these two stages from another angle we may say that Heidegger attacks the problem of authentic being-unto-death by seeking the answers to two questions: (1) If authentic being-unto-death is possible, what must be its existential or ontological structure? (2) Is there a phenomenon in Dasein which guarantees the existentiell possibility of this hypothetically projected structure?

A. *The Structure of Advancing*

The existential outline or project of authentic being-unto-death takes its orientation from the structures of the existential concept of death. Death is an existential, a possibility of Dasein, indeed the possibility of totality, of being itself in a total way, since it is the one possibility which includes all other possibilities. Authentic being-unto-death will be that understanding and comportment which holds firm to the true nature of death, refusing to ignore it as an existential possibility. It will be, as Heidegger says, a view which endures the possibility of death precisely as a possibility (*die Möglichkeit des Todes als Möglichkeit aushalten*). This enduring, or holding out against the possibility of death Heidegger calls "advancing" or "running forward" toward death (*Vorlaufen in den Tod*). It thus represents the exact opposite of the flight from death which epitomizes inauthenticity.[18]

The distinctive characteristic of advancing is that it stubbornly confronts the possibility of death as a possibility. Thus it is distinguished from several other conceivable attitudes, such as pondering, meditating on, brooding over, wondering about, or awaiting death as an event due to occur at some particular point in time. In all of these attitudes the pure possibility-character of death becomes mingled with actuality, and thus the essential nature of death as an existential, as a possibility-to-be, is lost sight of (SZ 261–62).

Combining the notion of advancing toward death in its full character as possibility with the elements of the existential concept of death already established, we uncover the following ontological structure of authentic being-unto-death. The understanding of death as the most proper and distinctive possibility of Dasein leads to the realization that it is precisely through death that Dasein is liberated from domination by the impersonal "someone" (*das Man*). Since death touches Dasein in its own reality, determining its existence individually and irreplaceably, the attitude of advancing toward death, of confronting it as an ever-present possibility of one's own being, is the first step toward recovery from the inauthentic condition of the someone-self, which lets itself be completely swayed by public opinion.

Death is also a nonrelational possibility of Dasein. Thus, the more resolutely we advance toward it, the more clearly we see the aspect of aloneness which characterizes Dasein in its being-unto-death. Advancing reveals that all being-with the other beings which make up one's world, whether in the mode of taking care of nonhuman things or caring for other men, fades away in the sight of death. The ever clearer realization that death cuts all one's innerworldly ties thus opens the way to the authentic acceptance of responsibility for one's own completely individualized being.

Advancing toward death as the unsurpassable possibility of Dasein brings it about that all one's other possibilities assume their proper place in the total picture of existence. These other possibilities are seen to be merely intermediate, since they lie "this side of" the outermost possibility of death and fall under its finalizing influence. They are all limited, determined, and in a sense defined by the fact that Dasein exists as being-unto-the-end. In the face of the unsurpassable, insuperable, and irretrievable possibility which is death, they are seen to be surpassable, repeatable, and thus, as compared with death, merely preliminary and secondary. Realizing this, Dasein is armed against the danger of absolutizing any of its intermediate possibilities or of becoming hardened at any state of existence already reached, since it knows that no stage can be definitive except that of death itself. Dasein remains a traveler, continually on the way toward its ultimate possibility-to-be, which is written existentially into its very being.

Advancing toward the unsurpassable possibility of death has also what may be called a social function, because it enables Dasein to understand and evaluate the possibilities of its fellowmen. Seeing that no possibility is absolutely definitive but that of death, and that this is accordingly the most important potentiality for all men, Dasein can more easily resist the temptation to ignore the existence-possibilities of others or to attempt to force them to serve its own. In this way Dasein not only becomes free to embrace its own ultimate possibility, but also makes itself free for the sake of others. Advancing toward death as the unsurpassable possibility thus produces a certain balance with respect to the sharp individualization revealed through advancing unto death as the completely nonrelational possibility of Dascin (SZ 263–64).

The comportment of advancing is the only possible way to ensure the existential certainty of death as an ontological structure constituting one's own being. Any other attitude, since it fails to face realistically the possibility of death as a possibility, as we have seen, glosses over the true nature of death. Anything less than such "enduring" of death robs this existential structure of its full reality by looking at it in its ontic actuality, which lies comfortably in the as yet unreal future. Only in the attitude of advancing unto death as the extreme possibility of its own being can Dasein see death "from within," i.e., from the viewpoint of its own internal structure. Only thus can it overcome the temptation to consider the certainty of death as being merely empirical and therefore external to one's own being. Dasein is in this way authentically certain of its own being-unto-death only insofar as it gives itself over to this possibility by advancing toward it (SZ 264–65).

Here we have an outstanding example of the hermeneutic circle intrinsic to Heidegger's methodology. On the one hand, the existential concept of death includes the certainty of death, and therefore, Dasein should advance toward it. But on the other hand, it is precisely the advancing which solidifies the certainty of being-unto-death. Is this a vicious circle? How can Dasein advance toward something which itself is rendered certain only through the advancing?

To find a way out of the impasse we must recall what the existential analysis is trying to do. Its purpose is not to uncover essential attributes or qualities of man's nature in the sense of traditional metaphysics, but rather to work out the structures of the concrete actions by which Dasein achieves its existence. Traditional metaphysics is concerned with the nature and essential properties of man, prescinding from the question of whether there really are existing men or not.[19] But the analysis of *Sein und Zeit* focuses upon the self-experience of an actually existing man in the concrete acts of his existence; thus it is rightly called an "existential" analysis. Accordingly, what might be a vicious circle in traditional metaphysics, which operates according to the laws of formal logic, is, in the existential analysis, an example of the reciprocal relationship of various factors frequently found in human activity. There is in man's actions such a thing as mutual causality, or, in the terminology of the existential analysis, there is in Dasein an ontological circle-structure.

In the present case, wherein the notion of death requires advancing toward it, and the advancing makes us all the more certain of the accuracy of our notion, the circular structure of existence becomes apparent. The phenomenon is common enough: in any matter of real existential importance, our conviction grows in proportion to the intensity of our dedication or commitment. In such phenomena as our response to another person in faith or love, for example, logic is not enough. One cannot wait until he is metaphysically certain of the worthiness of another before giving himself in love; otherwise love would never start. Rather, love is born and grows in direct proportion to the strength of one's commitment, just as one's commitment grows in direct proportion to the strength of one's love.

In like manner, one's certainty of death as a possibility of one's own being grows in the measure in which one embraces it by "advancing" toward it, just as one advances toward it in the measure in which one is certain of its ever-present existential possibility. Without the active acceptance of death which is implied by advancing, Dasein's certainty of death remains merely empirical, external, temporally distant, personally inconsequential, and therefore inauthentic. Only the attitude of advancing can secure and solidify the certainty of death which was already implicitly understood in the existential concept.

The last characteristic of the existential concept of death is indefiniteness regarding its "when." How does advancing illuminate this aspect? By enduring the ever-present possibility of death Dasein holds itself open to a continual insecurity, a constant threat. Authentic being-unto-death must hold out against this threat; in fact, it must even increase it by a continually growing understanding. How is this possible? What structure enables Dasein to hold itself open in this way? Heidegger answers: the fundamental disposition of anxiety (*Angst*).

Anxiety is for Heidegger a privileged locus of revelation of the being of Dasein. In the experience of anxiety all the innerworldly beings subside into insignificance. Anxiety reveals to Dasein that it is radically "not at home" in the midst of beings, since these can become meaningless and even completely vanish from him. In contrast to fear, which always has a definite object, anxiety is a disposition caused by no particular object at all, but rather by the very fact of one's being-in-the-world. In anxiety Dasein is anxious not about any particular being, but about the total horizon within which all its encounters with beings take place; furthermore, this horizon itself is no particular being, in fact not a being at all, but rather a "no-thing." Anxiety thus brings Dasein face to face with the seeming unreality, the "nothingness" of its own being-in-the-world (SZ 184–91).

But this experience of the radical tenuousness, even the apparent ultimate unreality, of existence is also characteristic of advancing unto death. Advancing brings death more and more clearly into focus as the constantly threatening possibility of the impossibility of existence. It uncovers the ever-present possibility of the fading away of all innerworldly beings. Thus, advancing toward death has an inner affinity with the phenomenon of anxiety. In fact, Heidegger sees anxiety as pertaining essentially to the structure of advancing, and therefore to authentic being-unto-death: "Being-unto-death is essentially anxiety" (SZ 265–66).

B. *Formulation of the Structure of Advancing*

Following the lead of the elements of the existential concept of death, we have elaborated the structural moments of advancing, which is the existentially projected outline of authentic being-unto-death. How can all this be drawn into a unity? Heidegger formulates the following conclusion: "Advancing reveals to Dasein its fallenness into the 'people-self' and brings it face to face with the possibility of being itself, radically unsupported by [the distraction of] taking-care-of [things] or caring-for [people], but rather being itself in impassioned freedom unto death, liberated from popular illusion, facticious, sure of itself, and anxious" (SZ 266).

This is an extremely dense and harsh sounding formulation. Let us attempt to pierce through the terminology to the ideas expressed, by describing each of these elements in terms of the preceding discussion of the structural elements of advancing.

(1) "Advancing reveals to Dasein its fallenness into the people-self": advancing shows death to be the most proper and distinctive and therefore the most individualizing possibility of Dasein; thus it counteracts the pernicious influence of merely external "public opinion"; (2) "and

brings it face to face with the possibility of being itself, radically unsupported by [the distraction of] taking-care-of [things] or caring-for [people]": insofar as it reveals death to be the completely nonrelational possibility of Dasein, advancing shows that the ultimate possibility is one in which all being-with other beings, both in the mode of taking-care-of and caring-for, must inevitably fade away, so that Dasein must accept itself, of itself, and for itself alone; (3) "being itself in impassioned," i.e., in an attitude of complete dedication and utter abandonment to its own most distinctive, nonrelational and unsurpassable possibility-to-be; (4) "freedom unto death": advancing makes it possible for Dasein to accept freely and thereby give itself over unreservedly to its own proper nature as being-in-the-world destined irretrievably for death; (5) "liberated from popular illusion," i.e., freed of the inauthentic popular misconception of death as a mere everyday event, and free to accept the authentic understanding of death as Dasein's most proper and distinctive possibility-to-be; (6) "facticious," as being-unto-death whose thrownness is revealed in the basic disposition of anxiety; (7) "sure of itself," that is, having solidified the existential certainty of death by actively accepting it as the structure embracing and guaranteeing the totality of its existence; (8) "and anxious": because of the indefiniteness of the when of death, Dasein must hold itself open to the ever-present possibility of the dissolution of its being-in-the-world, and must thus keep itself in the disposition of continual anxiety.

It must be borne in mind that this formulation is the summary of an existential projection, which Heidegger accordingly intends to be understood always in an ontological sense. Many of the terms used are charged with ontic, even emotional, overtones—"running forward toward death," "impassioned," "freedom unto death," "liberated from popular illusion," and "anxious." Thus there may be a strong temptation to interpret these terms ontically, especially since some of them are used here for the first time, without any previous preparation to guarantee their ontological purity. But Heidegger's intention is clear enough. The total context in which this somewhat startling formulation occurs is an existential-ontological one, namely, the existential outline or projection of human authenticity, which in turn takes place within the broader existential-ontological horizon of the entire investigation being carried out in the pages of *Sein und Zeit*.

Of course there is the further question of whether Heidegger has always chosen the most felicitous terms to express his thought. But this question is a literary rather than a philosophical one, and need not detain us here. Suffice it to say that Heidegger himself was quite aware of the terminological difficulties involved in trying to give expression to new modes of thought. He saw that new uses of language, even such as might seem to do violence to accepted usage, could not be avoided, if one were really to blaze new trails in the articulation of human existence: "The terminological delimitation of primordial and authentic phenomena struggles against the same difficulty which keeps all ontological terminology in its grip. When violences are done in this field of investigation, they are not arbitrary but have a necessity grounded in the facts" (SZ 326–27; cf. similar remarks, 39, 269, 309, 311).

C. Comparison with Inauthentic Being-unto-Death

Heidegger's concept of advancing in the face of death can be further clarified by contrasting it with its opposite, inauthentic being-unto-death. Again taking our orientation from the three moments of concern, as these have been elaborated above, we ask: how does advancing compare with inauthentic being-unto-death, in regard to existence, thrownness and fallenness?

In inauthentic being-unto-death Dasein does not understand itself in terms of the exclusivity (the "mineness") of its own existence, whose uttermost possibility is death. On the contrary, Dasein sees itself as a living human organism, as something present-at-hand which is—happily—still alive, as a being for whom death is not yet a reality, but stands politely out of sight, waiting offstage. Death appears only as an ordinary everyday happening, something reported daily in the newspapers, "a case." Moreover, a case of death is always someone else's, never my own. They die, but not I; or rather, everybody dies, but not yet I. The inauthentic attitude to death thus shows the characteristics of inconspicuousness and equivocation. Dasein learns to ignore its own death and occupy itself with what it thinks are the more immediate and pressing demands of everyday living (SZ 252–53).

The attitude of advancing toward death, on the other hand, makes it possible to understand death as the most intimate and most individual possibility of one's own existence. Instead of falling prey to the inauthentic inconspicuousness of death, Dasein recognizes death as its own ever-present, uttermost possibility-to-be, a potentiality which towers over and embraces all the other possibilities of its being, and is thus of quite a different order from the limited concerns of "everyday living." Death is even seen to be the possibility which gives all one's other possibilities their goal and final meaning, since they all flow into it, converge upon it, and find in it their completion. Thus death, far from being ordinary and inconspicuous, is Dasein's most important and all-pervasive possibility-to-be. Moreover, contrary to the equivocation which marks the inauthentic attitude, advancing acquires an ever clearer and sharper view of death as the most proper, unique, and individualizing possibility of the being of Dasein (SZ 263, 258).

The second element of concern, thrownness or facticity, is revealed by the ontological disposition of Dasein. Using this element as a touchstone to distinguish inauthentic being-unto-death from the existentially projected advancing toward death, we find that the difference may be expressed as that between ontic fear and ontological anxiety. The disposition characterizing the inauthentic attitude toward death is that of fear in the face of an event which has yet to happen. This fear comes to light in the very attempt to conceal it by falsely tranquilizing oneself and others with regard to death, by offering empty and insincere consolation to the bereaved, and by overeager efforts to distract one's thoughts from the morbid unpleasantness of death (SZ 253–54). On the other hand, advancing toward death is accompanied by the basic ontological disposition of anxiety. This consists in freely, consciously, maturely, and soberly holding oneself open to death as a continually imminent, ever-present possibility of one's own being. Anxiety brings Dasein face to face with its total self in the form of its uttermost possibility, and thereby opens the way to authenticity by the acceptance of one's own basic structure as being-unto-death (SZ 265–66).

Inauthentic being-unto-death is, finally, a surrender to the fallenness in which Dasein at first and usually finds itself. This takes the form of an evasive flight, which conceals the true nature of death (SZ 254).

But advancing toward death offers an authentic response to the human condition of fallenness among innerworldly beings. Recognizing fallenness as an existential component of its being, which can therefore never be completely rooted out but at best overcome and controlled, Dasein sees the flimsiness of all the possibilities of self-realization arising from its being-with other beings, since these possibilities are all intermediate or secondary when compared with the ultimate and toweringly transcendent possibility of death.

Thus Dasein can resolve to retrieve itself from fallenness by enduring the possibility of death precisely as an ever-present possibility. It is then in a position to offer constant battle against the distracting influence of everyday activities and concerns. By advancing toward death, it will remain in constant tension between the strong enticements of inner-worldly beings and the clear claim of authentic selfhood. Advancing thus makes it possible for Dasein to exist in dynamic equilibrium between these two poles, to maintain an authentic balance and achieve a true freedom with regard to death as the most decisive structure of its own being.[20]

V. Authentic Being-unto-Death: The Existentiell Realization

The discussion of death in the existential analysis grew out of the attempt to grasp Dasein's being in its totality. Having first formulated the existential concept of death and then briefly investigated the inauthentic attitude toward it, we went on to present Heidegger's "existential project" or hypothetical outline of authentic being-unto-death, by working out the ontological structure of such an attitude. It is now time to test the hypothesis: can authentic being-unto-death be experientially verified in Dasein? Is there a phenomenon that can bring the hypothetically projected authentic being-unto-death into the realm of actuality, or at least show it to be realizable? Heidegger finds such a phenomenon in the call of conscience.

A. Conscience and the Guilt of Dasein

In the traditional understanding, conscience is one of the subjective conditions of human morality, consisting in the knowledge of the moral or ethical value of human acts. According to one modern author, it involves three distinct moments with correspondingly different functions, before, during and after a human act: (1) *before:* conscience proclaims that an act would be honorable or not; thus it commands or forbids, counsels or dissuades; (2) *during:* it makes the subject aware that he is here and now acting well or ill; it is a concomitant aspect of the psychological awareness of the act, insofar as the act is concretely apprehended under the aspect of its ethical value; (3) *after:* it reveals the act to have been morally good or bad; it thus approves or reproves, praises or blames, induces satisfaction or uneasiness.[21]

Heidegger understands conscience somewhat differently. For him it pertains not so much to the realm of knowledge as to that of existence. It is an existential, a determination of Dasein in its concrete being-in-the-world. This interpretation arises not from any arbitrary rejection of tradition, but from the attempt to reduce the popular and metaphysical notions of conscience to their phenomenological-existential ground. As always in the existential-ontological analysis, Heidegger is attempting to uncover the underlying structures which form the foundations for all the manifestations of human existence. In the present matter he proposes to "trace conscience back to its existential foundations and structures and make it visible *as* a phenomenon of Dasein" (SZ 268–69).

How does conscience operate as an existential of Dasein? It is constantly and persistently issuing its call, not in the noisy, overly busy, and equivocating manner of the uncritical "someone," but quietly, clearly, and without concession to mere curiosity. This call has the same triple structure which was previously discovered in the analysis of Dasein's being-in-the-world. The one who is called is Dasein in its fallenness into the inauthenticity of the "anyone-self." That to which conscience calls is authentic existence, in which Dasein understands itself in terms of its own proper possibility-to-be. The one calling is Dasein in its state of "exile," in the homelessness of its thrown facticity. Fallenness, existence, and facticity —these are, once again, the structural moments of concern. Thus the call of conscience (and therefore conscience itself) has its ontological possibility in the fact that Dasein, in the roots and foundations of its being, is concern. Conscience is, existentially speaking, the call of concern (SZ 270–78).

Strictly speaking, conscience has no content; "the call 'says' *nothing* which might be talked about, gives no information about events" (SZ 280). It does not call *from* anywhere or *about* anything, but *to* something, namely to authentic selfhood. And yet, while conscience in this existential sense does not involve any ontic content, it does give one to understand something: that there is a gap between what Dasein is and what it should be. More exactly, conscience transmits the message of the distance between Dasein in its everyday fallenness and Dasein in its possible authenticity. It reveals the gulf between the anyone-self, the mask which Dasein usually wears, and the authentic self which it is challenging Dasein to achieve. In revealing this gap it is showing Dasein the wound of its existential guilt. This is the nonobjective, nonontic "content" of the call of conscience.

The call of conscience is thus for Heidegger the revelation of the guilt of Dasein. Compared with the classical conception, this is a decidedly narrower notion, since for Heidegger conscience is not active before an act or during an act, but only afterwards. Conscience in the existential sense shows up a condition which has already been existing in the very fundamental structure of Dasein. There is also a further departure from the classical view. Traditionally the post factum element of conscience can be either positive or negative, either approving or disapproving, giving either peace or remorse. For Heidegger, however, conscience reveals only a negativity: the guilt of Dasein.

True to his method Heidegger tries to reduce the classical concept of guilt to its existential ground. In scholastic metaphysics guilt is a kind of evil. Evil is a privation of good, a lack of some due perfection; guilt is such a lack in the area of free human acts. Thus, according to Thomas Aquinas, "evil . . . is a privation of good. . . . Now the evil which consists in the lack of proper operation in matters involving the will has the nature of guilt. For guilt is imputed to someone when there is a deficiency in an action of which his will is the author."[22]

Heidegger's existential analysis, however, views guilt not as a privation or lack of something which should be present, for such determinations fall within the area of things which are merely present-at-hand, rather than the transcendental region of Dasein's existence as concern and as the there of being. He finds two elements in the concept of guilt which provide the basis for an existential definition: negativity, since guilt means *not* being or doing what one should; and responsibility or "being-the-basis-for" some thing or action. He accordingly formulates the existential concept of guilt as follows: "being the basis for something determined by a 'not'—that is, *being the basis of a negativity*" (SZ 283).

Is Dasein guilty in this sense? We have seen that Dasein is necessarily concerned about its own being. Its being is handed over to it as a responsibility which it has to take over; it not only is, it has to be. Thus Dasein is a basis for something, namely, its own power-to-be.

Moreover Dasein is deeply affected by a "not." Its thrownness means that it did not bring itself into existence and never becomes complete master of its own being, even though it has the unavoidable task of taking over its own being by existing. As existence Dasein projects itself against the limited horizon of its own possibilities, into which it has been thrown, and each of which necessarily excludes other possibilities. As being-with, it has the tendency to fall into inauthenticity. Thrownness, existence, fallenness—once again we meet the moments of concern. Their negativity means that concern itself, which forms the being of Dasein, is essentially affected by a "not," is necessarily negativized. Dasein as concern is thus the basis of its own negativity; as such it is existentially guilty (SZ 284–85).

B. *Resoluteness: Hearing the Call of Conscience*

The correlative of calling is hearing. The proper hearing of the call of conscience consists in the willingness to be called, and, in the context of the existential guilt of Dasein, this means understanding and choosing oneself in the basic negativity of one's being. Hearing the call of conscience thus involves the affirmation of oneself precisely in one's own existential guilt.

The basic disposition corresponding to such self-understanding is anxiety, for existential guilt does not touch any particular aspect of Dasein, but rather its being-in-the-world as such. The mode of expression belonging to this type of anxious self-understanding is, paradoxically, silence. Since conscience issues its call soundlessly in order to summon Dasein back to the stillness of its true self, it can be perceived only if Dasein is not clogging the airwaves with noise. Heidegger thus describes the proper hearing of the call of conscience as "the understanding of oneself in terms of one's [existential] guilt, which is quiet and ready for anxiety." This he sums up in one word: "resoluteness" (*Entschlossenheit*) (SZ 296–97).

Resoluteness is not a psychological attitude or habit, not a conscious desire or determination, not "an empty '*habitus*' or an indefinite 'velleity,' " not "a special mode of behaviour of the practical faculty as opposed to the theoretical" (SZ 300). It is simply the existential structure of proper listening to the call of conscience, the attitude arising from willingness to acknowledge and accept one's own existential guilt, and to be summoned back to authenticity. Resoluteness is required if Dasein is to find its way back to its true self. It is thus a necessary condition of authentic existence.

Is this to be understood as a justification of solipsism, as if Dasein should become totally self-enclosed in the stubborn affirmation of its own faulty structure and cut itself off from all other beings? Solipsism can never be an authentic mode of existence for Dasein, since Dasein is essentially being-in-the-world; it exists necessarily among other beings. Resoluteness even calls special attention to this fact, since it hears the message of conscience about Dasein's inauthentic existence among these beings, and thus implicitly affirms its structure of being-with. Thus, instead of isolating Dasein from its world, resoluteness rather brings it face to face with this world, since it summons Dasein into its true situation as the being which exists as existentially guilty and as being-with other beings.

The term "situation" must also be understood existentially. It is not meant ontically, as a network of things, circumstances, events, and happenings which constitute the external framework of Dasein's activity, but rather as the internal ontological structure which makes such activity possible. Dasein's situation is his own being-in-the-world, insofar as this is the ground of all his actual decisions and actions. Moreover, his situation becomes clearer and more manifest in proportion to the degree of resoluteness with which he accepts and affirms his own basic three-dimensional structure. Situation is thus part of the existential self-knowledge which is contained in resoluteness (SZ 297–301).

C. Advancing Resoluteness

As the proper hearing of the call of conscience, resoluteness is one of the conditions of possibility of authentic existence. As such, it must have a relation to the entire basic structure of Dasein, to all three of the moments of concern. As readiness to accept one's own existential guilt, resoluteness enables Dasein to assume an authentic attitude to the moment of thrownness or facticity, since it consists precisely in the acknowledgment of Dasein's already-being-in the world. Moreover, insofar as resoluteness summons Dasein into its situation, it is the ground of authenticity in regard to the moment of being-with, or the aspect of Dasein's fallenness. But what is its relation to the moment of being-ahead-of-itself, to Dasein's projecting and understanding of itself against the background of its authentic possibilities-to-be?

The asking of this question leads us once again to the theme of death, since death is Dasein's existential of totality, its extreme and most all-embracing possibility. In Heidegger's construction of the existentiell realization of authenticity, resoluteness accepts guilt as an ever-present existential structure of Dasein. Moreover, this constant guilt extends to the entire being of Dasein, even unto its end. Resoluteness is thus full and authentic only insofar as it acknowledges and accepts being-guilty up to the end, that is, insofar as it coincides with a being-unto-death which simultaneously accepts the being-guilty of Dasein.

Thus it may be said that resoluteness reaches its own authenticity only by being combined with advancing toward death. Through advancing, resoluteness receives the existentiell modality which brings it to full authenticity. On the other hand, advancing, which up to now has been seen merely as a hypothetical existential projection, receives its existentiell guarantee and verification through the addition of resoluteness. The combination of these two thus gives Heidegger what he is looking for. Advancing plus resoluteness adds up to the existentially structured (by advancing) and the existentielly guaranteed (by resoluteness) authentic power-to-be of Dasein (SZ 305–306, 309).

It may be asked whether the combination of advancing and resoluteness is not an external adding together of two elements which have no real internal connection. Closer inspection, however, reveals that it is much more than that; the combination is a natural one, arising from the inner dynamics of resoluteness itself. Resoluteness, as we have seen, performs the function of listening properly to the call of conscience. By so doing it recalls Dasein away from its lost condition as a mere "anybody-self" to the possibility of being its authentic self; advancing then enters the picture and makes this power to be one's real self completely authentic by revealing death to Dasein as its own most proper power-to-be. Second, the call of conscience individualizes Dasein by reducing it to its own being-guilty; advancing further sharpens and completes this individualizing process by introducing the awareness of death as the nonrelational power-to-be of Dasein. Third, resoluteness opens to view the constant guilt of Dasein, which antecedes every incurrence of factual guilt through concrete acts, and therefore cannot be eliminated by any individual act of atonement or recompense; advancing, in turn, uncovers the final and most fundamental ground of this irretrievability of guilt, by incorporating the existential guilt into the absolutely irretrievable possibility of death (SZ 307).

Carrying further the parallel between resoluteness, as the response to the call of conscience, and the existential analysis of death, we find that resoluteness has its own type of certitude just as the existential concept of death has. Resoluteness is sure of the existential guilt of Dasein. It is, as it were, certain about its own uncertainty, sure of its own insecurity. For in resoluteness Dasein becomes more and more aware that it cannot absolutize any one situation or hold on forever to any one decision, but must keep itself continually open to change, revision, disappointment, renunciation.

This attitude might seem to be the opposite of resoluteness in that it forces man to refrain from all decisiveness. But in actual fact, it is merely the acknowledgment of things as they are, and is thus the confirmation of authentic resoluteness. For by remaining ever open to unforeseen events and influences, Dasein remains ever aware of its own negativity, of the lack of control implied by its own existential guilt.

But what does this have to do with death? The certainty contained in resoluteness tends toward holding oneself open for any and all possibilities, and eventually for the totality of its possibilities-to-be. But again, the last of these possibilities is death. The certainty implied in resoluteness is thus crowned and completed by the certainty contained in advancing toward death as the extreme power-to-be of Dasein, for death is the existentially certain possibility in which Dasein gathers itself together and gives itself up in its totality (SZ 307–308).

Insofar as resoluteness makes Dasein painfully transparent to itself in its guilty negativity, it brings with it the knowledge of the indeterminacy prevailing throughout the whole of Dasein's existence, which consists precisely in the alternative possibility of living authentically or inauthentically. But it is advancing toward death which reveals the fullness of this indeterminacy, for it opens to view the greatest indeterminacy of one's power-to-be—death. Thus the anxiety included in resoluteness reaches its term in advancing toward death; the anxiety of resoluteness, which is the basic disposition of Dasein in the face of its own guilty negativity, achieves its fullness in the anxiety attendant upon advancing, since this is anxiety arising not from any particular aspect of Dasein, but from the indeterminately certain possibility of the impossibility of existence itself (SZ 308).

This comparative analysis of resoluteness and advancing is revealing from still another point of view. It shows that the moments of the existential concept of death are primordial tendencies which lie implicitly concealed in the attitude of resoluteness and come to their fulfillment in the attitude of advancing toward death. Thus, resoluteness is authentically and completely what it should be, only if it is an advancing resoluteness: only by including the attitude of a free acceptance of death can resoluteness become the authentic power-to-be-whole (*Ganzseinkönnen*) of Dasein.

Thereby it also becomes clear that the question of the possible power-to-be-whole of Dasein, which came up originally merely as a methodological requirement, has now taken on a more realistic character. The question was first raised in order to guarantee the completeness of the existential analysis of Dasein, but now it is seen to reach not only into the existential-ontological structure but also into the ontic-existentiell realization of Dasein's concrete existence, since it is decisive for the actual achievement of Dasein's authenticity (SZ 309).

Advancing resoluteness or resolute advancing is thus the authentic being-unto-death we have been seeking. The combining of the constitutive elements of the two concepts of advancing and resoluteness enables us to formulate the following description of authentic being-unto-death: it is the understanding and acceptance of oneself in terms of the negativity of death as one's own most proper and distinctive possibility-to-be (which is nonrelational, irretrievable, and unsurpassable, certain and yet indeterminate as to its when), which negativity first announces itself through the call of conscience to the silent and unprotestingly anxious acknowledgment of one's own existential guilt; this self-understanding reveals to Dasein its condition of being lost in the inauthentic state of the anyone-self, and brings it face to face with the possibility of being its own true self by accepting and affirming its negativity in an impassioned freedom unto death, liberated from popular illusion, facticious, sure of itself, and anxious (cf. SZ 258–59, 266, 296–97).

One final question remains: is this authentic being-unto-death merely a partial aspect of the total authenticity of Dasein? Or are these two "authenticities" identical? Basically they are one and the same. Death, as we have seen, is not merely one possibility-to-be among others, but the extreme, final, and all-embracing possibility of Dasein; it is *sui generis*, towering above and containing all other merely intermediate possibilities. Therefore the conscious acceptance of death in resolute advancing is meant to permeate one's whole existence. Since only death is the most proper, intimate, and individual possibility of Dasein, only death can confer its own authenticity on every other attitude of Dasein. As death is the only existential of totality, so resolute advancing is Dasein's only

46

authentic power-to-be-whole. Outside of authentic being-unto-death, Dasein has no other authenticity. Authentic being-unto-death and the authenticity of Dasein are thus one and the same: advancing resoluteness.

VI. *The Ontological Meaning of Being-unto-Death*

Our investigation began with a question about the meaning of being. In order to ask this question properly, we investigated the mode of being of the particular being which asks this question—man considered as Dasein. Since we have uncovered the basic existential structures of this being—Dasein as guilty being-unto-death, whose authenticity is advancing resoluteness—we are now in a position to ask the question of the meaning of Dasein to determine the meaning of the being of *this* being, in order thereafter to be able to ask the question of the meaning of being itself.

A. *Temporality as the Meaning of Being-unto-Death*

The question of meaning has been previously formulated in the following terms: what do we really mean when we say such and such? At this point of the analysis Heidegger works out more exactly what is contained in that formulation. He defines the concept of meaning in the following steps. In common parlance the meaning of something is that which makes it intelligible, understandable. But for phenomenology meaning is that which makes something understandable without being thematically understood, or even explicitly seen in itself. Moreover, this meaning makes something understandable by revealing it in its enabling ground or condition of possibility. Meaning in this sense, however, is nothing else but the *being* of a being. Meaning and being thus coincide. The meaning of something is accordingly its being as its ground of possibility, insofar as this remains unthematic and yet renders the being in question accessible to understanding (SZ 323–25).

When Heidegger seeks the meaning of Dasein in the context of his existential phenomenology, he can only look for an immanent meaning, i.e., one contained within the phenomenon itself, for his method consists in letting that be seen which shows itself of itself, and in the way in which it shows itself. Accordingly, he understands meaning as the interior ground of a being which enables it to be understood, in clear distinction from the broader sense of the term, which would define meaning as a goal or purpose lying outside the being in question, toward which it is directed, or for the sake of which it exists, or which it is meant to serve; for instance, the meaning of war as the eventual reestablishment of peace. Heidegger prescinds completely from any consideration of such extrinsic meaning. His existential-ontological meaning-question is rather this: what is the ultimate interior ground which makes the existence of Dasein possible and understandable? (SZ 325)

Authentic existence has been seen to consist of advancing resoluteness. This has a triple structure, corresponding to the structure of concern whose authenticity it represents. Advancing toward death is the concretion of the moment of concern which we have described as being-ahead-of-itself; resoluteness in the face of one's own guilt concretizes the moment of already-being-in; and the summons into one's situation is the concrete expression of the moment of being-with. In a bold analysis, Heidegger now brings these three moments of authentic existence into a unity which he calls "temporality," which in its turn constitutes the ontological meaning of Dasein in the sense explained above.

According to the constitutive moment of being-ahead-of-itself, Dasein understands itself by projecting itself against the background of its possibilities-to-be. In advancing resoluteness Dasein understands itself in terms of its own most proper and distinctive possibility, death, and endures this possibility as a possibility. Thus it stands before itself in its own most extreme power-to-be, or, looking at it from the other direction, it allows itself in its own extreme possibility to come to itself. This "coming to" is an advent, an approaching of the future into the present. Heidegger calls the meeting with oneself in one's own extreme possibility-to-be the primordial phenomenon of futurity. It is the revelation of the dimension of the future in the heart of Dasein's existence.

Second, in advancing resoluteness Dasein accepts its own existential guilt, which consists of the negativity of its thrown facticity or its already-being-in. It comes back to itself and recognizes itself for what it has always been; it comes back to its already-having-been. Here we have the roots of another common time dimension, the past. Finally, advancing resoluteness is a summons to a situation, to the authentic acceptance of fallenness or being-with, the structure through which Dasein encounters the beings surrounding it in its world. This encounter is made possible by the presence of beings within the world, and thus represents the primordial phenomenon of the present (SZ 325–26).

Advancing toward death, resoluteness with regard to existential guilt, summons into a situation: these three moments of authentic existence are possible only on the basis of the three primordial phenomena we have just discovered: letting oneself come to oneself, coming back upon oneself, and encounter. These, says Heidegger, are the three basic existential phenomena which give rise to temporality. Corresponding to these are the three commonly accepted dimensions of time. In other words, authentic existence is made possible and meaningful by the fact that Dasein in its basic existential-ontological structure is futural, having-been, and presencing: in short, by the fact that it is fundamentally temporal. The ultimate ground of authentic existence, and thereby the ontological meaning of the being of Dasein, is accordingly temporality.

Is temporality, thus understood, another structure of Dasein besides concern and being-unto-death? Heidegger calls temporality the *meaning of concern*. It is thus not a structure added to concern but rather its interior ground, the most basic structure which makes concern possible and understandable. This also means that temporality is the innermost meaning of being-unto-death, for being-unto-death in its full reality as the unity of the three moments of death, guilt, and situation—as the triple unity of orientation toward death, existential guilt, and existing in a situation—constitutes the whole being of Dasein and is thus identical with concern. Temporality, as the meaning of concern, is at the same time the meaning of being-unto-death and of the being of Dasein itself.

B. *Temporality and Authentic Being-unto-Death*

The analysis of advancing resoluteness has led to the discovery of temporality as the meaning and ground of the existential-ontological structure of being-unto-death. What is the relation of this temporality to the ontic-existentiell accomplishment of advancing resoluteness, to authentic being-unto-death in its existentiell realization?

In advancing resoluteness, Dasein lets itself come to itself in its extreme possibility-to-be. But this is possible only insofar as Dasein *can* come to itself—insofar as Dasein is futural in its very being. Thus the ontic-existentiell accomplishment of advancing is grounded in the ontological temporality of Dasein. Conversely, however, it is advancing which leads the ontological temporality to its own ontic-existentiell authenticity; advancing makes Dasein authentically futural by the very fact that in advancing Dasein consciously affirms its own deepest and most fundamental futurity, the ultimate possibility which is coming to it: death.

Second, advancing resoluteness is the appropriate listening to the call of conscience as it summons Dasein to the acknowledgment of its own guilt. This takes place insofar as Dasein comes back to itself as the ground of its own negativity. But this presupposes that Dasein has the ability to come back to itself, to exist as already "having been." Thus the existential-ontological past of Dasein is the ground of possibility of the ontic-existentiell affirmation of one's guilt. On the other hand, this aspect of authentic being-unto-death, namely, the acceptance of guilt, brings the ontological temporality of Dasein to its existentiell authenticity, by the fact that it lets Dasein come back to itself in the true negativity of its thrownness, and thus lets it exist authentically as "having been."

Further, advancing resoluteness entails the summons into a situation. But this is rendered possible only by the fact that Dasein can encounter other beings in its world, or, in other words, that Dasein exists in the way of "presencing." It is this existential-ontological presence-structure which forms the basis of possibility for Dasein's ontically and existentielly giving itself over to its situation. And again conversely, it is precisely the advancing and resolute dedication to a situation which constitutes the authentic realization of the existential present of Dasein.

There thus appears a remarkable relation of reciprocity between temporality and authentic being-unto-death. On the one hand, temporality is the ontological meaning and the enabling ground of authentic being-unto-death. Dasein can let itself come to itself in its extreme possibility through advancing, come back upon its guilt resolutely, and respond to its situation authentically, only insofar as it exists in the roots of its being as futural, having-been, and presencing. In other words, Dasein can exist as authentic being-unto-death only insofar as its innermost ontological meaning comprises the three aspects of futurity, past, and present. On the other hand, the ontic-existentiell realization of authentic being-unto-death produces the authenticity of Dasein's temporality. The illuminative power contained in advancing resoluteness brings Dasein to the awareness of its own deepest structure and this structure's ontological meaning. Advancing resoluteness causes Dasein to become increasingly conscious of its three-dimensional and three-directional structure, thus leading to the understanding of temporality as the fundamental inner meaning of existence (SZ 325–26).

C. *Temporality and Inauthentic Being-unto-Death*

If temporality is the meaning and ground of authentic being-unto-death, one may legitimately ask: is it also the meaning of *inauthentic* being-unto-death? The answer is yes, and, as might be expected, the meaning of inauthentic being-unto-death is inauthentic temporality, the concealing or disguising of authentic temporality by the ordinary everyday understanding of time.

The popular unreflective concept of time corresponds to the inauthentic mode of Dasein's everyday existence, according to which it exists as an anonymous anyone-self. In this manner of thinking, time is conceived as something external to man, part of the extrinsic framework in which he exists. Time is pictured as a line, along a particular stretch of which a man's life moves. The line itself is composed of a series of time points, which succeed each other like chain links emerging limitlessly out of a machine up ahead, and passing irretrievably and irreversibly into the darkness behind. On the time-line, only the immediately present now is real; the future now's have not yet arrived, and the past now's are no more.[23]

As this conception sees the now or the present as the primary dimension of time, it provides the basis for the inauthentic mode of existence in which Dasein loses its true self in the immediate concerns of everyday life. Under the pressures of the present, Dasein generally tends to devote its energies to the affairs immediately confronting it; it busies itself with details and often with mere trivialities, so that it all but disappears in the here and now. In this state of fallenness among the beings making up its immediate world, Dasein loses sight of its even more primordial structure of being-ahead-of-itself. It ignores the future and lives for the day. It misreads its own being as something merely given, static, bluntly here and now, instead of something stretched toward the future, something to be achieved, something yet to come. As a consequence, Dasein blinds itself to its own most important and uttermost future possibility, death. This seemingly natural tendency is further fortified by the unpleasantness of death, so that Dasein not only mistakes its own being as being-unto-end, but also seeks refuge in the distractions of the present by an evasive flight from death. Thus the inauthentic understanding of temporality is the reason for—the ground and meaning of—inauthentic being-unto-death (SZ 424–26).

Conversely, the inauthentic flight from death solidifies the everyday misunderstanding of the true nature of time. By allowing itself to be taken up with the details of everyday life and thus to be distracted from its being-unto-end, Dasein readily succumbs to the illusion that "there is always time left." Since "everyone dies some day, but of course, it's not my turn yet," Dasein in its inauthenticity aspires to the amassing of as much time as possible for itself, hoping to lay claim to as great an amount of the unlimited supply of now-points as possible. Thus the misconception is strengthened that time is an infinite succession of points without beginning and without end, of which every man receives his definite allotment. As long as Dasein remains a prisoner of this inauthentic view of time, the true origin of this conception from the authentic intrinsic temporality of Dasein remains unknown (SZ 424–25).

However, we saw earlier that the inauthentic flight from death unwittingly reveals what it tries to conceal—the true nature of death as an ever-present existential of Dasein. The very fact of flight makes known the presence of that from which one is fleeing. Likewise the inauthentic understanding of time contains within itself the roots of authentic temporality. Even the most naïve men know that "time passes." Regarding this platitude Heidegger asks: "why do we say that time *passes* and not, with just as much emphasis, that it arises?" (SZ 425). Obviously, it is because Dasein even in its inauthenticity knows more about time than it wants to admit. From its "fleeing" knowledge of death, it knows too that time is "fleeing" or "passing away." It is aware that time is moving toward an end, a finish, and thus that it is finite. "In the kind of talk which emphasizes the passing of time, there is plainly reflected the *finite futurity* of Dasein's temporality" (SZ 425).

Moreover, the everyday interpretation of time sees the time-line flowing irreversibly in only one direction. Although the image of time as a line is inauthentic, still the perception of irreversibility conceals within itself an understanding of primordial authentic time. Why should the succession of now's be irreversible if it were merely a set of absolutely similar, completely equal now-points? If this were the case, the points would be wholly undifferentiated from each other, and then what could account for their differentiation in direction? The reason must come not from the nature of the imaginary "time-line," which is really a fiction, but from the nature of Dasein, the being who recognizes time and who consciously and reflexively lives in time. The reason for the irreversibility of the "time-line" stems from the fact that this conception of time is a secondary, derivative mode of authentic primordial time, namely, the temporality of Dasein, which is in a real sense irreversible, because Dasein is primarily and undeniably futural, passing away by moving toward an end or finish, i.e., fin-ite. Insofar as Dasein is being-unto-end, temporality is also "unto-end," and therefore the "flow" of time is irreversible (SZ 426).

Here we see another example of the reciprocal relation between Dasein's temporality and being-unto-death. Inauthentic temporality (time as a succession of now-points, of which only the present point is real) is the ontological meaning and ground of inauthentic being-unto-death (the flight from the future into the present). On the other hand, inauthentic being-unto-death in its ontic-existentiell realization uncovers the inauthenticity of the everyday conception of time, and thereby offers the opportunity of overcoming this condition and arriving at an authentic understanding of temporality.

For an appreciation of Heidegger's understanding of Dasein, it is important to note that the reciprocal relation between existential-ontological and ontic-existentiell mirrors the fundamental circularity characteristic of Dasein's whole structure. This double movement has recurred several times throughout the existential analysis, for instance, in the existential projection of authentic being-unto-death, in the existentiell realization of authentic being-unto-death, in the relation between temporality and being-unto-death in the mode of authenticity as well as in that of inauthenticity, and, as will be seen below, in the relation between temporality and the historicity of Dasein. There can be no doubt that the circularity of Dasein, reflected in Heidegger's hermeneutic methodology, is one of the key concepts for the proper understanding of the existential analysis, and thereby of *Sein und Zeit*.[24]

D. *Historicity and Being-unto-Death*

History, as it is commonly understood, is a consequence of man's living in time. This is also true on the existential-ontological level: an existential type of historicity is intimately connected with Dasein's temporality, so that "the interpretation of Dasein's historicity is . . . just a more concrete working out of [its] temporality" (SZ 382). From Heidegger's analysis of historicity we shall single out two points which will serve to illuminate further the theme of death: historicity in the ontological structure of Dasein, and historicity in the ontic-existentiell dimension of authentic being-unto-death.

It could perhaps be objected that the existential analysis has up to now been one-sided, for it has fixed its attention exclusively on death, saying nothing at all about Dasein's relation to its birth. After all, death is only one of the two extremes of a man's life-line; shouldn't birth, as the other limit, be given equal consideration? Moreover, the prolonged discussion of being-unto-death has ignored the extent of Dasein's existence *between* birth and death. Shouldn't something be said about Dasein's being-unto-beginning, and about the extension of its existence between birth and death? (SZ 372–73)

This objection arises from the everyday understanding of time and history, according to which time is a succession of neutral now-points and history is a chain of events or human experiences occurring at individual points along the time-line. The history of an individual man in this conception is a determined series of events, filling up a particular stretch of the time-line. And only the event which is present-at-hand in any particular now is real; past experiences exist no longer and future experiences have not yet arrived. Thus a man stands always at a particular now-point, which is circumscribed on both sides by the unreal points leading backward and forward to the unreal limit-points of his birth and death.

That this is a possible and, in its own way, legitimate image of a man's life history, need not here be disputed. But from the foregoing discussion of Dasein's existential temporality, it should be evident that this is a derivative image, and an essentially defective one at that. For in this conception neither a man's death nor his birth receives any serious consideration. Birth is simply something once experienced, a past happening which is no longer real, just as death is something to be experienced someday, but now by no means real. This neutral view ignores any real influence of birth or death upon Dasein's present existence. It is at best a very pale and lifeless notion of time and history.

The existential analysis, on the other hand, shows the significance of death as an ever-present existential structure, which determines Dasein's being as a whole and at every moment of its existence, just as it leaves the door open for considering the profound significance of birth, by bringing to light the thrown facticity of Dasein. Understood existentially, birth is by no means merely a past fact which is no longer real, but

54

something taken up into the ontological structure of Dasein as an aspect of its thrownness. Indeed, it can be said that both birth and death are always present in the concrete realization of Dasein's existence: "Facticious Dasein exists as born, and, as born, it is already dying in the sense of being-unto-death" (SZ 374).

Accordingly, the historicity of Dasein does not consist in the fact that its existence is stretched out on the time-line between the two points of birth and death, but much more in the fact that it *is*, in the ground of its being, this very extension, or, to take liberties with language again, Dasein *is* this very stretched-outness. Dasein exists as temporality spread out three-dimensionally, extended forward toward the futurity of death and backward toward the pastness of its thrown facticity, thus being held in dynamic suspension in the presentness of its situation. Dasein is historical not because it stands at a particular point on the time-line between the two end-points of birth and death, but because it is existentially-ontologically temporal. Dasein is itself an event, a happening, insofar as temporality happens or comes-to-be in it.[25]

Because of the existential historicity of Dasein, the existentiell realization of authentic being-unto-death is also historical. Advancing resoluteness is a happening, an event, in which Dasein accepts as its own the tripartite structure of temporality, and affirms it in the concrete form of being-unto-death, existential guilt, and situation. At this point Heidegger raises the question: whence does Dasein draw the concrete possibilities-to-be which constitute its particular situation, and what is the relation between these possibilities and the possibility of death? (SZ 382–83)

Of itself, advancing toward death has no power to open to view the facticious possibilities of authentic existence, since this is concerned exclusively with the ultimate possibility-to-be of death itself. These possibilities are rather revealed in the process of coming-back-upon-itself which constitutes resoluteness; furthermore, they are seen to arise from the heritage of one's thrown existence. However, the advancing exercises a decisive influence upon these possibilities, playing both a constitutive and a regulative or normative role.

Advancing toward death is constitutive of the facticious possibilities of authentic existence insofar as these are possibilities of a Dasein which is itself destined for death as its own ultimate possibility; just as Dasein itself, so all of Dasein's day-to-day possibilities are touched at their core by the possibility of death. Moreover, death is normative for all the other

possibilities of Dasein, insofar as these can only be authentically understood and brought to realization if they are seen in the light and perspective of the preeminent possibility of death. The unity of Dasein as
being-unto-death requires that all of its retrievable, repeatable, intermediate, and thus secondary possibilities be built into the primary, unrepeat-
able, and irretrievable possibility of death. Death is not merely one of the
de facto possibilities of Dasein but rather *the* 'transcendental' possibility,
towering over all others in such a way as to include and enter into all of
them as part of their very structure. Death is therefore structurally constitutive of all other possibilities of Dasein, as well as normative for their
authentic realization.[26]

Advancing toward death as the transcendental possibility of Dasein is
thus the decisive element of the three-membered authenticity of existence
(advancing toward death, resoluteness toward guilt, summons into situation). It is thus also the aspect which guarantees the authentic wholeness
of any particular, actual realization of existence. "Only advancing toward
death drives out every accidental and 'provisional' possibility . . . ,
snatches one back from the endless multiplicity of possibilities which
easily suggest themselves, such as comfortableness, taking things lightly,
shrinking back, and brings Dasein into the simplicity of its *fate*" (SZ
384).

By "fate" (*Schicksal*) Heidegger means the authentic grasping of the
particular concrete situation in which Dasein finds itself, "handing oneself
over to the there of the moment" (SZ 386). It is essential to note that the
"moment" in which man achieves his authenticity is not the blind now-
point of the everyday inauthentic conception of time, but rather a moment
of vision, insight, and understanding, when Dasein senses its responsibility
to exist as the "there" of being.[27]

Advancing thus brings it about that Dasein "is in a moment of vision
for what is world-historical in its current situation" (SZ 391). By taking
seriously the ongoing process of its existence as being-in-the-world and
reacting responsibly to the concrete possibilities of its situation as finite
being-unto-death, Dasein can exist in an authentically historical way. In
this manner, advancing is the ground of the authentic realization of
Dasein's historicity: "Authentic being-unto-death . . . is the hidden
ground of the historicity of Dasein" (SZ 386).

Having reached this point, we may consider as completed the existential analysis of *Sein und Zeit* under the particular aspect of the problem of

56

death. Dasein exists as being-unto-death; the ontological ground and meaning of this is temporality, which expresses itself as historicity; existence is a three-dimensional, temporal, historical happening. On the one hand, temporality-historicity is the ontological ground of being-unto-death, since the three-directional stretched-outness which constitutes temporality is pointed inevitably toward an end. On the other hand, the authenticity of the temporal-historical structure of Dasein lies in the adequate existentiell achievement of being-unto-death, in tripartite advancing resoluteness. In its existential-ontological structure Dasein is temporality, concern, and guilty being-unto-death existing in-the-world. It exists authentically in the measure in which it accepts and ontically-existentielly realizes these structures in advancing resoluteness.

VII. *Death and the Image of Man in* Sein und Zeit

Having completed our sketch of this bold and often disturbing picture, we must step back and look at it again. What kind of an image of man is projected by Heidegger's existential analysis? What precisely is the role of death in this image? And finally, does it leave the way open for the further pursuit of Heidegger's main intent, to pose the question of the meaning of being?

First we must recall that Heidegger insists more than once that it is *not* his purpose to construct an anthropology, but exclusively to clear the ground for the proper posing of the question of being; thus it is not his intent to project an image of man. However, it would be hard to deny that a very definite picture does, as a matter of fact, arise from the existential analysis of *Sein und Zeit*.

Is man according to Heidegger a heroic-tragic figure, bearing the cruel but inescapable wounds of finitude, negativity, and even nullity, whose picture is finished off by the final stroke of death? Does Dasein exist as being-unto-nothingness? And is the analysis of death really nothing but a desperate attempt to overcome death by stubbornly facing it down?

Heidegger would answer no to these questions. Authentic being-unto-death does not propose to overcome death, but rather to grant it its proper freedom through the adequate understanding of it, so that it can assume its proper, controlling place in Dasein's existence. Moreover, this "freedom unto death" through advancing resoluteness is not a heroic-tragic gesture of despair, but rather "springs from a sober understanding of what are *de facto* the basic possibilities of Dasein"; it is accompanied not by fear or terror, but by "fortified joy" (SZ 310).

However, many of Heidegger's critics find these assurances far from comforting. They interpret the analysis of death, as well as the entire existential analysis in *Sein und Zeit,* as heroic, tragic, pessimistic, nihilistic. To cite one such critic among many, Rudolf Beerling calls Heidegger's conception a "tragic world-view"[28] and sees the condition of Dasein, hemmed in between the two nothingnesses of thrownness and being-unto-end, as evidence of a "basic conviction [which is] nihilistic";[29] moreover, nothingness is the *basso continuo* sounding amid all the variations on the theme of Dasein.[30] He sums up the Heideggerian image of man in a provocative pun, calling it a "deadly realism": "All that remains is man in the scaffolding of his essential finitude, with no possibility of refuge in any metaphysical context of meaning and no interior shelter in any order of society, liberated but at the same time robbed of all illusory ties to 'here' and 'hereafter,' a spiritual being sunk in the abyss of nihilism, but, without a trace of pessimistic apathy, responding to the summons of this lot through the acceptance of his own possibilities, which he clearly recognizes as negativized, in an attitude of, literally speaking, *deadly realism.*"[31]

Critics such as Beerling are doubtless correct in concluding that the practically unavoidable impression produced by the first reading of *Sein und Zeit* is one of pessimism and tragedy. Nevertheless, Heidegger holds fast to his assertion that the existential analysis is a purely ontological investigation. As such it lies before and outside the scope of ontic attitudes such as optimism and pessimism; in its existential purity it is ontically quite neutral. Thus he writes: "the existential definition of concepts must be unaccompanied by any existentiell commitments, especially with regard to death. . . . The existential problematic aims only at setting forth the ontological structure of Dasein's being-unto-end" (SZ 248–49). On the one hand we have the assertion that the existential analysis is tragic, pessimistic, even nihilistic in tone; on the other, Heidegger claims it is ontically neutral, pure, noncommittal. What are we to think?

A. *The Two Sides of* Sein und Zeit

Beerling himself gives a hint toward a solution of this seeming contradiction by pointing out a certain two-sidedness in *Sein und Zeit*. He thinks that Heidegger's thought in *Sein und Zeit* purports to be a philosophy of being, while in reality it is a philosophy of man, an existentiell anthropology. Accordingly, the ontology of Dasein as a preparation for the posing of the being-question would be nothing more than a mask for Heidegger's real intent to construct an emotionally colored ontic-existentiell anthropology of the existentialist school.

The hypothesis that *Sein und Zeit* has two sides is most helpful in that it suggests the possibility of an authentic and inauthentic understanding of the book, perhaps even in Heidegger's own mind. But it seems that this hypothesis must be applied in the opposite direction from the one taken by Beerling. The *authentic* philosophy of *Sein und Zeit,* what the book really intends and accomplishes at its most profound level, even though this may not adequately come to light, is the philosophy of being, the ontology of Dasein in terms of its usefulness for the question of being itself. The fact that Heidegger is primarily aiming at the being-question is clear from the numerous references to this question as the goal and horizon of all the individual analyses of *Sein und Zeit.*

The fact that the book does not first appear to be a philosophy of being follows from its exclusive preoccupation with the analysis of Dasein, which, according to the original plan, should have constituted only the first two sections of the first half of the total work.[32] Since neither the last section of the first half nor the second half ever appeared, there has arisen, perhaps unavoidably, a distortion in the interpretation of *Sein und Zeit.* It has been looked upon as a book complete in itself, and Dasein has correspondingly been understood as being completely closed in upon itself and sufficient unto itself so that even *being* seems to be completely subordinated to it. But this is a superficial understanding of *Sein und Zeit;* it considers only the face which the book shows at first sight, but which does not correspond to its true purpose. The authentic *Sein und Zeit* is a projected ontology, a philosophy of being, which is being prepared for by the preliminary analysis of the particular being which asks the being-question.

It is the inauthentic side, the existential analysis insofar as it creates the impression of being an ontic-existentiell theory of man, that gives rise to the dark and forbidding picture of a being who achieves his true greatness by the joyfully stubborn affirmation of his own nothingness. Insofar as the book produces such an image, the characterizations "pessimistic, tragic, heroic, nihilistic" are justified, but an accurate understanding of the book's true purpose demands that these be applied only to its *inauthentic* philosophy.

The confusion of these two aspects has produced the "existentiell misunderstanding" to which many of Heidegger's critics have fallen prey. One of the German commentators favorable to Heidegger, Max Müller, has declared that the missing third section of the first half of *Sein und Zeit* would have achieved the original intention of going beyond Dasein to being itself, and would thus have established the primacy of being in Heidegger's thought by showing that time and everything connected with temporality receives its meaning only from being itself. Thus the authentic meaning of the book would have come to light, a meaning which unfortunately now can only be drawn out of the "profound and laborious words of the Hölderlin interpretations and the various epilogues and prologues to the other published lectures."[33]

Heidegger himself later makes explicit reference to the missing section of *Sein und Zeit*: "The section in question was held back because [my] thought failed in the adequate expression of this turning, and did not come through successfully with the aid of the language of metaphysics."[34]

Another recent commentator, Walter Schulz, confirms the connection between the existentiell misunderstanding and the newness of the path along which Heidegger was attempting to move: "Contrary to the 'existentiell misunderstanding,' as if Heidegger were trying to describe, if not even to proclaim, the nihilistic-heroic man of the period after the first World War, those who were able to penetrate more deeply into this work recognized that here a new beginning was being sought for philosophy."[35]

The "new beginning," which made it impossible for Heidegger to complete *Sein und Zeit* at the time of its original publication, and which has consequently led many critics into the "existentialist" misinterpretation of the book, consists in the fact that Heidegger is attempting to give an *ontic* foundation to *ontology*, to ground the philosophy of being in an ontic point of departure—in the particular being who asks the being-question, man or Dasein (SZ 13, 436). The tension which is thus set up between the ontic and the ontological in the analysis of Dasein is no more than an echo of the fundamental tension between the two poles of Heidegger's entire project. There is the ever-recurring question whether ontology or its ontic foundation is primary, whether being or Dasein is in command. At the heart of Heidegger's very methodology, in the fact that he approaches the question of being through the analysis of Dasein, lies the seed of a struggle for primacy between these two elements. This contest is not resolved in *Sein und Zeit,* but continues in Heidegger's succeeding works.

But granting that the ontic image of man projected by *Sein und Zeit* is the inauthentic side of the book, it may still be asked why this image turns out to be a pessimistic, heroic-tragic one. Here, it seems, one must admit that the picture is decidedly influenced by a particular ideal of human existence lying at the basis of the existential-ontological analysis. Heidegger admits freely that there is such an ontic ideal at work in *Sein und Zeit*: "But isn't there a definite ontic conception of authentic existence, a facticious ideal of Dasein underlying our ontological interpretation of Dasein's existence? This is indeed so. . . . Philosophy should never try to deny its 'presuppositions,' but neither may it simply admit them. It grasps them, and unfolds with more and more penetration both the presuppositions themselves and that for which they are presuppositions" (SZ 310). This general principle is applied explicitly to the analysis of death in the following words: "The fact that an existential analysis of death contains overtones of the existentiell possibilities of being-unto-death, lies in the nature of all ontological investigation" (SZ 248).

What were the influences contributing to the somberness in tone of the image of man created by *Sein und Zeit?* While a complete enumeration is perhaps impossible, there is good evidence that the following factors were at work.

First of all, the thought of Nietzsche played an important role. One of the sharpest of Heidegger's critics, Adolf Sternberger, has documented this influence in great detail, pointing especially to the similarity between Heidegger's advancing toward death and Nietzsche's *amor fati,* as well as between Heidegger's authentic existence and Nietzsche's "superman."[36] A more favorable commentator, Peter Fürstenau, also points out the great significance which Heidegger attributed to Nietzsche, whom he considered the "last thinker of the West."[37]

Second, Heidegger was certainly stimulated by the writings of Kierkegaard. Several commentators, among them Rudolf Beerling and Alphonse de Waelhens, give extended analyses of the Kierkegaardian elements which found their way into Heidegger's thought, there to undergo a certain transformation. According to the majority of these critics, the transformation consisted in the fact that Heidegger rigorously excluded all theological elements for the sake of his purely philosophical-phenomenological analysis, and thereby cut out the dimension of religious hope which is found in Kierkegaard.[38]

Third, like any other being, the book *Sein und Zeit* is a historical phenomenon. This means that one cannot expect it to have no relation at all to the times in which it was thought out and written, i.e., the uncertain and often chaotic period after the First World War, which was filled with political, economic, social, and intellectual turmoil in Europe, when practically all the accumulated wisdom of previous generations seemed discredited and thus capable of offering little or no support to men's minds and spirits. Undoubtedly this atmosphere exercised its influence on the composition of *Sein und Zeit*. Nevertheless it is still possible to agree with the assertion of Walter Schulz, that Heidegger was not endeavoring to "describe, if not even to proclaim, the nihilistic-heroic man of the period after the first World War."[39] This was indeed not Heidegger's intention, for his authentic philosophy, even in the existential analysis of Dasein, is a philosophy of being, an ontology. But the fact that such a "nihilistic-heroic" description arises from the pages of the book is undeniable. This aspect forms, as stated above, the inauthentic philosophy of *Sein und Zeit*.[40]

B. *The Role of Death in* Sein und Zeit

As we have seen, the theme of death is introduced to guarantee the completeness of the analysis of Dasein. Thus death is not considered ontically, as an event which enters into existence at a particular point, but rather ontologically, as an ever-present possibility of Dasein. Instead of ontic death, Heidegger is primarily concerned with death as an ontological structure, that is to say, with man's being-unto-death, or with death as a constitutive element of the being of Dasein.

Moreover, since death is the extreme or uttermost possibility of Dasein, it is the key to authentic selfhood. Once Dasein recognizes this as an existential structure of its own being, in fact as its own most proper and distinctive, nonrelational, unsurpassable, and irretrievable possibility, for which it cannot delegate anyone else as its representative, all false sense of security and all chance of evasion disappear. Death thus throws Dasein back upon its own resources and forces it to assume responsibility for its own authenticity. The proper understanding of this possibility is therefore capable of snatching Dasein out of the illusory refuge it finds among the beings of its world and of freeing it from the domination of "what everybody thinks," from the inauthentic someone-self. In this sense the adequate appreciation of being-unto-death is the ground of possibility of authentic existence.

But if man can understand himself authentically only by accepting the nonrelational possibility of death, in which he must stand completely alone, must not every other realization of existence be done absolutely nonrelationally, so that solipsism becomes the only plausible philosophy? Isn't Dasein in its being-unto-death so completely reduced to its own resources that it is entirely closed in, self-sufficient, autonomous, and even posited as something absolute? Furthermore, doesn't Heidegger's analysis cause the hard and irreducible fact of ontic death to disappear in the intangible realm of the "ontology" of Dasein, where it ceases to be a real threat by being swallowed up as part of the underlying "structure"? Doesn't Heidegger succeed in so "ontologizing" death that it loses its inexorable power over man and is thus rendered harmless?[41]

Even though there are aspects of the existential analysis which seem to lend support to such charges—one is reminded of the harsh-sounding formulation of the meaning of advancing toward death: "radically unsupported," "impassioned freedom unto death," "liberated from popular illusion," "sure of itself and anxious"—still it is apparent that this interpretation does not do justice to the complete thought of *Sein und Zeit*. It seems to overestimate the importance of death by attributing to it not merely a decisive, but an exclusively decisive role.

Death is indeed the extreme possibility of Dasein, and the understanding of man's being-unto-death is consequently the indispensable condition of authentic selfhood, but death is not the only element of Dasein's structure, which is always tripartite, nor is the understanding of being-unto-death the only prerequisite for authentic selfhood, since this comprises not only advancing unto death but also resoluteness with regard to one's existential guilt and responsiveness to one's situation. It must be remembered that the ontological ground and meaning of Dasein, that which gives Dasein its ultimate and most profound unity, is not death alone, but three-dimensional temporality. Death is the uttermost concretization of futurity, only one of these three dimensions.

Therefore one cannot simply fasten upon the analysis of advancing as if this constituted the whole of authenticity. The complete being of

63

Dasein and the full authenticity of existence comprise all three moments: being-unto-death, existential guilt, situation. If the being of Dasein is simply referred to as being-unto-death, this is merely an abbreviated way of speaking, a *denominatio per partem principaliorem,* in which the three-membered totality is referred to under the name of its most important, but not its only, constitutive element.

Consequently, Heidegger does not simply call authentic existence "advancing unto death," but rather "advancing resoluteness," a term which refers explicitly to two of the three moments, but which is meant to include all three. Authentic existence consists in the process whereby Dasein, through advancing toward death, is thrown back upon its own existential guilt, in order to be able to exist authentically in its situation. All three moments of this process are indispensable. Advancing eliminates neither guilt nor the structure of being-with, but rather provides the necessary basis for these two moments and thereby for the entire structure.

But one might further object: doesn't authenticity mean that Dasein stands alone as a completely autonomous judge, seeing everything from its own point of view and in reference to its own self? Does not Dasein thus become something absolute, a law unto itself, the sole norm of its own existence? Doesn't *Sein und Zeit* declare explicitly: "Dasein can be authentically itself only if it makes this possible for itself of its own accord"? (SZ 263)

Again it must be admitted that there is some evidence for this interpretation. But it seems that these words are susceptible of a deeper meaning which does not necessarily involve an unrealistic autonomy of man—that all norms of authentic existence must become operative from within, must be accepted and affirmed personally and individually. Extrinsic norms, such as the heritage of family, race, nation, culture, and even religion, are of no value for the attaining of authentic existence unless a man interiorizes them, consciously makes them his own. It can even be said that the achievement of authentic existence does have something absolute about it; even though the individual self receives profound influences from its environment, still, when all is said and done, the conscious acceptance of oneself and one's own existential responsibility is the absolutely necessary condition, the first moment of the process of realizing authentic existence, and it can be done by absolutely no one else but oneself.

Understood in this way, Heidegger's analysis is not proclaiming the

64

absolute autonomy of the individual, but pointing out the radical nature and unfathomable depth of man's responsibility for his own being. The realization of this responsibility is the necessary basis for all concrete norms of existing, whatever they may be. This fundamental acceptance of oneself, it must be noted, does not of itself provide a particular set of ethical norms, but merely lays the existential-ontological foundation upon which an ethic must be built. Accordingly, far from being closed up within itself and cut off from other beings, Dasein is actually "opened up" to authentic existence in the world by advancing toward death. Once it begins the process of advancing resoluteness, it begins to be authentically present for its ontic-existentiell association with other beings.

It is precisely in the analysis of death, which so many Heidegger critics have seen as setting the final seal upon the absolute closedness of Dasein, that this openness best comes to light. There are, in fact, many expressions in *Sein und Zeit* which can only be understood as referring to death as something other than Dasein, which Dasein is simply not able to manage or control. Thus, for example, death is said to "enter into" Dasein (*hereinsteht*, SZ 248); Dasein is "delivered over" to its death (*überantwortet*, SZ 251); death is something regarding which Dasein has to take a stand, assume an attitude (*sich verhält*, SZ 250, 260); Dasein has to "take over" its death, for death "lays claim" to it (*übernehmen, beansprucht*, SZ 263); in advancing Dasein "goes under the eyes of death" (*dem Tod unter die Augen geht*, SZ 382), "shattering itself" against it (*an ihm zerschellend*, SZ 385).

These citations should suffice to show that the ontic reality of death is not swallowed up by Heidegger's "ontologizing." Further evidence that ontic death retains its threatening power comes from the indeterminacy regarding "when," which Heidegger has elucidated as an element in the existential concept of death. As another commentator, W. Müller-Lauter, has pointed out, the "when" aspect can refer only to ontic-existentiell death which breaks into existence at a particular point and as a definite event. It is this ontic death of which Heidegger often uses the expression "as long as"; for example: "Dasein, however, can pass away only as long as it is dying" (SZ 247). In such expressions it is clear that the limit of the period of time indicated by the expression "as long as" can be defined only by death in its ontic reality.[42]

But how is death in its otherness and uncontrollability to be understood? Needless to say, it must not be hypostatized as an independent agent or force existing outside Dasein, nor, on the other hand, can it be lightly brushed aside as a mere occurrence breaking in from the outside and having no intrinsic relation to existence. Such conceptions would be merely ontic, and would rob death of its ontological dimension. As something which pertains essentially, and indeed exclusively, to Dasein, death can never be merely ontic, but is something both ontic and ontological.[43] As Heidegger has stated of Dasein itself, so also we must declare of death: its ontic distinction lies in the fact that it is ontological, that is to say, insofar as death is, it is in Dasein and exists as belonging to the very structure of existence.

Thus the existential-ontological analysis leaves the dual character of death intact. Without death as an ontic reality there would be no ontology of death, just as, on the other hand, without death as an ontological structure there would be no ontic death, but at most a blind, unintelligible, nonhuman, purely organic ceasing-to-be. The specific quality of death lies in the fact that it is a structure of human existence and therefore something both ontic *and* ontological. Death thus manifests the tension between the ontic and the ontological which expresses the absolute distinctiveness of human existence, and which lies at the very heart of Heidegger's methodological intent to ground ontology upon a firm ontic base.

C. *The Problem of Being-in-Death*

Reference has already been made to the fact that Heidegger is searching for the immanent meaning of the being of Dasein, which naturally entails the inner meaning of being-unto-death. This meaning he finds in temporality. But particularly with regard to the problem of death, the question of transcendent meaning demands to be raised. Does death have any significance exterior to itself as an existential, a meaning which does not simply coincide with the interior structure of Dasein itself?

Here we are confronted by the age-old problem of immortality, the possibility of life after death, or, in more Heideggerian terms, of the being of Dasein beyond its phenomenologically accessible being. Even the terminological formulation reveals its complexity. If one speaks of life "beyond" death, or of life in the "hereafter" as opposed to life "here," the question is obscured by spatial imagery which does not really suit the problematic of death. Or if one asks about what will come "after" death, one is locating death at a point on a time-line which runs on after death in exactly the same way as before; but this is inadequate because death is itself the outermost limit of Dasein's time-line. As Rudolf Berlinger has remarked, death "is removed from time and can only be thought by detemporalizing one's own thinking"; thus, instead of asking what comes *after* death, one should rather phrase the question: "What is in death, when a man has died?"[44] Following Berlinger's lead, we shall refer to the question of the "after-life" as the problem of Dasein's *being-in-death*.

In Heidegger's view this is a merely ontic question, since it deals only with a particular state of a particular being, rather than with that being's underlying ontological structures, or with being itself. It asks merely: will Dasein continue to be after the occurrence of its ontic-existentiell death? Accordingly it does not fall within the scope of the existential-ontological analysis, and Heidegger can say: "our analysis of death remains purely 'this-worldly' insofar as it interprets this phenomenon merely in terms of the way it enters into a particular Dasein as a possibility of its being" (SZ 248).

Does this mean that Heidegger is answering the question of a possible being-in-death negatively? Adolf Sternberger thinks so; he asserts that Heidegger renders life after death impossible: "Death is the 'total nullification' (*die schlechthinnige Nichtigkeit*) of Dasein, by which it is so completely permeated that nothing at all can be salvaged from it. For if Dasein is 'totally negative' (*schlechthin nichtig*), what could possibly be rescued from annihilation?"[45]

But this judgment seems somewhat rash. Heidegger does not consider death as the dissolution of man, as the separation of soul and body, but rather as a structural determination which serves the function of gathering Dasein into its total existential unity. Death in the existential analysis is not viewed as the "end of the line" for Dasein, but as a possibility-to-be which enables a man both to exist and to understand himself completely. In this context there can be no question of salvaging a part of man out of the destruction of the whole, but only of the significance of death for man's existence. In this perspective, which sees death "re-flexively," by *looking back* from the outermost possibility of existence to the structures which make such existence possible and intelligible, nothing at all is said about the destiny of man after the ontic-existentiell conclusion of life.[46]

Moreover, Sternberger's objection arises out of the everyday understanding of time as a continuous line, which runs on after existentiell death just as before. While this concept of time is useful in speaking of beings and events which are merely present-at-hand, it does not suit the condition of Dasein, which is not merely present-at-hand but existent. Because of its unique character, Dasein does not simply exist "in time" or "on the time-line." Understood existentially, time is not the external framework of Dasein's activity, but its basic interior ontological structure; Dasein exists as three-dimensional temporality.[47]

But what of Heidegger's characterization of death as the total nullification (*die schlechthinnige Nichtigkeit*) of Dasein? Doesn't this amount to a denial of any possibility of a continued being-in-death? The dictionary lists several meanings of *Nichtigkeit*: nullity; nothingness; futility; vanity; perishableness. Actually, the word is a substantive formed upon the base of the negative adverb *nicht,* meaning simply "not." Thus, the most fundamental meaning of *Nichtigkeit* is the condition of being affected by a "not," by a negation of some sort. Death is said to be the total negation of Dasein, because it negates not just one or another aspect, but Dasein's very existence.

Since Heidegger is not thinking of ontic death, this negation is not one which takes effect only at the temporal end-point of existence, but one which coexists with Dasein from the very beginning; it is death as an ever-present existential determination or ontological structure. The negation constituted by death is thus nothing more nor less than the fatal flaw of finitude, about which philosophers have been talking at least since the time of Parmenides and Heraclitus, if not earlier. Heidegger's view is that death is the seal of this finitude written into the very structure of existence, so that man, as finite, exists as being-unto-death. This, however, says nothing at all about the question of survival "after" death, or about Dasein's possible being-in-death.[48]

In other words, the expression "total nullification" really expresses the thoroughgoing negativity induced by death as an existential; it says nothing more than that death is an ever-present structure of Dasein's existence. And yet, in spite of this negativity, Dasein *is.* One could say, perhaps paradoxically, that while Dasein is totally negativized by its being-unto-death, it is, on the other hand, totally *being* because of the power of its existence. Just as everything in Dasein is negativized by its being-unto-death, so also everything in Dasein is positive by virtue of its being. Negativity and positive being, remarkably enough, do not exclude, but rather demand, each other. They exist together and permeate each other so thoroughly that Dasein is just as much "being negativity" as it is "negativized being."

This is precisely the enigma of human finitude, which Heidegger is attempting to grasp. This mysterious duality will turn up again in *Kant und das Problem der Metaphysik* in the form of "finite transcendence." Moreover, it will continue to occupy a central position in all of Heidegger's further writings, with various nuances and under several different names.

We can perhaps discover a further consequence of this duality in the present context. If Dasein is already negativized, insofar as it is completely permeated by the negativity of death, and nevertheless *is,* then it can by no means be concluded that death is incompatible with the existence of Dasein, and must completely annihilate it. The coexistence of these two features seems to prove the opposite—that the existential of death is perfectly compatible with the being of Dasein. If this is so during life, before the occurrence of Dasein's ontic death, then there is no reason to suppose it is not possible after ontic death. The argument thus ends up by indicating not the impossibility, but rather the plausibility of Dasein's continued being-in-death.

It must be pointed out, however, that the above reasoning is based not upon any phenomenological evidence, but upon a postulated parallellism between Dasein's being before and after ontic death. Since this is a postulate and not a conclusion drawn from the phenomena, it has no real binding force in Heidegger's existential analysis. Heidegger, rather, seems justified in asserting that his analysis requires neither the one conclusion nor the other, neither the affirmation nor the negation of the continuance of Dasein: "If death is defined as the 'end' of Dasein . . . , this does not imply any ontic decision as to whether 'after death' still another being is possible, either higher or lower, or whether Dasein 'lives on' or 'survives' and is 'immortal' " (SZ 247–48).

A similar interpretation must be given to Heidegger's designation of death as "the possibility of the impossibility of existence" (SZ 262). What is the "existence" which death renders impossible? As we have seen, existence in the strict sense is the first of the three elements composing the basic structure of concern; by virtue of existence, Dasein is always ahead-of-itself, projecting its self-understanding against the horizon of its various possibilities-to-be. Obviously, *this* mode of being is no longer possible after ontic death, because death is the extreme and outermost of these possibilities. The "impossibility of existence" caused by death could thus mean that Dasein no longer exists in *this* mode of being but in another. It no longer exists in the sense of being ahead-of-itself, because it no longer needs to project itself against its possibilities, but has already reached the stage of definitiveness, in which it is completely identical with its possibilities and with its fully realized self. Thus, death renders existence impossible not because Dasein is completely annihilated, but rather because, after death, Dasein no longer has to be, but simply is its own being.[40]

The existential analysis takes no position with regard to this question, since there is no phenomenological evidence available on which to base an answer. But it is important to note that the question remains open. Heidegger's phenomenology neither denies the "immortality of the soul" nor affirms it. *Sein und Zeit*, because of its method and scope, remains neutral.

If the question of being-in-death cannot be suitably handled in a phenomenology of human existence, where can it be handled? Is it a philosophical problem or does it belong exclusively to theology? Heidegger declines to pronounce upon the issue: "Whether such a question is a possible *theoretical* question at all, will not be decided here" (SZ 248). He is interested exclusively in the existential-ontological understanding of death within the framework of Dasein. Heidegger says the underlying being-structure of Dasein must first be worked out before the problem of ontic-existentiell death can be properly posed: "Only when death is grasped in its full ontological essence can we meaningfully and properly and with methodological assurance even *ask* what may be *after death*" (SZ 248). Thus it seems clear that, for Heidegger, the ontological problematic of death is necessarily antecedent to any consideration of the ontic question: "The this-worldly ontological interpretation of death lies before any ontic other-worldly speculation" (SZ 248).

But, we may ask, what does this "before" mean? Does it indicate a temporal priority, so that a man can only begin to take an attitude to the question of his being-in-death after he has grasped death's "full ontological essence"?

Heidegger cannot mean this, for many, if not indeed the vast majority of men, never succeed in arriving at such a complete ontological grasp, and yet they are forced by the demands of authenticity to assume *some* attitude to their own most distinctive possibility-to-be and its necessary consequences. Thus the "before" must signify an ontological precedence, a priority in being. Accordingly, from the standpoint of ontological thinking or phenomenological questioning about the meaning of being, the ontological problematic of death enjoys primacy over the ontic, since it is foundational with regard to the latter.

VIII. *Summary*

The analysis of death contained in *Sein und Zeit* forms a part of the analysis of Dasein, which in turn is undertaken for the sake of working out the question of the meaning of being. We shall now gather together in propositional form the results of the foregoing interpretation, in order to see what significance they may have for the understanding of the being of Dasein, and thereby for the question of being itself.

1. The discussion of death serves the specific purpose of guaranteeing the completeness of the existential analysis of Dasein.

2. Death as an existential is Dasein's most proper and distinctive possibility-to-be, which is nonrelational, unsurpassable, certain, and yet indeterminate with respect to its "when."

3. Inauthentic being-unto-death consists in an evasive flight from death, marked by the characteristics of inconspicuousness, equivocation, temptation, tranquilizing, and estrangement.

4. Authentic being-unto-death, as a hypothetical existential projection, consists in advancing toward death, in enduring the possibility of death precisely as possibility.

5. Authentic being-unto-death in its existentiell realization, the possibility of which is attested by the phenomenon of the call of conscience, is the combination of advancing toward death and resoluteness with regard to one's existential guilt, i.e., advancing resoluteness.

6. The ontological meaning of being-unto-death is temporality. To the three-dimensionality of temporality there corresponds a triad in the structure of advancing resoluteness: advancing toward death, resoluteness toward guilt, summons into one's situation. The historicity of Dasein consists in the fact that it exists as temporal being-unto-death.

7. The analysis of Dasein manifests a two-sidedness, insofar as it presents the inauthentic appearance of a heroic-tragic philosophy of man as well as the authentic appearance of a preliminary phase of an ontology of being. This duality grows out of Heidegger's intention to provide an

ontic grounding for ontology. The tension thereby created between the ontic and ontological dimensions becomes most pronounced in the analysis of death, which lends itself to two quite different interpretations: (a) death ultimately closes Dasein up within itself, rendering it totally self-sufficient and autonomous; (b) death is the condition of possibility for the authentic openness of Dasein as being-in-the-world. Death itself is both ontic and ontological, since it is both an internal existential structure of the being of Dasein, and an "other" over which Dasein has ultimately no control. Since Heidegger is interested only in the existential ontological interpretation of death, he takes no position with respect to the ontic question of being-in-death.

What does the analysis of death contribute to the understanding of the being of Dasein? It shows Dasein in its totality, in its extreme possibility-to-be, which hovers over all other possibilities and permeates every concrete realization of existence. Likewise, the analysis of death reveals authentic existence to be the enduring of death as the ever-present transcendental possibility of Dasein. This enduring is a process by which Dasein, through advancing toward death, is forced back into the acceptance of its own thrownness, and is then called forth into the situation of its facticious being-in-the-world. In this way the analysis of death offers a penetrating look into the interior structure and the deepest immanent meaning of the being of Dasein, which consists in three-dimensional temporality.

In other words, the analysis of death yields an existential understanding of the *finitude* of Dasein. This finitude appears existentially as being-unto-end, which entails the guilt of thrownness and the fallenness of being-with innerworldly beings. Finitude in the existential sense thus does not mean the limitation of man in his knowing, willing, and acting, nor does it signify existing within the confines of space and time, nor is it simply creatureliness or contingency. Rather it means that Dasein exists *fin-itely*—or, if we were to attempt to reproduce in English the linguistic artifice possible to Heidegger in German—*finish*-ingly or *end*-ingly (*endlich*), as being-unto-end, as three-dimensional, temporal being-unto-death.[50]

The analysis of death produces a second positive result with regard to the being of Dasein and the question of being itself. Insofar as Heidegger's investigation reveals death to be the possibility of the impossibility of existence, i.e., of the impossibility of any comportment of Dasein with the other beings confronting it, it lays open the possibility of the complete disappearance of all the beings in Dasein's world. Thus it gives us a view of "nothingness" or nonbeing. But it must immediately be added, in order to forestall illegitimate criticism of Heidegger as a nihilist, that this "nothingness" is *not* meant as *nihil absolutum* or total emptiness, but rather as the complete negation of innerworldly beings—the disappearance of the network of beings confronting Dasein within its world. This is the "nothing ready-at-hand within-the-world" revealed to Dasein in the experience of anxiety (*nichts von dem innerweltlichen Zuhandenen,* SZ 187). But as Heidegger immediately adds, "this nothing ready-at-hand . . . is not totally nothing. The nothing of readiness-at-hand is grounded in the most primordial 'something,' in the *world*" (SZ 187).

Certainly there are questions which remain unanswered here. What is the difference between "total nothingness" and "nothing ready-at-hand"? Why is the negation of anything ready-at-hand not identical with total nothingness? Further light will be shed upon these questions as our study progresses. But the thing to be noted here is that the nothingness revealed by anxiety and concomitant with death is grounded in "something," so that it can be spoken of only in the context of being, and indeed points to being. Thus, the analysis of death directs our view toward nonbeing, which in turn opens up the prospect of being itself. The death analysis thereby takes the first step toward the question of being, precisely by making a detour through the land of nonbeing.

These two results of the analysis of death, the existential finitude of Dasein and the directing of our gaze toward the veil of nothingness which hides being, are the two signposts pointing the way toward the next stage of Heidegger's thought, the further development of the relation between man and being, which constitutes the horizon of the problematic of death.

3

Broadening the
Horizon

In order to see Heidegger's philosophy of death in true perspective, we have treated it in connection with the leitmotiv which he originally espoused: the question of the meaning of being. After the detailed discussion of *Sein und Zeit* we now turn to the subsequent writings in order to work out the development of our theme. Since death is spoken of only incidentally in these texts, the principal significance of this stage of the investigation lies in the unfolding of the thematic of being which forms the remote context of the theme of death.

The present chapter will focus upon four works dating from the years 1929 and 1930: the interpretation of Kant, *Kant und das Problem der Metaphysik*; the treatise *Vom Wesen des Grundes*; the official address given on the occasion of Heidegger's assuming a professorship at the University of Freiburg, *Was Ist Metaphysik?*; and the lecture *Vom Wesen der Wahrheit*, first delivered in 1930 but not published until 1943. The unity of these four writings lies not merely in their contemporaneity but, more importantly, in their content. Each extends the line of thought of *Sein und Zeit*, and each witnesses to a gradual evolution in Heidegger's view of the relation of man and being.

I. *Finite Transcendence*

Sein und Zeit was chiefly concerned with working out the presupposition for the question of being. To that end, an analysis of Dasein as the locus of the preontological understanding of being was undertaken. The being of Dasein revealed itself as temporality, the three dimensions of which achieve their concretion in the triple structure of being-unto-death, existential guilt, and existing in a situation. Since this finitely structured being is marked by its understanding of being and its inquiring about the meaning of being, the question arises: what is the significance for the meaning of being itself that a finite temporal being poses the being-question? This, however, presupposes the prior, not yet fully elaborated question: how are finitude and the understanding of being related to each other in Dasein? The writings now to be discussed treat of the temporal understanding of being, or the question of *finite transcendence*. The clarification of the relationship between finitude and transcendence in Dasein will more adequately equip us to ask the question of the meaning of being itself.

A. *Transcendence and the Foundation of Metaphysics*

Heidegger's Kant interpretation, *Kant und das Problem der Metaphysik,* appeared just two years after the publication of *Sein und Zeit.* The book gives clear evidence that Heidegger has not lost sight of the question of being as the basic philosophical question, despite his apparent preoccupation with the analysis of Dasein. In the study of Kant, as in *Sein und Zeit,* Heidegger is concerned with "fundamental ontology," the analysis of Dasein for the sake of the correct posing of the question of being.

Heidegger finds this intention anticipated in Kant. Instead of viewing the *Critique of Pure Reason* as an epistemological treatise, as so many Kantian scholars do, Heidegger sees it as a search for the foundation of metaphysics, a quest for the clarification of the basis of ontology, which is the science of being. Here is the novelty of Heidegger's interpretation of Kant: Kant is not primarily interested in exhibiting the conditions of possibility of human knowledge, particularly of the synthetic a priori judgment, but in showing, with the help of these, where, how, and why metaphysics, which is something belonging to the essential structure of

75

man, arises. Thus Kant himself writes: "Now the real task of pure reason is contained in the question: how are synthetic a priori judgments possible? . . . Metaphysics stands or falls . . . with the solution of this problem."[1]

Heidegger sees his affinity with Kant not only in a common basic ontological goal, but also in the means of realizing it. Kant also wished to ground metaphysics through an analysis of man, by focusing on the conditions of man's knowledge. Kant's *Critique* asks about the possibility of synthetic a priori judgments, which are the conditions of possibility of all experience. Insofar as these judgments are antecedent to all ontic knowledge, as the prerequisites which make it possible, they constitute pure, nonempirical, ontological knowledge. According to Heidegger, however, this ontological knowledge is nothing more than the preontological understanding of being—now broadly named 'transcendence'—which appears in *Sein und Zeit* as the prior and enabling ground of all ontic encounter with beings. Thus, for both Kant and Heidegger, the foundation of metaphysics comes down to the problem of transcendence, i.e., the understanding of being which is prior to all experience with individual beings, and which renders such experience possible.

But the problem of transcendence is simultaneously the problem of *finitude*, for human knowledge is profoundly limited. Kant explains this by contrasting human with divine knowledge. Infinite knowledge is not dependent upon beings already in existence, but is such that the known is created by the very act of knowing. In contrast to this *intuitus originarius,* which causes a being to come-to-be in the very knowing of it, man possesses merely an *intuitus derivativus* which can only know beings which already are. Thus, man cannot cause things to 'arise' or 'stand-out' (*ent-stehen*) from nothingness, but only to 'stand-over-against' (*gegen-ste-hen*) himself. While the thing known is for God a 'thing arisen' (*Entstand*), it is for man only a thing standing over against him, an object (*Gegen-stand,* KM 30–31).

Nonetheless, man understands beings in their being. Furthermore, he understands being a priori, prior to any encounter with beings. How is this possible? How can a finite being, which is wholly dependent upon beings for its knowledge, understand a priori the being of beings without itself being their creator? How can a being which is thrown being-unto-death, which possesses no evocative, but only receptive knowledge, nonetheless go beyond beings to their being, and accomplish this prior to all experience? How must man be structured in order to be antecedently attuned to the being of beings? (KM 30–31, 42, 46)

Kant responds by deriving the synthetic a priori judgment from the transcendental imagination. This is the 'constitutive medium' (*die bildende Mitte*) of ontological knowledge; it makes possible the pure synthesis of the synthetic a priori judgment through its 'schemata,' which are "nothing but a priori temporal determinations according to rules."[2]

Heidegger eagerly takes up this statement, in order to stress particularly the role of time. Since the schemata are temporal determinations of the transcendental imagination, this imagination has an intrinsically temporal character; indeed as the enabling ground of the triple pure synthesis (sense intuition, reproductive imagination, thought) it is that primordial time which corresponds to the temporality of Dasein discovered in *Sein und Zeit*. Thus, primordial time or the temporality of Dasein is the ground of possibility of a priori ontological knowledge or finite transcendence. By virtue of his temporality man can project beings against the background of their being; on the basis of his inner three-dimensional structure, he can understand being and thereby know beings. Temporality, by enabling man to reach out and ahead to being, is the condition of possibility for his receptively knowing beings. In short, man can be finite transcendence precisely because he exists as temporality (KM 156–84).

For the sake of clarification we can once again compare this sort of knowledge with infinite knowledge. Infinite knowledge brings beings into being; it produces beings *together with* their being, in one simple, instantaneous act. Finite knowledge, on the other hand, knows beings only because it understands being a priori, i.e., insofar as it has antecedently projected being as the horizon within which beings can be encountered.

This 'indirectness' of our knowledge, the necessity of a previous projection of the horizon of being in order to be able to know beings, is the mark of finitude. Consequently, the understanding of being is not a special privilege elevating man beyond his finitude; it is rather the expression of his transcendental poverty (cf. KM 213). His finitude means that he knows beings only in this indirect, noncreative way. Man not only can, he must, understand being a priori so that he can know the beings upon which his whole existence depends.

Thus, the understanding of being is intimately bound up with finitude in Dasein; indeed the understanding of being is itself "the innermost essence of finitude" (KM 208). Man understands being because he is finite. But this finitude is grounded in the fact that he is thrown being-unto-death existing among beings, and possesses the three-fold structure of already-being-in, being-ahead-of-himself, and being-with. In other words, man understands being because he exists as temporality.

Thus, Heidegger stands once more where he stood at the conclusion of the analysis of Dasein: the basic ground and meaning of Dasein, which makes the being-question and the understanding of being both possible and intelligible, is temporality. Heidegger's study of Kant thus provides a cogent confirmation of the results of *Sein und Zeit*. Conversely, insofar as Heidegger employs Kant to bring into sharp focus the problem of the foundation of metaphysics, the study is an illuminating introduction to the problematic of the existential analysis.[3]

B. *Transcendence as Grounding*

The problem of finite transcendence as the question of the foundation of metaphysics leads to a thematic discussion of the problem of *ground* in the essay *Vom Wesen des Grundes*.

Here transcendence is viewed as the process of "grounding" and, corresponding to the three-sided structure of Dasein as temporality, it is divided into three modes. "Originating" (*stiftende*) grounding is the broad projection of possibilities of its own existence, by which Dasein forms the peculiar understanding of itself and of being which constitutes its world. In grounding as "taking ground" (*Boden-nehmen*) Dasein comes back to its facticious thrownness; its actual possibilities are limited by the beings in the midst of which it exists, either because certain possibilities are simply not afforded or are for some reason withdrawn. Third, grounding as "founding" (*Begründen*) provides the basis for ontic truth, for the opening-up to Dasein of the beings it encounters within its world, and thereby makes possible the basic human question "why" (WG 44–49).

The "essence of ground" is the unity of these three modes of grounding. It is the three-phased event of transcendence, whereby Dasein projects itself and being against the possibilities of its world, comes back upon its thrown facticity, and lets the beings it encounters reveal themselves to it. Heidegger calls these three moments of transcendence "the projection of world, being caught up among beings, and ontological founding of beings" (WG 50). Thus the problem of finite transcendence is once again resolved through a reduction to the three-fold structure of Dasein—to temporality as the ontological meaning of the being of Dasein (WG 50–51).

C. Result: Finite Transcendence as Temporality

Thus we have found an answer to the question posed above concerning the relation between Dasein's finitude and its understanding of being. The understanding of being must be viewed in connection with finitude, and vice versa. These two determinations belong together as two aspects of one and the same basic structure of Dasein: temporality. Consequently Heidegger can say: "We have no need of first inquiring about a relation of the understanding of being to finitude in man; the understanding of being is itself the innermost essence of finitude" (KM 207).

It must be remarked that the concept of finitude now appears somewhat differently from the way it appeared in *Sein und Zeit*. There finitude was understood as the being of Dasein unto its end: Dasein was said to be finite because it exists fin-ally, i.e., as temporal being unto death. But here in the context of the Kantian problematic, the concept of finitude seems to be limited to the realm of knowledge. How are these two "finitudes" related?

The finitude described in *Sein und Zeit* is the limitation of Dasein's possibilities because it is being-unto-death. Death is the extreme possibility by which man understands himself and in view of which he exists ahead-of-himself; thus death is the outermost concretization of the structural moment of futurity in the temporal structure of Dasein. Consequently, the finitude of Dasein as being-unto-death means limitation with respect to the structural element of futurity or being-ahead-of-itself in the being of Dasein.

On the other hand, the finitude which is spoken of in connection with the Kantian problematic is related to man as knower, and consists of Dasein's necessity of an antecedent projection of being as the horizon in which it can encounter beings. The knowledge which is under consideration here, however, is not just one human activity alongside others, but it is the basic encounter with the being of beings which is demanded by man's existence as being-in-the-world, and is grounded in the structural element of being-with, or being-present-to, the beings making up one's world. The finitude of this knowledge means limitation with respect to the existential present, to the aspect of being-with in the basic structure of Dasein.

Thus, both concepts of finitude are expressions of the fundamental limitation of Dasein in its ontological structure, each with respect to a different aspect of this structure. The similarity and the difference of these two finitudes can perhaps be formulated as follows: both signify the limitation of the three-membered fundamental structure of Dasein, the first in regard to the aspect of being-ahead of itself or futurity, the second in regard to the aspect of being-with or the existential present of Dasein.

It is time now to evaluate the result of these reflections in relation to the question of being. Thus we inquire: what is the significance for the question of the meaning of being and for the meaning of being itself, that the one raising the question exists as finite temporality?

II. *Being*

In the course of the writings which we are now discussing, the emphasis shifts gradually from the transcendence of Dasein to the horizon of this transcendence. This development brings us ever closer to the question of the meaning of being itself.

A. *Being as the Horizon of Transcendence*

Heidegger's purpose in the Kant book is to thematize the problem of the possibility of ontology, by inquiring about "the nature of this transcendence of the understanding of being" (KM 25). He finds that this transcendence goes beyond particular beings, penetrating to their being, to that which makes them be. Thus the being of beings is viewed as a moment in the process of transcendence, or as the 'object' of ontological knowledge. It is important to point out that this 'object' is completely different from any object of ontic knowledge, which always knows particular beings. This is not a being but, in Kantian terminology, "the non-empirical object = X," the "transcendental object," the "object *par excellence*" (*der Gegenstand überhaupt*), which can perhaps be said to consist of 'object-ness' itself (KM 114–15).

Heidegger now calls this "X" the pure horizon of the knowledge of beings. The horizon is being as the object of transcendence, and, as such, the condition of possibility of the revelation of beings in and for Dasein. As such a horizon, being itself is not *a* being. What is it then? Heidegger replies: "A nothing," i.e., "not a being, but still 'something' " (*Ein Nichts . . . nicht ein Seiendes, aber gleichwohl 'Etwas,'* KM 114; cf. 71, 128, 204). This conception of the horizon as a nothing is expanded upon in *Was Ist Metaphysik?*: "The nothing is the rendering possible of the revelation of beings as such for human Dasein" (WM 35); transcendence is accordingly Dasein's "condition of being thrust into the nothing" (*Hineingehaltenheit in das Nichts,* WM 38).[4]

Thus, being and nothing as the horizon of the understanding of being are in some manner the same.[5] Yet this sameness is not a simple identity in the logical sense. There is a distinction between the two which can be described somewhat as follows: Dasein does not experience being as such because human experience is always of beings; the nothing however *does* make itself known in the basic disposition of anxiety, which causes the totality of beings to fade away and thus brings Dasein face to face with 'nothing' (WM 30–32, 34; cf. SZ 184–91). Anxiety thus exposes the essential fragility and basic questionableness of beings as such and in their totality. They seem so infected with nonbeing, so apt to slip away into the abyss of nothingness that their hold on being is not only tenuous, but ultimately entirely ineffectual. The question thus arises: how is it that beings *are* at all? Whence and why do they derive their *being*? From here it is an easy step to the question: what is the meaning of *being* itself? In this way the 'nothing' revealed by the experience of anxiety points beyond itself to the totality of beings, and still further to being itself. The nothing is thus a step on the way to being, or to use another metaphor, "the veil of being" (WM 51).[6]

Being as the transcendental horizon of the encounter with beings manifests certain characteristics which are important for the development of Heidegger's problematic. First, it is and remains unthematic in Dasein's encounter with beings. As horizon, it must be seen concomitantly, but "precisely not as that which is uniquely and directly meant" (KM 115); otherwise it must lose the character of a pure horizon and become *a* being, for which still another horizon would have to be sought. Second, it is *not able to be conceptualized,* for it is itself the preconceptual understanding of being which makes possible the grasping of particular beings through concepts. Moreover, as unthematic and nonconceptualizable, it tends to be taken for granted, if not forgotten or overlooked entirely (KM 205). This tendency manifests itself in the revelation of the nothing through anxiety: the nothing draws the attention of the anxious man not to itself but to the beings which are slipping away; it modestly draws back as if wishing to remain concealed (WM 34). This characteristic of self-withdrawal is explicitly attributed to being in the treatise *Vom Wesen der Wahrheit*, in which being is seen as something profoundly mysterious (WW 19–23).

Finally, being as horizon is *finite*. There are two principal reasons for this assertion, which at the same time explain what it means. First, being is essentially linked up with negativity, for it shows itself only through the 'nothing,' i.e., through the negation of beings in their totality which characterizes anxiety. Thus, being in its appearing is essentially negative, and in this sense, finite. Second, being is considered phenomenologically, according to its manifestation in beings and in Dasein. Thus it is tied to the temporal-finite structure of Dasein, and can manifest itself only as temporal and therefore finite (WM 39–40). The latter argument Heidegger finds confirmed in ancient Greek metaphysics. Being was understood by the Greeks in terms of time: *aei on, ousia, parousia, to ti en einai;* but time categories are categories of finitude; therefore the Greeks originally understood being as finite (KM 216–18).

B. *Being and World*

The essay *Vom Wesen des Grundes* contains a detailed explanation of the formal structure of transcendence, which leads to a further discussion of the object of transcendence (WG 18–21, 21–38). The act of transcending means a going-beyond or surpassing; the being which achieves this going-beyond is Dasein. Particular beings as such are surpassed and that toward which Dasein surpasses beings, which could be called the object of transcendence, is—surprisingly enough—not the being of beings, as we might expect, but rather 'the world': "We call that *toward which* Dasein as such transcends: the *world,* and we now define transcendence as *being-in-the-world*" (WG 20). What does 'world' mean here, and how is it related to being?

True to his method, Heidegger reduces the concept 'world' to its phenomenological-existential content. This means that he considers world in its relation to Dasein, and specifically to Dasein in its most characteristic act of transcending particular beings by its preontological and preexperiential understanding of being. Thus, world has the basic characteristic of being "for the sake of" (*umwillen*). It is the preunderstood totality of beings, insofar as this totality is considered from the viewpoint of Dasein, and as something belonging to Dasein's basic structure (WG 37–38).

This explanation of 'world' corresponds to the analysis contained in *Sein und Zeit*, where the world consists of the total complex of relations of the beings confronting Dasein (SZ 83–88). In this manner of thinking, Dasein appears as the central point of a network of relations to particular beings, insofar as these are 'ready-at-hand' (*zuhanden*), or meaningful for the accomplishment of Dasein's existence. World in the existential sense is thus the totality of whatever is of importance for Dasein at a given point of its existence, or whatever occupies a place in the horizon of its existential fulfillment.[7]

World and being are intimately connected with the horizon of transcendence. In *Kant und das Problem der Metaphysik* the horizon was said to be the nothing (KM 114); in *Was Ist Metaphysik?* the nothing was seen to point necessarily beyond itself to being, since it is being's "veil" (WM 5). But in *Vom Wesen des Grundes* the horizon is called the world, and indeed this is the horizon in which being is understood, since it is "the projection of world [which] makes possible . . . the prior understanding of the being of beings" (WG 47). Heidegger leaves the question of how world and being are related in the structure of transcendence unanswered —"something which cannot be shown here" (WG 47). To clarify the point, we hazard the following explanation. Beings *are*; this means that being reigns and appears only in and through beings. But beings confront Dasein in a definite relational structure, which is composed of many beings, and, by extension, of the totality of beings. This total relational structure is the 'world,' and its center is always Dasein. Thus, being can appear only in the context of a 'world' of beings, which is always the world of a particular Dasein. 'World' is therefore a condition of possibility for the appearing of being in beings; moreover it is a prerequisite which is projected by Dasein itself.[8]

In this context being is clearly not considered as the horizon of transcendence, but as the ground which makes its presence felt in a hidden way in the beings which Dasein encounters within its own world; being is "that which determines beings as beings, that in terms of which beings . . . are already [primordially] understood" (SZ 6), and, we must add, understood within a world which is already at hand. What is significant for our present discussion is the fact that being is always bound up with a world, and this world is always a definite, particular world of a definite, individual Dasein. Thus, being can appear only in a determined, limited, 'historical' way, or, to speak in metaphysical terms, being appears only as *finite*.

C. Being as the Open

The chief interest of the treatise *Vom Wesen der Wahrheit* lies once again in the problem of the horizon of transcendence. Here in connection with the question of truth, being acquires an important new determination: it is called "the open" (WW 11). According to Heidegger, the original meaning of the Greek word *aletheia*, generally translated as "truth," is more accurately expressed by the word "unconcealment"; being, or "the open," since it lies at the base of all truth, is that which is primordially "unconcealed" (*das Unverborgene*, WW 15).[9]

As that which is originally unconcealed, being is the ultimate basis enabling beings to be revealed to and encountered by Dasein. Thus it is the ground and source of all truth; in fact, it is primordial truth itself. But since it is the ground which makes the truth of beings possible, it is itself *not* exposed in the revelation of beings, but rather withdraws; in the very revealing of beings being itself remains *concealed*. Thus being is not only the primordially unconcealed or open, but it is also that which is originally concealed or hidden (WW 19).

The hiddenness of being extends so far that the concealment itself is concealed: Dasein, in relating to a being revealing itself, is so fully preoccupied that it pays no attention to the concealment of the horizon of this revelation. This double concealment of being—the concealment of the concealment itself—is called by Heidegger "the mystery" of being. Being as mystery is accordingly "the first and broadest unrevealedness, the authentic 'untruth,'" or the "unessence of truth" (WW 19–20). However, the "unessence" of truth is meant neither as falsehood nor as inauthenticity nor as the opposite of truth, but as something belonging to the full essence of truth itself, and indeed as that which is most proper to it. By a peculiarity of the German language, the prefix 'un-' is used not in the sense of negation, but of sublimation, as, for example, in the German word

"*Untiefe*," which can mean not only a shallow, but also an unfathomable depth. Thus 'un-' in the present usage points "toward the not yet experienced realm of the truth of being" (WW 20), the hidden mystery of *lethe* prior to the occurrence of *aletheia*.[10]

The fact that the concealment of the horizon goes unnoticed cannot be merely ascribed to human frailty; it belongs to the very essence of truth. On this point the present analysis shows a marked difference from that of *Sein und Zeit*. There the complete preoccupation of Dasein with beings was explained solely on the basis of the structure of Dasein, particularly the structural element of fallenness; here, however, this structural aspect is seen to be reinforced by and ultimately grounded in the mysterious nature of being itself. Because being as mystery remains doubly hidden from man, it keeps him in ignorance of this concealment. Heidegger calls this forgottenness of the mystery "errance" (*die Irre*). On the one hand, errance belongs to the intrinsic constitution of Dasein, and on the other, to the primordial essence of truth, whose 'antiessence' or negative pole it is. The complete essence of truth, therefore, consists in the intertwining of unconcealment, mystery and errance: "The concealment of that which is concealed and errance belong to the primordial essence of truth" (WW 23).

Why such an involved structure? Why speak of both positive and negative aspects of truth? Is not truth pure positivity, pure transparency? Heidegger's discussion must be seen from its phenomenological point of departure: in this view truth is not something isolated and standing by itself, but something which is present in Dasein, in the confrontation of Dasein with beings. Truth in this sense has the same double structure as Dasein itself; insofar as it appears in Dasein, it not only determines Dasein's structure but is itself determined by that structure. Just as Dasein exists as the combination of the understanding of being and being-unto-death, as temporally structured finite transcendence, so truth presents itself as both unconcealment and concealment, as the mystery which reveals all beings and at the same time conceals itself. Truth is thus something negatively positive; it appears only in a *finite* way. And since primordial truth, as the ground of the revelation of beings to Dasein, is clearly another facet of being as the horizon of transcendence, we have here a further confirmation of what has already been established: in the essence of truth being reveals itself as finite.

D. Result: The Finite Essence of Being

The end-result of the foregoing may be formulated as follows: being, which is preontologically understood by finite-temporal Dasein, is itself finite. As the horizon which is not *a* being, being is linked with the nothing and with finite Dasein's transcendence. It appears within the particular world of a finite Dasein; it comes to light in truth both positively and negatively as both unconcealment and concealment. The conclusion thus seems inevitable: being itself is finite.

But a serious difficulty immediately presents itself: is finitude compatible with the concept of a horizon? Admittedly, a horizon is always a horizon for something contained within it; thus it is bound up with this something and is in this sense limited or finite. But on the other hand, it is essential to the concept of horizon that it itself does not belong within its own finite realm but rather transcends everything contained within itself. Should we not thus designate it as infinite? The difficulty becomes even stronger when we conceive of the horizon as the open: is not the concept of a finite open intrinsically contradictory? Is not the open, proceeding from its very definition, unbounded and as a consequence nonfinite or infinite?[11]

We are here entangled in something like Kant's antinomies of reason. It seems necessary to conclude that the concepts 'finite' and 'infinite' are inadequate for discourse about being in the Heideggerian sense. They are categories derived from the realm of beings and thus applicable only to this realm. Only beings can be finite or infinite, for only beings *are*. Being for its part is neither finite nor infinite, for strictly speaking, being cannot be said *to be* at all. If we say 'is' of being itself, we constitute it as a being; such a predication is thus a violation of the first and most certain statement possible about being: being is not *a* being (cf. SZ 6).

This is not to espouse any form of nihilism, as if there were no such thing as being. Certainly beings are, and this means that being appears, or comes to light, or is present in them; thus, in some way being 'is.' But the present discussion serves to emphasize once again the irreducible difference between being and beings, and to underline the fact that when we speak of being, we are in a quite different realm of thought and discourse than when we speak of beings. Remembering this radical difference, we may say that being, as the horizon of human transcendence, presents itself as finite; it appears within finite Dasein's world; it does not show itself in pure unbounded positivity, but concealing and revealing at the same time. In this sense, being may be said to 'be' finite. This is what is meant in discussions about the 'finitude of being' or when we use the inaccurate but unavoidable expression, "being *is* finite."[12]

This formulation answers the question posed above: what is the significance for the being-question and for the meaning of being itself that a finite being poses the question? It means that being presents itself as finite, and that what we really mean when we say 'being,' is the finite coming-to-presence of being in and for Dasein. We are admittedly still far from a complete answer to the being-question; we have merely staked out more precisely the area in which the answer must be sought, thus giving a formal delimitation which should aid in the further search for the desired material content.

III. *From Transcendence to Being: The Turning*

By now it should be clear that the Heideggerian problematic has undergone a decisive change. In *Sein und Zeit* and *Kant und das Problem der Metaphysik* the transcendence of man stands in the foreground, while being as the horizon of transcendence is scarcely spoken of. But in *Vom Wesen des Grundes,* although transcendence as grounding is the real theme, the world, as that toward which transcendence is aimed, comes in for extensive discussion. And in *Was Ist Metaphysik?* the horizon is explicitly thematized under the title of the nothing, while being as primordial truth or as the open is the central point of the entire treatise *Vom Wesen der Wahrheit.*

This development is not wholly unexpected, since from the beginning the question of being has been the unique leitmotiv of the Heideggerian effort. Thus one might think that Heidegger is simply arriving at the goal he originally intended, that he is now treating directly what he had previously seen only indirectly and from a distance. But the development is more complicated than this. What has occurred is not merely a shifting of the focus from Dasein to being, but also a profound change in the ontological roles of being and Dasein. These writings reflect a struggle for dominance between being and Dasein, the result of which becomes finally clear in the essay on truth.

A. *Dasein and Being*

In *Kant und das Problem der Metaphysik* being is still the pure projected horizon of the preontological understanding of being, and as such is to a certain extent dependent upon Dasein. Nonetheless, the primacy of Dasein is not wholly uncontested, for Heidegger designates being as the "area of opposedness" (*Dawider*) of transcendence, as that which renders possible the standing-over-against of objects: "the realm of opposedness visible in and through transcendence as its horizon" (KM 144, cf. 99, 102). It is also stated that transcendence is concerned with "the prior opposedness of being" (KM 72).

In *Vom Wesen des Grundes* the dominance of Dasein is reflected in the assertion that "there is being (not *a* being) only in transcendence" (WG 51). Moreover, transcendence is the "ground of the ontological difference," i.e., the difference between being and beings (WG 16); this seems to imply a radical dependence of being upon Dasein. But being begins to assert its own dominance in a discussion of the Platonic ideas. Here Heidegger points out that these ideas must be considered as both the most subjective and most objective elements of thought, for they are in one instance said to be innate or inborn in the human subject, whereas they are again spoken of as dwelling in a celestial, transhuman realm. This ambivalence holds also for the question of the primacy between being and Dasein, for "the world is as much something held up before Dasein (and therefore something beyond it), as it is something which at the same time constitutes itself in Dasein" (WG 41). Heidegger seems to have this beyondness or externality in mind when he writes that "the world gives itself to Dasein" (WG 43).

The remarkable interweaving of dependence and beyondness in being's role with regard to man is again mirrored in Heidegger's characterization of transcendence as an "unveiling projection of being" (WG 40). The ambivalence of this expression is to be understood as follows: insofar as being is projected, it is necessarily dependent on man, but insofar as it is unveiled in the projecting process, it is prior to and independent of the human act of transcendence.

B. *Being and Dasein*

In *Was Ist Metaphysik?* being clearly begins to assert its primacy. Although being continues to need Dasein to be able to reveal itself, it is ever more the determining element in the structure of transcendence. The nothing which is the "veil of being" (WM 51) "discloses itself" in anxiety, without being grasped in it (WM 33); the nothing is originally revealed in Dasein as the condition of possibility not only of human relations with beings, but also of the authentic selfhood and freedom of man (WM 34–35); transcendence makes man an attendant "holding a place for the nothing," i.e., for being (*Platzhalter des Nichts*, WM 38).

The growing dominance of being is confirmed in an epilog added several years later to the text of *Was Ist Metaphysik?*, where mention is made of being's "claim" upon man (*Anspruch*) and its "voice" (*Stimme*) calling and challenging him (WM 46). Here Heidegger explicitly states that "being is not a product of thought. Quite to the contrary, foundational thought (*das wesentliche Denken*) is an event (*Ereignis*) of being" (WM 47).[13] In an introduction to the same work written still later, being is presented as the light in which beings are known in Dasein, and as the source of thought (WM 7, 10).

Further verifications of the new position of being with regard to Dasein are found in *Vom Wesen der Wahrheit*. Mystery, as the double concealment of being, "governs" (*durchwaltet*) Dasein (WW 19); errance "thoroughly rules" (*durchherrscht*) man (WW 22); man is "subjected to the reign of mystery and the pressure of errance" (WW 23). Human freedom, which Heidegger understands as openness to the revelation of being in beings, derives from the "original essence of truth" (WW 23); it receives "its own essence from the more primordial essence of the uniquely essential truth" (WW 14). Philosophy is not the autonomous "proprietor of its own laws" (*Selbsthalterin ihrer Gesetze*) as Kant maintained, but is "itself first possessed . . . by the truth of that, of which its laws are even laws" (WW 25).

The primacy of being has thus become unmistakably clear. It would still be an error to represent this precedence as a simple independence of being from Dasein; the relation remains always one of mutual interdependence. The truth of being is the "reign of mystery and the pressure of errance" which "keeps Dasein in need by a constant back and forth motion [between the one and the other]" (WW 23); on the other hand, being 'needs' Dasein, for the assertion of *Was Ist Metaphysik?* remains in force, that "being . . . reveals itself only in Dasein's transcendence" (WM 40).

Hence philosophical thought must both respect the concealment of being and attempt to bring this out into the open, into its own full truth.

Such thinking, says Heidegger, is "the relaxed calm of a gentleness which does not refuse [its service to] the concealedness of beings on the whole . . . [and is] at the same time the resoluteness of a severity which, while not bursting open the concealment, still forces its unviolated nature into the openness of understanding, and thus into its own proper truth" (WW 24). This paradoxical reciprocal relation is just what the name 'Dasein' is meant to express: "In order to state simultaneously in *one* word the relation of being to the essence of man, as well as the essential relation of man to the openness (the 'there') of being as such, the name 'Dasein' was chosen to designate the essential region in which man stands as man" (WM 13–14).

Thus the Heideggerian turning has been accomplished. At the close of *Vom Wesen der Wahrheit* Heidegger himself points out that his thought has experienced a "transformation of the relation to being" (WW 27). The full import of this change will become apparent only in subsequent works; thus, a more precise elaboration of what has transpired must be reserved for succeeding chapters. At this point, however, two aspects of the turning are abundantly clear: the purely ontic shift of the focus of interest from Dasein to being, and the more profound ontological transformation in the relation of primacy between being and Dasein.[14]

IV. *Summary*

The four works following *Sein und Zeit* manifest two trends important to the investigation of Heidegger's philosophy of death: first, the analysis of Dasein is carried further by the answering of the preliminary question of the relation between finitude and the understanding of being in Dasein, and by the clarification of the significance for the being-question of Dasein's finite-temporal structure; second, Heidegger's thought undergoes the turning from Dasein to being. The results of the present chapter can accordingly be formulated as follows:

1. Transcendence and finitude, or the understanding of being and being-unto-death, are two moments of one and the same basic structure of Dasein, namely, temporality.

2. Being, whose meaning is sought by the temporal-finite Dasein which understands it, appears as the horizon of transcendence, which is itself not a being. It is understood within the context of a particular 'world'

and shows itself in the revelation of beings as revealing and concealing. In all these ways being presents itself as finite.

3. The turning in Heidegger's thought is (a) a change of perspective, in which the focus moves from the transcendence of Dasein to being as the horizon of this transcendence, and (b) a change in the relation between being and Dasein, in which being assumes the role of ontological primacy in the process of transcendence.

It will be the task of succeeding discussions to elaborate in greater detail the impact of the turning upon the question of the meaning of being and to give a more exact interpretation of that turning. We shall then be in a position to consider the meaning of the new perspective for the theme of death. We shall have to ask: is death also drawn into the transformation worked by the turning? Will it now play a different role in the thought of Heidegger?

4

Being, Man, & Death
in the New Position

Having witnessed the critical turning in Heidegger's thought accomplished in the four writings *Kant und das Problem der Metaphysik, Vom Wesen des Grundes, Was Ist Metaphysik?* and *Vom Wesen der Wahrheit,* we shall now trace the consolidation of the newly won position in the subsequent work, *Einführung in die Metaphysik (Introduction to Metaphysics),* originally delivered as a university lecture course in 1935.[1]

Here, being is definitively established in a position of precedence. Also, the further determinations of being are worked out, which lay the foundation for the entire later development of the Heideggerian problematic. We shall discuss first the assertions about being, passing then to the new relation between man and being which becomes constantly clearer, so that we can finally formulate an interpretation of the turning. This will enable us to treat in context those passages of *Einführung in die Metaphysik* which are important for the theme of death.

I. *Being Itself*

As a consequence of the turning, the desire to think being itself, as distinguished from thinking about the being of beings, came to the fore in *Vom Wesen der Wahrheit* (WW 25). Heidegger now explicitly pursues this desire, and thereby sharply distinguishes his philosophy from traditional metaphysics. Whereas previous metaphysics had only considered beings as such, or the being of beings, Heidegger proposes to inquire about being itself. The title *Einführung in die Metaphysik* is thus consciously ambivalent: Heidegger does not intend his work to be an introduction to the traditional metaphysics of beings, but to the new thinking of being (EM 14–15). Consequently, the title would be more accurate if it read: *Introduction to the Thinking of Being.*[2]

But have the philosophers of the western tradition never considered being itself? Not explicitly and thematically, Heidegger contends, although the early Greek thinkers, especially the greatest of the pre-Socratics, Heraclitus and Parmenides, came very close. They still enjoyed a primordial relation to being, which was unfortunately lost with Plato's and Aristotle's initiation of the metaphysics of beings. Heraclitus and Parmenides indeed spoke of the being of beings, but in such a way that being itself shone through their words: "Here in this great time, the speaking about the being of beings contained within itself the (hidden) essence of being, of which it spoke" (EM 74).

Heidegger attributes the originality of the relation between man and being to the fact that Heraclitus and Parmenides antedated the division between thought and being, between subject and object, which determined—one might almost say, vitiated—the whole course of western philosophy from Plato and Aristotle to Hegel and Nietzsche. The consequence of this division has been the primacy of thought, particularly logical thought, over being. In this metaphysics dominated by logic, being has traditionally received its entire meaning, even its very possibility, from thought. This is shown by the fact that being is made to conform to the 'principle of contradiction,' which is a law of formal logic, to such an extent that anything which conflicts with this law is called impossible (EM 88–89, 143).

Heidegger wishes to overcome the domination of thought over being by turning the tables: thought should again become subordinate to, and indeed determined by being. One could hardly wish for a more decisive confirmation of the new position of primacy won by being in the turning than the ringing summons to a new effort "to overcome the traditional logic" (EM 92) by a "return to the question of the essential relation of thinking to being, . . . [through] a more original, stricter kind of thinking proper to being" (EM 94).[3]

A. *Being as Physis and Ousia*

What did the early Greeks really mean when they said "being"? For them, being was *physis*. Originally this expression did not mean "nature" in the sense of the sum of material things, as it came to be translated later, but the totality of beings. The force of the term *physis* is described by Heidegger as follows: "What does the word *physis* convey? It means something emerging of itself (e.g., the emerging of a rose), a self-opening unfolding, a coming into view by means of such an unfolding and a remaining in view, in short, an emerging and abiding holding sway" (EM 11).

In this conception of *physis* two elements should be noted: the emerging itself, which is not an ordinary occurrence like other everyday events, but a basic entrance into existence, a coming into view out of the darkness of nonbeing, a primordial stepping out of concealment into the light of the real (EM 11–12); and second, the abiding of what has come forth; beings not only step out, but remain, assume a posture, and become something substantial. This moment of continuing presence is expressed by another Greek word for being, *ousia*, or more completely, *parousia* (EM 46). For the Greeks, being thus signified presence or perdurance, specifically in the double sense of arising or standing up (*physis*) and enduring or standing (*ousia*) (EM 48). Both senses are expressed in the Heideggerian formula: being as *physis* is "an emerging and abiding holding sway" (EM 11).

As *physis* being has universal power. It rules inexhaustibly and irresistibly in the totality of beings. It permeates and circumscribes everything; it is the *deinon*, the awesome, the mighty, the overwhelming (EM 114–15). Accordingly, it is also called *dike*, not in the sense of moral justice, but as the arrangement which arranges everything, the powerful organizing process and relational pattern of beings on the whole (EM 122–23).

B. *Being as Logos and Polemos (Heraclitus)*

Heraclitus has experienced and spoken of being as *logos*. Is it something other than being as *physis*? From the first two Heraclitean fragments Heidegger deduces the following about *logos*: it is constant, abiding; it presents itself as the 'together,' as the collecting force among beings; it prevails in everything that happens, i.e., in everything that comes into being. Thus he formulates the essence of *logos* as "constant, self-prevailing, primordial, collecting collectedness" (EM 98). Whence comes this remarkable collecting character of *logos*? Heidegger points out that *legein*, from which the substantive *logos* is derived, originally meant "the placing of one thing next to another, bringing together into a unity, or, in brief, collecting" (EM 95). Thus, *logos* is "the constant collecting, the autonomous (*in sich stehende*) collectedness of beings" and, as such, it is that which makes a being to be what it is. Thus, *logos* and *physis* are basically the same: the being of beings as such in their totality (EM 100).

The collecting character of being as *logos* appears clearly in the Heraclitean concept of *polemos*, usually translated as battle, fight, war. Fragment 53 calls *polemos* the father and king of all; he has made some to be gods, others men, some slaves, others free. Heidegger translates *polemos* as "putting asunder," *pater* (father) as "progenitor (who permits things to emerge)," and *basileus* (king) as "governing preserver." *Polemos* is the primordial battle, not in the sense of a war between men, but "a prevailing contention antedating both gods and men," the primordial putting asunder which unites within itself all contraries, and gathers together all things striving against each other (EM 47). As such, *polemos* is another facet of the being of beings. *Polemos*, *logos*, and *physis* are basically the same thing under three different aspects: putting asunder, collecting, and emerging and abiding holding sway.

C. *Being as Noein–Einai (Parmenides)*

What was being for the other great pre-Socratic thinker, Parmenides? Contradicting the widely held opinion that the teaching of Parmenides is diametrically opposed to that of Heraclitus, Heidegger maintains that both thinkers really shared the same philosophical standpoint: "Where should these two Greek thinkers, the founders of all thought, take their stand but in the being of beings? For Parmenides too, being is the *hen, xyneches,* that which holds itself together in itself, *mounon,* that which uniquely unites, *oulon,* that which is complete, the constantly self-manifesting holding sway" (EM 104).

If it is true that Parmenides conceives being as *hen,* "the one," or primordial unity, he does not mean this in a static, but a dynamic sense. It is "never empty uniformity, nor sameness in the sense of mere equality

. . . [but rather] the interdependent correlation of things mutually opposed" (*Zusammengehörigkeit des Gegenstrebigen,* EM 106). In other words, being as *hen* is basically the same as being under the aspects of *physis, logos,* and *polemos.*

Perhaps the best known saying of Parmenides is the one usually interpreted as an affirmation of a radical subjectivism: *to gar auto noein estin te kai einai* (Fragment 5). This can be literally rendered as: "For the same is both to think and to be." Certainly this proposition expresses some type of correlation between being and thinking, some form of belonging together. But the real question is: which of the two belongs to the other? Which enjoys ontological primacy? According to the traditional interpretation, which Heidegger rejects as thoroughly "un-Greek," Parmenides is expressing a kind of rationalism, saying that being belongs to thought, in such a way that "the thinking of the subject determines what being is. Being is nothing other than what is thought in thinking (*das Gedachte des Denkens*). . . . There are no beings in themselves" (EM 104).

In contrast to this interpretation, Heidegger attempts to show that the direction of the belonging-together of thought and being must be reversed. He claims that Parmenides intends just the opposite of the above opinion, meaning in fact that thought belongs to being, and not vice versa.

Heidegger's analysis fastens upon the three elements of the saying: the same, to think, and to be. What does Parmenides mean by *to auto,* "the same"? Not identity in the sense of uniformity, numerical unity or sheer equality, but rather the correlation or belonging-together of things mutually opposed. Thus, *to auto* must be understood in the sense of Parmenides' theory of being as *hen,* "the one," as outlined above. It is also seen in its similarity to Heraclitus' view of being as *logos* and *polemos.* *To auto* is thus also that which gathers together into unity, and that which originally sets asunder the elements of *noein* and *einai,* enabling them to play their distinctive and complementary roles in dynamic combination (EM 106).[4]

What does *einai,* "to be," mean? This is undoubtedly being in the basic Greek sense of *physis,* emerging and abiding holding sway (EM 105).

The third element, *noein,* is the most difficult to grasp and consequently the most widely misunderstood. It cannot simply be translated "to think," for thinking in the history of western metaphysics is something *distinguished from* being, rather than something belonging to it. The *noein* which is "the same" as "to be" must accordingly be something antecedent to the distinction between thinking and being.

Heidegger thus translates *noein* as "to perceive" (*vernehmen*). This includes two essential elements: first of all, it means acceptance, i.e., receiving that which is allowed to approach and reveal itself; second, it means accepting in an active sense, as a judge takes the testimony of a witness, bringing it out and examining it and thereby establishing the facts of a case. Heidegger clarifies this double meaning by the use of a military example: "When troops take up a position, they wish to receive the approaching enemy, and in such a way that they will at least bring him to a halt" (EM 105). Similarly, *noein* for the Greeks is as much a receiving of what is revealing itself as an active position-taking with regard to it. Briefly, it is an accepting bringing-to-a-standstill of that which appears. In this way perceiving belongs to the taking-place or the coming-into-position of beings as such.

Is this a subjectivistic explanation? Does it mean that beings are real only through human thinking, that the being of beings is merely an object of thought? If one understands man and beings as subject and object, as two completely independent, separate entities standing opposite each other, there is indeed the danger of such an interpretation. Perceiving could be construed as the activity of a subject constituting the real being of beings as object. But Heidegger is here concerned with the relation between *noein* and *einai* in pre-Socratic thought, and therefore *before* the distinction between subject and object was first made. In this primordial context, 'to perceive' and 'to be' constitute an original unity which is the presupposition for any subject-object distinction at all. Thus, Heidegger's interpretation is not subjectivistic but rather *transcendental,* reaching back to the presubjective and preobjective realm of transcendence in the sense previously explained, to the ground of possibility for the primordial occurrence of the illumination of being.[5]

Let us recall once more: for the Greeks, being is basically *physis,* emerging and abiding holding sway, or emergence as appearing, standing in the light, stepping forth from concealment into unconcealment. The accepting bringing-to-a-standstill which we have called perceiving belongs to the holding sway of being understood in this way. The emerging sway of being consequently denotes a simultaneous and concomitant occurrence of perceiving; *noein* belongs to *physis,* i.e., to *einai.* Being holds sway as appearing, and "because it holds sway and insofar as it holds sway and

97

appears, it necessarily occurs *along with* appearing and perceiving" (EM 106). Thus, being and thinking, *einai* and *noein*, "are united in the sense of a mutual opposition, i.e., the same *as* correlative" (*zusammengehörig*, EM 106).

D. *Being before and after the Turning*

Is being now the same as it was in the previous writings? The term certainly has acquired new aspects and nuances: in the language of the pre-Socratics, it is now conceived as *physis, ousia, logos, polemos, einai-noein, deinon,* and *dike.* It is that which is emerging and holding sway among all beings as constant presence, collecting collectedness, the primordial putting-asunder, that which takes place in perceiving, that which is overwhelmingly uncanny, universally organizing organization. These new expressions mark a definite broadening of Heidegger's concept of being.

But although there has been an enrichment in content, still the formal framework of the meaning of being has not changed. Echoing determinations established in the works before *Einführung in die Metaphysik,* being continues to appear as that "in virtue of which beings become and remain observable" (EM 11), that which we antecedently understand in every confrontation with beings (EM 59, 65), the most unique, the incomparable (EM 60), the primordially manifest (EM 65), that "which is not a being nor an entitative component of a being" (EM 67), that which "is, in a certain way, a nothing" (EM 155), that to whose essence truth belongs (EM 78), that which is called "coming-into-unconcealment" (EM 130) in such a way that it simultaneously conceals its own primordial truth (EM 79, 83), that whose essence includes both the arising from concealment and the tendency to return to concealment (EM 87).

Is being still conceived as the horizon of human transcendence? Fundamentally, yes; but by now it has far surpassed its role as horizon. Being is no longer considered from the standpoint of man, but vice versa: transcendence, or, more precisely, human existence on the whole is considered from the standpoint of being. Being takes the initiative in revealing itself to man in order to be transformed into history, to be put to work, to be set asunder into beings, to be overpowered, to be brought to a position (EM 110, 122, 123, 125). This new direction of the relation is expressed quite strongly and explicitly: "being is the fundamental event on the basis of which historical Dasein is given a place at all in the midst of the luminescent totality of beings" (EM 153–54). Thus, the primacy of being with respect to man is definitively established.

In this new view, however, there could arise the disturbing question of whether being has not now been reduced to the status of *a being* standing over against man, i.e., to a mere object confronting man as subject. Such a reduction would surely be the betrayal of the whole Heideggerian project, which consists in the effort to think being precisely in its difference from beings and prior to the division of subject and object. Thus, expressions which might seem to apply to the ontic realm of beings must be understood in their intended ontological and transcendental meaning.

In emphasizing the primacy of being, Heidegger is attempting to point out as clearly as possible the nonsubordination of being to man, by showing in various ways and from several starting-points that man is not lord over the totality of beings. This insight compels him to concede to being a clear initiative in relation to man. The initiative, however, is not that of one being dealing with another, not that of a subject confronting an object, but a sign of the nondisponibility and nonsubordination, or in other words, the ontological primacy, of being over man, who nevertheless is entrusted with the task of bringing being to a halt and putting it to work in the concrete forms of history.

Thus it would be a mistake to conceive the reversed relationship of man and being in ontic terms. In the writings after the turning it remains true that being is not *a* being, but is rather that which is present and holds sway in all beings, making possible their self-revelation to man. In order to preserve this inexpressible character of being, Heidegger has pointed out the mysterious tendency of being to conceal itself in the revelation of beings. Being sends or presents itself precisely by withdrawing. We accordingly understand it best when we recognize it as incomprehensible. This is the paradoxical nature of being which Heidegger's investigations are gradually discovering.

Thus, one must not fall prey to the snares of language. Even when Heidegger speaks of being *itself*, "being" is not meant to designate a substantive entity or an objective force standing in front of or over against man, but is only the unavoidably human expression for the inexpressible something which reveals itself in beings without being a being itself.[6]

II. *Man*

Parmenides' saying chiefly concerns being and is considered here from that viewpoint, for being was the determining factor in early Greek thought. Only secondarily does he speak of man or of the role of human perceiving in the coming-to-be of beings. Granting this, we now ask: what was the pre-Socratic view of man in relation to being?

A. *Man according to Parmenides*

The saying of Parmenides indicates that man shares essentially in the event of the emergence of being. Man belongs to being not only because he himself *is,* but also because in the emergence and coming-to-position of being he plays the role of the one perceiving, the one bringing being to a halt and thus bringing beings to be. Herein Heidegger sees the first, primordial intimation of the essential definition of man. He insists that we should not bring a predetermined definition of man to the interpretation of this text, but must work out a definition from the text itself. Thus, it would be inappropriate to say that according to Parmenides, man is a being equipped with the faculty of perceiving, since the full import of the text is that man is originally constituted by this very perceiving; without this, man is not man in the full sense. "Perceiving is not a mode of comportment which man possesses as a property, but the opposite is true: perceiving is that event which possesses man" (EM 108). Since perceiving belongs to being, as we have seen, the essence of man, to whom the task of perceiving is entrusted in the event of being, can be defined only in terms of the essence of being (EM 106–107).

What, then, is man in this perspective? He is the perceiver in the combination of emerging holding sway and perceiving bringing-to-position which constitutes the event of being amidst beings. In this sense he is essentially the "guardian of being" (*Verwahrer des Seins,* EM 108).

B. *Man according to Sophocles*

The preceding interpretation of human existence finds confirmation in Heidegger's explanation of the first chorus of Sophocles' *Antigone.* Here man is named the uncanniest of all things uncanny in the world of beings; many things in creation are strange and wondrous (*deinon*), but man is the strangest of all (*to deinotaton*).

The Greek adjective *deinon,* translatable generally as wondrous, marvelous, strange, contains two elements which explain the kind of strangeness intended: first, it means capable of inspiring fear or dread, thus fearful, terrible, dreadful, dire, awesome; second, it conveys the notion of force or power, thus mighty, powerful.

The totality of beings is *deinon* in this twofold sense. It is awesome since it is all-encompassing, omnipresent, indefatigable and yet elusive, mysterious, never wholly transparent. It is also strangely powerful, since the might of being seems indomitable and inexhaustible; *physis* manifests its power all around us, before us and beyond us, even within us. Being is thus not only wondrously powerful; it is truly overpowering (EM 112–15).

But man is also wondrous in this double manner. He is awesome insofar as he himself is a being and thus belongs to this strange realm of mystery; he is also wondrously powerful, asserting by his great technical and cultural achievements his mastery over beings on the whole. In fact, he often seems to pit his power against the overwhelming power of being itself. Moreover, this is not merely one arbitrary aspect of his existence; rather, it is his essential and natural activity to wrest for himself a place of power in the midst of the overwhelming power of being. He is thus *to deinotaton,* the most awesome, most powerful, most strange and uncanny of all beings (EM 114–15).

The activity of man is also designated as *techne,* which Heidegger translates as "knowledge" (*Wissen*). By this he does not mean theoretical knowledge, but a practical, working knowledge, the ability to exploit "the capacity of being to be put-to-work as such and such a being," or "the conscious forcing of being, previously locked up within itself, into the open of appearance as a particular being" (EM 122).

Does this mean that man is the master of being? Not at all. While it is true that he dominates the sea, the earth, and the rest of beings below his own human level, his domination is never complete. He might think he is master of everything, but the opposite is really true; the totality of beings holds sway invincibly around him. He might also imagine that he is the master and even the inventor of language, of knowledge and of the *polis* which is the seedbed of history, but in reality all of this is again the overwhelming power of being, which dominates him and completely permeates all he does. Finally, all his actions reach an inexorable limit over which he has no control: "All power-activity (*Gewalt-tätigkeit*) runs aground at only one point. This is death" (EM 121). Death overtakes all man's accomplishments and is thus the most certain sign of his limited power against the overwhelming might of being (EM 116–21).

What is the relation between the might of man and the overwhelming power of being? Man is the most uncanny of all things. He sets out to do battle in the midst of being's almighty holding sway, carries out his essential power-activity, splinters being into beings, puts being to work, brings it to a halt in some particular being (EM 122–23). His essential task is to transform being into history and, by so doing, to attain his own authentic selfhood (EM 110).

Still he will never gain complete mastery over being. Even in his power-activity, the initiative is not his, but lies entirely on the side of being. The overwhelming power that surrounds man needs him, in order that it may itself come to presence in beings, for man is the stage on which being appears, the lighting-up place, or the there of being (EM 124). Man's task is to "put [being] to work and thereby hold the totality of beings open" (EM 125). Thus, for Sophocles, man is the wielder of overwhelming power, but even in his very might he is a servant, because the power is not his own, but that of being (EM 132).

C. Man before and after the Turning

Is this still the same picture of man as that encountered in Heidegger's earlier writings? Is man still finite transcendence, the being-unto-death which understands being, whose meaning is temporality?

Although the expression 'transcendence' is not found in *Einführung in die Metaphysik*,[7] man is still the being who, going beyond beings, is open to being. This is clear from the designation of man as the most uncanny of all things. Man indeed exists in the midst of beings and is at home among them. But the overwhelming power which surrounds him will not permit him to remain at home among particular beings; from time to time it shows the inadequacy of this preoccupation by invading his existence directly. Man is then torn out of his familiar surroundings and propelled toward the uncanny strangeness of being itself. "Man is the strangest of all things . . . because he steps out, marches beyond his ordinary, customary, familiar boundaries, because, as active-power, he goes beyond the limit of the familiar, precisely in the direction of the uncanny in the sense of the overwhelming" (EM 116). This means that man is distinguished among all beings by the fact that he transcends the beings he meets in everyday experience and penetrates, to some extent, the mystery of being itself. In short, he exists as transcendence.

However, man is still seen as *finite* transcendence in this work. The earlier signs of finitude—thrownness, fallenness, being-unto-death, knowledge of being which is simultaneously concealing and revealing—all these reappear in *Einführung in die Metaphysik*. Thus Heidegger writes that "being itself throws man" (EM 125); man is "forced [to exist] as Dasein, thrown into the necessity of such [a mode of] being" (EM 124); he is "thrown to and fro between organization and disarray" (EM 123). Though his power-activity blazes trails in being, still he is "constantly thrown back into the pathways he himself has made, by getting bogged down in his tracks and caught up in what is familiar to him, drawing the circle of his world in this captivity, entangling himself in mere appearance and thus cutting himself off from being" (EM 121).

In order to overcome the "continually cramping entanglement in customary, everyday affairs," Dasein must use force in the form of a "decisive march on the way to the being of beings . . . out of the familiarity of the usual, of the things closest to him" (EM 128). This exercise of power eventually runs aground in death; insofar as he exists, man stands inevitably under the sentence of mortality (EM 121). He must wrest being into beings in a continual struggle against mere seeming, for the possibility of seeming belongs essentially to the appearing of being in Dasein (EM 79–80).

Finally, the meaning of Dasein is still temporality, as was demonstrated in *Sein und Zeit*. This assertion receives a more precise determination in *Einführung in die Metaphysik*, in that Heidegger speaks now not only of time, but of history. The power-activity commanded by being itself, whereby man forces being into beings by bringing it to a concrete, epochal halt, is the genesis of history; man stands in the service of being, because being transforms itself into history through him. This is the essential task of man, constituting his selfhood but also finally shattering him. Thus history, or the task of transforming being into history, is the deepest meaning of human existence (EM 110, 124–25, 130).

Consequently, man remains Dasein after the turning—he is the 'there' or the place of illumination of being in the midst of beings. But the fact that everything is now viewed from the new standpoint of being itself, means that this term too takes on a new accent. Heidegger even writes it in a new way, inserting a hyphen between the two parts of the term, to emphasize that 'man' and 'Da-sein' are not simply identical and interchangeable. Da-sein might loosely be called the essential aspect or the phenomenological heart of man, the ground in man which makes possible his openness toward the being of beings (WW 15). As such, it is even more primordial than man himself, it "possesses" him (WW 16). Thus man begins to live an authentic historical life only when he penetrates to this ground, takes it over and assumes responsibility for it, ontically achieving his orientation to the being of beings (WW 22, 23). Da-sein is the 'place' in man where being itself draws near to him, where he finds being in himself (WW 27). Indeed Da-sein is being itself, insofar as being comes to its own illumination in man. Thus one can now say that Da-sein is both man as the 'there' of being, and also being itself as 'being-in-man.'[8]

Although man remains basically the same after the turning—Da-sein or finite transcendence, whose ontological meaning is temporality—he has also become something else; his essence is now broadened and deepened by the fact that he is completely defined by his relation to being. He is no longer one who acts autonomously (as in *Sein und Zeit*), but one whose essential task is the projecting of being into history, and this task is imposed on him by being itself. Correspondingly, his finitude is no longer defined in terms of his internal structure, but more importantly in terms of his relation to being. Da-sein is finite not only because it exists as being-unto-end, but because it is placed in the service of being. The autonomous sounding character of man's finitude thus gives way to the note of subordination to being. Man indeed remains the finite-temporal transcending being, but this now means that he is the strange and uncanny guardian, the mighty administrator, the worker who puts being to work, the servant who transforms being into history.

This concept is crystallized in a bold turnabout of the traditional definition of man as a rational animal, or, more literally, an animal having reason. The new formulation summarizes pregnantly and succinctly the Heideggerian interpretation of early Greek thought. Significantly, the term which stands in the beginning of the definition is not 'man,' but 'being' as the Greeks understood it, *physis*. The classical definition, formulated from the viewpoint of man, reads: "*anthropos = zoon logon echon*: man, the living being, which has reason as its essential portion" (EM

134). Heidegger's definition, formulated from the standpoint of being, reads: "*physis = logos anthropon echon*: being, the overwhelming coming-to-appearance, compels the gathering which possesses and grounds human being" (EM 134).[9]

III. *Interpretation of the Turning*

What has actually happened between Heidegger's initial thrust in *Sein und Zeit* and the point of view reached in *Einführung in die Metaphysik?* Has Heidegger turned from man to being in the sense of a shift from subject to object? Has he thus broken out of the modern trap of subjectivism? Where does he stand now in relation to his thought before the turning? Where does he stand with respect to the Kantian transcendental philosophy?

A. *A Turning to the Object?*

The turning is definitely a shift in emphasis from Dasein to being. But to understand this development properly, we must ask if the turning means that Heidegger has burst the bonds of subjectivism and broken through to an affirmation of the reality of objects independently of knowing subjects.

At first it might seem so, for in *Sein und Zeit* Heidegger proclaimed more than once that being *is* only in the understanding of man, that there is being only insofar as there is Dasein (SZ 183, 207–08, 212, 230, 316). But a deeper reading of *Sein und Zeit* and a study of the subsequent writings show conclusively that Heidegger, from the beginning, has never been a subjectivist. *Sein und Zeit* treats extensively of the epistemological problem of the reality of the external world, in a way which unhesitatingly acknowledges the objective existence of beings (SZ 202–08). The Kant study adds that man, as finite transcendence, in no way creates or can create the objects of his ontic knowledge (KM 112–13). If man were creative in this fashion, there would be no problem of finite transcendence at all, since this problem consists precisely in the fact that man understands the being of beings even though he is not capable of making beings come to be, but only of making them stand over against him as *ob-jects* (KM 30–31, 36–37).

But does not man create the object of his *ontological* knowledge, i.e., *being,* as the horizon of his encounter with beings? This impression might well arise in *Sein und Zeit* and in the Kant book, where being is primarily spoken of in connection with human projection. But the subsequent writings have conclusively established the fact that being enjoys the position of primacy, that it is being which "gives itself" to man (WG 43). Being indeed 'needs' man so that it can give itself to him, so that it can come to appearance at all, but the initiative remains undeniably on the side of being.

This change in precedence should not be understood as if man and being were two things confronting each other as the opposite poles of a relation in which dominance has now passed from one to the other, from subject to object. On the contrary, the whole question of transcendence, or the relation between man and being in the preontological understanding of being, occurs in a dimension which antecedes the distinction between subject and object, and indeed constitutes the ground of possibility for this distinction. We are not here concerned with the ontic, empirical encounter between a knowing human subject and beings which are known, but with the preontic and preempirical understanding of being which makes such encounters possible. Heidegger is speaking from the standpoint of Kant's transcendental position, which concerns the a priori conditions of possibility of human comportment with beings. Accordingly, he views being within the context of the transcendental problematic, and not within the confines of subjectivism or objectivism.[10]

Thus the turning takes place completely on the transcendental level. It is not an explosion of subjectivism, which is an ontic position, but much more a decisive shift of accent on the plane of transcendentality itself. Far from being a mere transition from subject to object, it is a change from 'Dasein' to 'Da-sein,' from man as the place of revelation of being to being as revealing itself in man. Succinctly formulated: before the turning, the whole consideration was from the standpoint of man; after the turning, the consideration is from the standpoint of being, but in both cases Heidegger's thought moves on the plane of transcendentality. This interpretation is confirmed by Otto Pöggeler: "Thus the turning is accomplished: no longer does Dasein as being-in-the-world stand in the center of the philosophical enterprise, but being in its meaning and in its truth and, consequently, in its role of rendering a 'world' possible. The direction of thought is no longer from beings to being, but from being to beings."[11]

Walter Schulz describes the turning as "a step from nothing to being."[12] His formulation summarizes the following process: Dasein's painstaking effort to ground itself in and from itself ends in the revelation of its own frailty and nothingness; Dasein sees that, of itself, it has and is nothing. Thus it is forced to the realization that it is exposed to existence, that existence is imposed on it, that it is borne along "by that which is not a being, but the ineffable ground of all beings, i.e. being itself."[13]

But this interpretation, as illuminating as it is, does not seem to describe adequately what is central in the turning. First of all, Heidegger's undertaking consists not so much in grounding Dasein in and from itself (which suggests an ontic grounding relation, which is not the proper concern of *Sein und Zeit*), but in understanding Dasein in and from itself ontologically, specifically on the transcendental level. Second, being does not make its first appearance in a sudden somersault of the argument from a preoccupation with nothingness, nor does it spring forth completely unexpectedly; rather it has been present from the very beginning of Heidegger's quest (cf. SZ 1). Schulz sees correctly that the discussion of nothingness is a necessary stage on the journey toward being, but he miscalculates the central thrust of the turning by placing the chief emphasis here. As our interpretation has tried to show, the essence of the turning lies in the change of the relation of primacy between Dasein and being, all of which takes place within the problematic of the transcendental being-question, to which nonbeing inseparably belongs as the first form of the appearance of being.[14]

Heinrich Ott's excellent book, *Denken und Sein* (*Thinking and Being*), follows Schulz's characterization of the turning as a change "from nonbeing to being."[15] But again this formulation does not seem to correspond to the inner dynamic of Heidegger's development, nor even to the central insights of Ott's own thought. He is more inclined to see the essence of the turning in the shift in the relation between being and Dasein: "The *name 'turning'* consequently may be grounded in the fact that . . . the consideration *no longer proceeds from Dasein but toward Dasein*."[16] Similarly he sees the new way of writing and the new meaning of 'existence' as an expression of the turning, wherein the 'before' corresponds to the Dasein phase, and the 'after' to the being phase of Heidegger's thought: "In this new way of writing and interpreting the word 'existence,' the 'turning' of Heideggerian thought finds expression in a most concise form: while 'existence' could possibly still be understood in a narrow 'anthropological' or 'existential' way, 'ek-sistence' immediately expresses the fact that man exists only as the one who perceives *being*."[17]

B. *Heidegger and Kant's Transcendental Position*

In understanding the turning it is important to note the relationship between the thought of the early Heidegger and that of Kant. Heidegger's approach in *Sein und Zeit* is entirely dominated by the Kantian transcendental problematic, as becomes clear in the Kant book. But his indebtedness to Kant is noticeable not only in *Kant und das Problem der Metaphysik.* In *Vom Wesen des Grundes,* for example, where he distinguishes his conception of ontology from various attempts at a 'realistic' ontology, he points out that it was "precisely Kant [who] in and through his *transcendental* problematic, was able to take the first decisive step since Plato and Aristotle towards an *explicit* foundation of ontology" (WG 15, note 14). The view that Kant is a true turning-point in the history of philosophy is expressed also when Heidegger writes that Kant's work "introduces the final turn of western metaphysics" (WW 25).

But Heidegger does not stop with Kant. In *Vom Wesen der Wahrheit,* it is already evident that he has begun to go his own way, even in the very conception of what philosophy is. Kant thinks that philosophy is the "mistress of her own laws" (*Selbsthalterin ihrer Gesetze*); Heidegger, on the contrary, sees it as "itself dominated . . . by the truth of that, of which its laws are even laws" (WW 25).

The most important aspect of this difference of outlook is the fact that it corresponds to the basic disagreement on the nature of the transcendental position itself. Heidegger points out that Kant, "according to his basic metaphysical position of subjectivity, could only conceive [the essence of philosophy] from this point of view" (WW 25). This undoubtedly indicates that Heidegger sees philosophy from another point of view, and according to a different "basic metaphysical position." What is this position? Has Heidegger abandoned the transcendental problematic and adopted a completely new approach? Or has he rather achieved a breakthrough of the Kantian position and overcome it by a further extension of its own proper internal dynamics?

The latter is undoubtedly the case. Heidegger's thought is a kind of explosion of Kant's transcendental philosophy, not in the sense of a demolition, but rather in the sense of a construction of a new position which emerges from the old, and for which the old is an indispensable prerequisite. The radical change in the relation of man to being which arises from the Heideggerian turning brings with it a decisive new nuancing of the transcendental problematic. This problematic has now evolved from a transcendental subjectivity to a transcendental posing of the question of being.

Heidegger's position remains a transcendental one, because the self-manifestation of being, as distinguished from beings, takes place in the transcendental domain, which thus necessarily remains the field within which all investigations in the direction of the question of being must be carried on. Nevertheless, this position is no longer Kantian, because a philosophy of being issues from it, something which was not possible for Kant himself. At best, the new being-oriented transcendental position is what Kant wanted to say, but not what he actually said. Heidegger's transcendental position is avowedly ontological, since it is a problematic which is explicitly directed toward, and preeminently determined by, being.[18]

C. Recapitulation of the Turning

The preceding interpretation of the turning can be summarized in the following points:

1. The central concepts 'being' and 'man' give evidence of both the continuity and the discontinuity in Heidegger's development: while remaining basically the same before and after the turning, they are both decisively amplified.

2. The essence of the turning, however, is not the enrichment in the content of these concepts, but the shift in the relation of man to being.

3. This change is not accomplished on the plane of the subject-object relation, but on the deeper dimension of the transcendental problematic; it is the development from 'Dasein' to 'Da-sein,' from man as the 'there' of being to being as 'being-in-man.'

4. This development effects a new breakthrough in the transcendental position itself, since this now becomes a transcendentality oriented not to man but to being.

The turning, then, does not imply a break in Heidegger's thought, but a development of the theme he originally set out to treat. The primary role of being was already basically adumbrated in the effort of *Sein und Zeit* to work out the prerequisites of properly posing the question of being.[19] Because of the nature of the phenomenological-existential analysis, however, the discussions of *Sein und Zeit* could give rise to the opposite impression of the primacy of Dasein, and thus lay Heidegger open to the charge of being an 'existentialist.'[20] Now, however, it has become clear that that which dominates man and history, and which man is appointed to serve as guardian and steward, is being, the overwhelming, the uncanny, the mysterious.

IV. *Death*

After this lengthy discussion of the horizon of our own more limited theme, we come now to the question of how death appears in *Einführung in die Metaphysik*, Heidegger's first work after the completion of the turning.

A. *Death as an Existential*

The inescapable power of death over man is acknowledged in the choral ode of the *Antigone* which we have treated above: "There is only one pressure he cannot resist or flee from, and that is death" (EM 113). Man can exercise his power over the totality of beings in many ways, but one thing frustrates all his might: death. This overpowers all his power, renders every perfection imperfect, and ultimately exiles man from everything with which he is familiar and at home (EM 121).

Moreover, death is not just another occurrence among the many varied events of human life, not merely the last in a series of experiences, all of which are of equal weight and value, but one which hovers constantly and essentially over man, accompanying him along the entire path of his existence: "insofar as man *is*, he stands in the inevitability of death" (EM 121). This thought comes to the fore also in relation to the teaching of Heraclitus: "The being of life is simultaneously death. Everything which enters life begins immediately to die, to head toward its death" (EM 100). In the language of *Sein und Zeit* this means that death is a continual determination, an existential of Dasein; Dasein is essentially being-unto-death.

This is assuredly only a confirmation of what has already been established concerning death. But *Einführung in die Metaphysik* also presents a new aspect of death in the remarkable notion of the shattering of Dasein against the overwhelming power of being.

B. *Shattering and Authentic Being-unto-Death*

The struggle between the power of Dasein and the overwhelming might of being is really an unequal fight, for there is no doubt as to its outcome. Being must triumph, because it presents itself as *physis,* the inexhaustible, emerging, abiding holding sway. This combat thus entails "the possibility of falling headlong into an abyss, in which there is no foothold and from which there is no exit," i.e., the unavoidable possibility of the ruination or the "shattering" of Dasein: "[Man's] power must be shattered against the superior power of being. . . . The Dasein of historical man means being set in position as the breach through which the superior power of being achieves its breakthrough and comes to appearance, so that the breach itself is shattered upon being" (EM 124).

Shattering is the direct consequence of Dasein's position as the steward of being. The service of Dasein consists in putting being to work, in enforcing the transformation of being into history, for Dasein is the place where being breaks in upon beings, the "breach" in which being "achieves its breakthrough and comes to appearance" (*erscheinend herein-bricht*). As such a breach, it must itself break asunder so that being can break in. In the concrete, this means that history, i.e., the advent of being among beings, presupposes the *transitoriness* of 'history-making' man. No history would be possible if men were eternal, immutable, and timeless, for they could not *become* anything; they would simply *be* what they are. Thus history, becoming, transitoriness, and temporality are all interconnected.

But the temporality of man is ultimately grounded in his three-dimensional structure, whose most basic feature is being-unto-death. Thus the "shattering against being," which is necessarily bound up with the history-making role of Dasein, means death as the fundamental structural element and the extreme possibility of Dasein. Since man exists as being-unto-death, the possibility of shattering necessarily belongs to his ontological constitution: Dasein *must* shatter against the overwhelming power of being.

In fact, man is forced into the position of Dasein so that he will shatter against being (EM 124); thus shattering belongs to the very teleology of Dasein. Moreover, this possibility is always present; it does not first set in "at the end, . . . but holds sway and waits fundamentally in the polarity of the overwhelming [power of being] and the power-activity [of man]" (EM 124). Thus shattering is not merely an event awaiting Dasein in the indeterminate future, but an existential determination which is part of its essential ontological makeup. Dasein is not only being-unto-death; it is also being-unto-shattering. Both are formulations of its being-unto-end.

Shattering is thus another term for the extreme and most characteristic possibility of Dasein. It is the accomplishment of the highest service which Dasein can render to being—its power-active 'cooperation' in the appearing of being in the midst of beings, or in history. The new aspect of this formulation of Dasein's being-unto-end lies in the fact that this existential is no longer merely present in Dasein but "holds sway . . . in the polarity" of being and man, i.e., in the relation between being and Dasein. To be sure, being-unto-shattering is a determination of Dasein, for it is Dasein which shatters against being. Nevertheless, man's being-unto-end is no longer defined merely from the viewpoint of Dasein, as was the case in *Sein und Zeit*, but from the viewpoint of the relation between Dasein and being. It is shattering of Dasein against being.

What is the significance of being-unto-shattering from the viewpoint of Dasein's relation to being and vice versa? The following can be said for being: being forces man into the position of a servant, sets him in position as the breach which is to be shattered, because it requires him for its irrupting appearance; thus it imparts to him his being-unto-shattering. This function of being is not to be understood as the ontic activity of an efficient cause, because the relation between man and being takes place in the preontological, transcendental realm. All that is claimed here is that being is the determining aspect within this relationship.

From the standpoint of man, being-unto-shattering can be considered as follows: man receives this determination from being, as a moment given with his existential constitution. His acceptance of this constitution is an act of service toward being. In fact, it is an outstanding service, since it is the total fulfillment of the assignment given him by being, and thus also the supreme recognition of the overwhelming might of being. This is how the hard saying is to be understood: "[His own] destruction is his most profound and broadest 'yes' to the overwhelming" (EM 125). In this acquiescence man reaches the highpoint of his existence. By relinquishing his claim to domination and acknowledging his subordination to being, he becomes existenti*elly* what he already is existenti*ally*: the sheltering steward of being. By his 'yes' to being, which means acceptance of the necessity of his own being shattered, he achieves the deepest authenticity of his own being.[21]

To summarize the foregoing:

1. Being-unto-shattering is an existential determination of Dasein; the phrase is a new formulation of the being of Dasein to its end, which in *Sein und Zeit* was called being-unto-death.

2. The new element in this formulation consists in the fact that it is considered from the standpoint of the relation of Dasein to being and not simply from the standpoint of Dasein itself, for the shattering in question is a shattering against being.

3. Being unto the end as being-unto-shattering is imparted to Dasein by being; in making this imparting its own, Dasein renders to being its supreme service and thereby achieves its own highest authenticity.

C. Death and the Transformation of the Image of Man

Sein und Zeit showed a double face: the existentialist side of the philosophy of human existence and the ontological side of the intended philosophy of being. The former we called the inauthentic, the latter the authentic philosophy of *Sein und Zeit*. The image of man emerging there was a heroic-tragic one, corresponding to the inauthentic side of the book; the image of man of the authentic philosophy of being did not appear. Now, immediately after the turning, the inauthentic image remains predominant; it even receives further amplification in the historical treatment of Greek thought. Nevertheless, a new image has begun to emerge, one more in conformity with Heidegger's philosophy.

The designation of Heidegger's early inauthentic image of man as heroic-tragic is supported both literarily and objectively by *Einführung in die Metaphysik*. Since Heidegger draws his interpretation of the Greek image of man from the poetic style of thought which found concrete expression in Greek tragedy, primarily from the first choral ode of Sophocles' *Antigone,* it seems fair to call this image a 'tragic' one. The objective features of the picture further bear out this designation. The adjective 'tragic' generally means characterized by, or involving death or calamity or suffering; terrible; calamitous. A tragedy is an event which excites pity or terror because of the miseries or misfortunes or catastrophe it entails.

These notions apply admirably to Greek man as seen by Heidegger in both the existentiell and the existential sense. In the concrete realization of his existence, Greek man typically suffers "death or calamity"; his life is one which "excites pity or terror by a succession of sorrowful events, miseries, or misfortunes, leading to a catastrophe." Moreover, the existential structure which provides the ground for these existentiell events is man's being-unto-end, which in the present context is called his being-unto-shattering, i.e., his existential proclivity toward the ultimate catastrophe of death.

Furthermore, man achieves the highpoint of his existence in calamity, since his shattering against the overwhelming power of being is his "most profound and broadest 'yes' to the overwhelming" (EM 125). Herein lies his true greatness, his proper authenticity; through acquiescence to the task assigned, even though it means catastrophe for him, he becomes a hero in the battle against (and for) being. Thus, according to Heidegger, the Greek image of man is not only tragic, but heroic. In this sense, it may legitimately be called heroic-tragic.

This concept of man even contains certain titanic or promethean features. It is essential to man that he rise up against all beings; he is necessarily a wielder of power, who forces his will on everything around him, breaking out against the sea and breaking into the earth, capturing and subduing other living creatures, rending being into beings (EM 118, 123). Man is "the worker who launches forth into the unspoken, breaks into the unthought, forces what has not yet occurred, and brings into view the unseen" (EM 123). But all of this is risky for him, because he is in contest with unfathomable powers: "Every violent subduing of the powerful is either victory or defeat. . . . [He] is always taking a chance. . . . In daring to try to subdue being, he must risk the counterpressure of nonbeing, *me kalon*, breaking apart, impermanence, unstructure and disorganization" (EM 123). In this dangerous battle there is no consolation and no rest; the war must go on: "Man as the wielder of power knows neither kindness nor pity (in the ordinary sense), neither soothing nor assuagement by success or prestige. . . . In desiring the unheard-of he throws all help away" (EM 125).

And in the end man suffers his final defeat: death, on which all his power runs aground (EM 121). Set in position as the breach of being, he must eventually be broken upon it (EM 124). This fateful task is allotted him by being itself: "Being itself throws man" (EM 125). He can thus do nothing but 'adjust' to his situation, by integrating himself into the overwhelming pattern: "In the shattering of the work he has done, in the knowledge that all is disarray and a *sarma* (dungheap), he leaves the overwhelming to its right" (EM 125).

With such bold strokes the titanic-heroic image of man is sketched. Of course, Heidegger would protest that everything is to be understood in an ontological rather than an ontic sense. Indeed, in the preface to *Was Ist Metaphysik?* written several years after *Einführung in die Metaphysik,* he explicitly denies ever having sought "to awaken surreptitiously the impression of a 'heroic philosophy'" (WM 47). No doubt this is true, for Heidegger wants his philosophy to be, right from the very beginning, a philosophy of being. Nevertheless, it is impossible to overlook the heroic-tragic, and even titanic, traits in the picture of human existence projected by the early writings, including the transitional work under discussion in the present chapter.

Still, the heroic-tragic element does not constitute the whole of the image of man in *Einführung in die Metaphysik.* Because of the turning, a new feature begins to emerge: a certain feeling of reverence before being. This characteristic makes its first appearance in an allusion to being as "that depth out of which the essential (*das Wesentliche*) ever approaches and indeed returns to man, thus compelling him to superiority" (EM 35). It is also hinted at in the characterization of being as "most worthy of all [our] questioning" (*das Fragwürdigste alles Fragens,* EM 63), which designation is meant literally, since only an attitude of respectful questioning pays due homage to the supremacy of being: "Questioning is the genuine and proper and only way to pay due respect to that which, from its position of supreme strength, holds our Dasein in [its] power" (EM 63). The new posture is also evident in the reference to 'shyness' (*die Scheu*) as an appropriate attitude with regard to being: "The uncanny (*deinon*) is fearsome in the sense of the overwhelming holding sway which commands not only panicky terror and true anxiety, but reflective, self-contained, reserved shyness as well" (EM 114–15).

The subject of death presents a concrete example of the emerging contest between the titanic and reverential tendencies in Heidegger's thought. In *Sein und Zeit* death was purely a phase in the existential analysis of Dasein; thus it could easily fit into the heroic-tragic mold of the total image of man. Now, however, it belongs to the context of the total relation of Dasein to being, and indeed offers Dasein the opportunity of rendering its supreme act of service to being. Death has thereby acquired a teleology which it did not explicitly have at first. The meaning of being-unto-death has been significantly enlarged in the direction of a "reflective, self-contained, reserved," rather than a heroic-tragic, acceptance of this existential necessity. Being-unto-death is no longer just the final sealing of the tomb of Dasein's finitude, but is now man's highest recognition of the overwhelming holding sway of being.

V. Summary

In *Einführung in die Metaphysik*, Heidegger inquires about the meaning of being as it presented itself to man's experience and thought at the dawn of western philosophy. What the early Greek thinkers meant when they spoke of 'being' was, in general, *physis* and *ousia*. In particular, however, 'being' meant *logos* and *polemos* for Heraclitus, and the correlation of *noein* and *einai* for Parmenides. These determinations enrich the concept of being with which Heidegger is concerned; however, 'being' remains fundamentally the same as in the earlier works.

Parmenides' famous saying, "For the same is both to think and to be," speaks primarily of being, secondarily of man. It means that the essence of man can be defined only from the standpoint of its correlation with being; accordingly, man is essentially the guardian of being. This view is confirmed and further explained by Sophocles' dramatic presentation of human existence. In *Antigone* the correlation of man and being is expressed as the relation between man as a wielder of power and the overwhelming power of being. Man's power is active against the totality of beings, but is ultimately shattered against the superior might of being.

This interpretation sheds further light on man's function in the 'lighting-up' of being. As the 'lighting-up-place' of being, man has the task of putting being to work, or, in the context of his temporality structure, of transforming being into history. Thus his subordinate position with respect to being is more sharply defined, but he remains basically what he was previously discovered to be: finite transcendence, whose meaning is temporality.

The turning in Heidegger's thought is not a change from subjectivism to objectivism, but takes place wholly on the level of the transcendental problematic which antecedes the distinction between subject and object. Through the turning, Heidegger achieves a new transcendental position, which indeed derives from the philosophy of Kant but is essentially distinguished from this by virtue of its radical orientation toward being. The turning is a legitimate continuation of the program originally announced in *Sein und Zeit*, but achieves a result which could not clearly be foreseen there: the ontological primacy of being.

In *Einführung in die Metaphysik*, death is once more presented as an existential structure of Dasein, indeed as the precise structure which requires that man's activity in the task of transforming being into history must ultimately be shattered. Being-unto-death now becomes being-unto-shattering. This new formulation indicates that death now occupies a new position: it is no longer located merely in the internal structure of Dasein, but in the relation of Dasein to being. It is an existential imparted to Dasein by being itself, for being sets Dasein in position as the necessarily shattering breach through which its holding sway is to appear. The acceptance of this situation is at one and the same time Dasein's supreme service to being and the achievement of its own authenticity.

Since man is defined by means of an interpretation of Greek tragedy, in which he necessarily ends tragically—by being shattered against the might of being and thereby attaining his true heroic greatness—the image of man sketched here can be called 'heroic-tragic.' Nonetheless, an opposing tendency begins to emerge in the picture, a certain serene reverence before being. This opposition opens up the horizon for a further development of the image of man and the role of death in the thought of Heidegger. We shall trace this development in subsequent chapters, first in the writings about poetry and language, and then in the exposition of the quadrate.

5

Death in History,
Poetry, & Language

In the course of our investigation, death has been discussed within the context of the crucial turning in Heidegger's thought. This development has been traced from its point of departure through its actual accomplishment to its definite consolidation. With the turning a far-reaching transformation occurs in the Heideggerian image of man, which affects the concept of death. Instead of merely being an existential, death becomes an element in man's relation to being, so that authentic being-unto-death signifies not only the affirmation of the structure proper to Dasein, but also the deepest possible 'yes' to being itself.

Because Heidegger's gaze after the turning is focused on being rather than man, his utterances concerning death, which belong essentially to the problematic of human existence, are sparse. Nevertheless, death does appear in four problem areas: history, poetry, language, and the essence of 'things.'

The writings of interest for Heidegger's discussion of poetry are the four Hölderlin interpretations from the years 1936 to 1943, collected under the title, *Erläuterungen zu Hölderlins Dichtung* (*Explanations of Hölderlin's Poetry*, HD), and the three articles, "Der Ursprung des Kunstwerkes" (1936), "Die Zeit des Weltbildes" (1938) and "Wozu

Dichter?" (1946), which were later published in the book *Holzwege* (*Woodland Trails,* HW). The writings in which the problem of language is articulated are the *Brief über den "Humanismus"* (*Letter on "Humanism,"* HB, 1947), the article "Logos" (1951) in the book *Vorträge und Aufsätze* (*Lectures and Essays,* VA), and the six essays of the book *Unterwegs zur Sprache* (*On the Way to Language,* US, 1959).

Also written in the first period after the consolidation of the turning, between 1936 and 1949, the following works cast additional light on the problems of poetry and language, and contain important statements on the central theme of the historicity of being: the two-volume work entitled simply *Nietzsche* (N I, N II), the sketch, "Überwindung der Metaphysik" contained in *Vorträge und Aufsätze,* the conversation "Zur Erörterung der Gelassenheit" appearing in *Gelassenheit* (*Serenity,* GL), *Aus der Erfahrung des Denkens* (*From the Experience of Thought,* ED), *Der Feldweg* (*The Country Lane,* FW), plus the epilogue to the fourth edition (1943) and the introduction to the fifth edition (1949) of *Was Ist Metaphysik?* (WM).

I. *Approaches to Being Itself*

Heidegger's principal concern after the turning is the thinking of being itself. He continues to ask about the meaning of being, a question which remains phenomenological, because it inquires about being insofar as being reveals itself to man. But the being question has undergone a two-fold change since *Sein und Zeit.* First, the question is considered less from the standpoint of man than from the standpoint of being. Consequently what *we mean* when we say 'being' is not the main point, but rather *what* we mean, in other words, what view of itself being affords when it reveals itself to us and permits us to understand it. The consideration of the being question has shifted its emphasis from the inquirer to that which is inquired about. Second, the questioning aims now at being itself, rather than at the being of beings. To be sure, being reveals itself only in beings, but "the decisive question is . . . no longer merely that of the basic characteristic shown by beings, how the being of beings may be characterized, but it is the question: What is this being itself? It is the question about the 'meaning of being,' not just about the being of beings" (N I 26).[1]

A. *The History of Western Thought*

In *Einführung in die Metaphysik,* Heidegger probed the thought of the pre-Socratics and concluded that while being itself was dimly present in the considerations of these great thinkers, still it was neither thought about thematically nor considered as itself (EM 74, VA 227–29). The subsequent period (which Heidegger calls the epoch of metaphysics) extending from Socrates, Plato, and Aristotle up to Nietzsche showed no essential advance, because being itself never became an explicit theme. Metaphysics considers beings in their being, but not being itself; it treats of the "leading question" of philosophy: What is a being?, but not the ultimate "basic question": What is being? (N I 13, 80, 455, N II 205; cf. N II 353–55, 371, 481–90, WM 8–11, 19–21)[2]

But the result of Heidegger's many thought-dialogs with the philosophers of the western tradition is by no means completely negative. Even though being itself does not speak in the pages of these great writers, still their thought is a record of the historical modes in which being has revealed itself. The "history of being" (*Seinsgeschichte*) is thus one of the privileged avenues of approach to being itself.

B. *Art*

If being itself is nowhere directly encountered in the history of western thought, where is it to be sought? Heidegger discovers an access in another realm of human activity, in an area which reflects an original relation of man to being—art. A true work of art is the product of the determining forces of a historical age. This means not only that the men of a particular era express their world view, i.e., their understanding of reality, existence, and the world, in their art, but also that the age itself appears and 'speaks' therein. The spirit or atmosphere of an age finds concrete, material expression in these achievements and writes a permanent record of itself in them. But this "spirit of the age" (GL 18) is really the all-encompassing horizon within which beings on the whole are seen, judged, and evaluated by the men of a certain period; in fact, the spirit of the age is the being of beings on the whole, or being itself, as it appears to man in a given era. Art is the deposit of a people's understanding of the totality of being; it is a reflection of being as it progressively reveals itself in history.

Accordingly, a work of art does not speak only of man, nor does it even speak of him primarily, but rather of being. Art is "a form of being on the whole, in fact . . . the preeminent form" (N I 94). It lets being reveal itself in a certain historical period and concretizes the unique relation of being to men in a certain time. Viewed from the standpoint of being, this means that through art being comes into the open, into unconcealment (truth); it puts itself to work by sending itself into the midst of historical beings. In fact, this is the most fundamental definition of art: the putting-itself-to-work of the truth of being (HW 25–28). Art is consequently a place where being is found at work, one of the privileged 'workshops' of being.

C. Poetry

In order to find being at work in art, Heidegger studies a Van Gogh painting and a Greek temple in the lecture "On the Origin of a Work of Art" (HW 22–24, 30–32). Later on in the same lecture, however, he awards the preeminent position among the various arts to poetry (HW 60, cf. N I 193). This special position rests on the direct relation of poetry to language, which, for Heidegger, is much more than a mere tool or instrument at man's disposal for the sake of communicating with others. Language is rather a primordial type of speaking in which being itself 'finds its voice,' expressing itself to and through man. As the art of language, poetry is the preeminent art form, in which being can most readily be found in the process of 'putting-itself-to-work.' From this point on, Heidegger accordingly restricts his discussion of art to poetry (HW 59–63).[3]

Heidegger's interest in poetry, at least insofar as his serious philosophical interpretations are concerned, is limited to the work of the controversial nineteenth century German poet, Friedrich Hölderlin. Although he has also written about other poets, including Rainer Maria Rilke, Eduard Mörike, Georg Trakl, Johann Peter Hebel, and Stefan George, Hölderlin remains for him the poet *par excellence*. This is no mere matter of personal preference or taste, but rather a judgment resting on the conviction that Hölderlin is the one poet who writes explicitly about poetry. In his work, poetry itself becomes thematic and problematical; of all the German poets, he is the one who explicitly reflects on poetry in his poems; he is accordingly the "poet of poets" (HD 32, 44, HW 251).

In Hölderlin's view, the poet's function consists in his standing between gods and men, in order to receive the joyful message from above, secure it in words, and pass it on to the care of his fellow men (HD 29–30, 43). Heidegger interprets this conception in the context of his view of the historical self-manifestation of being. The receiving, securing, and passing on of the message from above takes place in a particular era and among a particular people. The concrete form of the message reflects the total world view of the people in which it is received, secured, and handed on. The poetic expression of the message is the appearance of being itself, as it reveals itself to this people at this historic time; it is the self-sending by which being puts itself to work and emerges into unconcealment.

Because Hölderlin has this understanding of poetry, he is the out-standing poet who "thinks poetically down to the ultimate ground and center of being" (HD 44). He is not only the poet of poets, but the poet of being. Heidegger sees in Hölderlin's poetry an unusually fertile field for the study of the self-revelation of being; Hölderlin is the ideal partner for the strenuous enterprise of trying to think being itself. Heidegger accordingly sets himself the task "of bringing Hölderlin's poetic word into the realm of thought" (VA 138).

D. *Language*

From its inception, Heidegger's thought has been concerned with the problem of the relation between language and being. The problem had already been grappled with in the early thesis which won Heidegger his first teaching post at the University of Freiburg, *Die Kategorien- und Bedeutungslehre des Duns Scotus* (*Duns Scotus' Theory of Categories and Meaning*), and again in *Sein und Zeit* in connection with speech as an existential structure (SZ 160–66, US 91–93). Through the interpretation of poetry as the art form of language, Heidegger once again raises the problem, this time in relation to the self-revelation of being. He undertakes several explicit discussions of language as part of the effort to think being itself.

Like a genuine work of art, language affords special access to being. The language of a people, like their art, is a key to their collective understanding of the world and of themselves, and thus of the way being appears to them. On the one hand, a particular people's understanding of being is historically concretized in its language, and on the other, being, insofar as it sends itself to a people for their experience and understanding, shows up in their language. Viewed from the standpoint of being, language is thus "the mode of the occurence [of being]" (US 267); it is "not [just] a collection of words designating various . . . things . . . , but the *primordial sounding of the truth of a world*" (N I 364). One can find being at work in language, then, as well as in art.

II. *Being*

At this stage of Heidegger's thought, being retains the predominance over man which resulted from the turning, but in this predominance remains dependent upon man as the indispensable locus of its 'lighting-up.'[4] Being shows itself once again as *physis, logos* and *polemos*.[5] And, as in previous works, it manifests the paradoxical characteristic of simultaneously revealing and concealing itself.[6] But new aspects of being come to light in Heidegger's discussions of poetry and language.

A. *"The Side Facing Us"*

In the works on history, poetry, and language now occupying our attention, being remains the all-encompassing horizon within which all beings are encountered. It "assembles . . . each to each and all to one another" (GL 41), so that there is "nothing outside [of it]" (GL 68), in such a way that "even the nothing is not present without being" (HD 141). Being is simply and uniquely transcendent; it underlies and overreaches everything; it is the ground and source of all beings, not in the sense of an efficient cause, but rather as the open horizon which makes it possible for beings to be known as beings, or as the primordial illumination which sheds its light on all beings enabling them to be seen.[7]

But Heidegger wants to consider being not only as the horizon of beings, but in itself. He speaks of "being itself" (VA 78), the "open itself" (GL 40, 44), "the open surrounding us, in itself" (GL 41), "the region itself" (GL 42), and "the expanse itself" (GL 52). What is decisive here is the view that the horizon-aspect of being does not constitute its full essence. Thus Heidegger writes: "The horizon-function is . . . only the side facing us of an open which surrounds us" (GL 39); and again: "The horizon is . . . the expanse's side turned to our re-presenting. As horizon, the expanse surrounds us and shows itself to us" (GL 50).

But what is the "expanse" in itself? And how are we to think of the side of the open which is turned away from us? The immediate reply is that it is simply not to be thought; for it is by definition the inaccessible side of being, turned away from our gaze and incapable of being grasped as a phenomenon. Heidegger attempts to delimit it negatively, by saying that the relation of the expanse in itself to man and to things can be grasped neither ontically as a causal connection, nor ontologically as a transcendental-horizon relation (GL 55).

There now appear to be three levels to be considered in the question of being itself: (1) the existentiell-ontic level of beings, (2) the existential-ontological dimension of being as the horizon of human transcendence and of beings on the whole, and (3) the ultratranscendental or metaontological realm of being in itself. If it can be said to constitute the side of being essentially turned away from us, the third realm confirms the element of mystery previously discovered in being, when it was observed that being withdraws in the very process of sending itself, and that it reveals itself precisely by retiring into concealment. The paradox is expressed in Heidegger's assertion: "Being is what is nearest. Yet nearness remains farthest from man" (HB 76).

B. *The Holy*

In the Hölderlin interpretations, in the article on Rilke "Wozu Dichter?" and in the important self-interpretation *Brief über den "Humanismus"* Heidegger's favorite name for being is "the holy."[8] Hölderlin calls nature "the holy" because it is "older than the ages" (HD 57). Heidegger interprets this phrase ontologically: nature is "older than the ages," "because as marvelously omnipresent, it sheds its primordial light upon all reality, and it is in the opening created by this light that all things are enabled to appear" (HD 57). Nature is thus the original illumination, the horizon which is not itself a being, but within which all beings appear "through the awakening of the illuminating light" (HD 57). It is being as the source of beings, the "holy chaos" in the original Greek meaning of the word: "the gaping, yawning cleft, the open primordially opening itself, in which all is engulfed" (HD 61).

As the holy chaos, being opens the horizon not for a static, but for a historical appearance of beings. It opens up space-time as the context of history, not once and for all, but each time a new historical epoch dawns: "In its advent the holy . . . grounds another beginning of another history"

(HD 73). The holy must accordingly be historical itself in a unique, metahistorical way. Heidegger says that it is "the one and only (*das Einstige*) in a twofold sense. It is the oldest of all former things and the youngest of all things to come" (HD 61) and "the first before all and the last after all, . . . that which goes on ahead of everything and contains everything within itself" (HD 71). Being as the holy is the primordial root of everything past and the primal spring of everything to come, simultaneously the oldest and the youngest. It is always "present as coming" (HD 65), "the ever beginning and, as such, the ever abiding" (HD 71).

The "abiding" of the holy is to be understood not as "the empty lingering of something ready at hand, but [as] the coming of a beginning . . . , the unforeseeable originality of an origin" (HD 72–73). Being is historical as the source of all history; it extends unlimitedly and all-encompassingly back into the past and forward into the future; it is the always coming and ever abiding primordial event which gives rise to each epoch of history. It is the inexhaustible font and the totality of all history. In fact, it is primordial history itself.

Being, as primordial history, merits the title 'the holy' and has the quality of the *numinous*[9] because first, it is a *mysterium tremendum*: a *mysterium* because it is something wholly other than beings, "older than the ages," the primeval chaos, the open primordially opening itself, which sheds light upon every being (HD 57, 61); *tremendum* because it is "the unapproachable [which] renders idle every attempt at crowding too close" (HD 61); it "jars all experience out of its customary path, and sweeps away all solid footing" (HD 62). As sheer beginning, it is full of danger, for it brings with it "the violent concussion of chaos which offers no foothold, the terror of the immediate which baffles every approach" (HD 68).

Further, the holy enjoys the *majestas* of the simply overwhelming, since it reigns both before and ahead of man as the ever-present advent of a new beginning, encompassing both gods and men (HD 72–74). Thus it is "the highest" and as such "the bright," "the joyous," "that which is previously present in every finite thing, . . . the 'infinite' " (HD 18, 66–67, 99). Moreover, the abiding of the holy is a kind of eternity, not in the sense of a removal from all history and change, but rather as the ever perduring ground which lies at the basis of all history and all mutability among beings, letting these things rise up from within itself (cf. "the eternal heart," HD 71). As "omnipresent nature," "the all-creative," as that which awakens, besouls and vivifies everything (HD 51, 58–59), being is the source of all dynamism and energy, the preeminent *energicum*.

Yet being is also a *mysterium fascinosum*, attractive, comforting, generous, and protective. It appears "as a still light" (HD 16), conceals its terrifying aspect "in the gentleness of a soft embrace" (HD 62), allows itself to be transformed "through the stillness of the protected poet . . . into the gentleness of mediate and mediating words" (HD 68–69). From its immeasurable riches being lavishes upon the poet's words "a super-abundance of meaning, almost beyond human expression" (HD 64). Being is superabundance, continually overflowing and surpassing itself (HD 125), unceasingly welling forth while remaining in its original source (HD 143). It affords man a home and nearness to the source (HD 21), since it is itself the nearest, even nearness itself (HD 16, 23–24, 138–39, HB 77–78).

It may be asked if Heidegger has not given being a religious quality; if he has not merely substituted being for God. It is true that being as the holy does exhibit some characteristics traditionally attributed to God as the object of religious faith. It is all-encompassing, full of mystery, reigning always and everywhere, ultimately beyond man's power to control or comprehend, and in this sense, worthy of respect and reverence. Certainly it fulfills Rudolf Otto's definition of the holy as *mysterium tremendum et fascinosum*. Nevertheless, being is not properly a religious object, if religion is taken in the strict sense as involving adoration, worship, and service of a transcendent being who enters into personal communication with man, makes moral demands upon him, and promises rewards and punishments according to man's response to his proffered friendship. The tone of Heidegger's writing makes it clear that he does not intend to endow being with a personal nature, that statements about the holy are meant tentatively rather than literally, and that the whole discussion moves on the existential-ontological level, not on the moral and religious level.

Moreover, Heidegger explicitly rejects an identification of being with God: " 'Being'—this is not God and not a ground of the world" (HB 76). He is not concerned either with an ascent to the highest being, a tracing back to the first being, or a thrust forward to the ultimate being. His aim is to penetrate to the ontological ground of beings, i.e., to being itself insofar as it appears in beings and in history. To use a spatial metaphor, which is admittedly oversimplified: the direction of Heidegger's thought is not upward, backward, or forward, but inward. He is struggling to understand and express not the first or highest being, nor the final cause of all things, but simply being as man encounters it in the world of phenomena.

Nevertheless, the problematic of being as the holy is certainly not devoid of any connection with the question of God. Heidegger is of the conviction that the experience of being as the holy is an indispensable prerequisite for the proper posing of the question of God, as well as for the possibility of perceiving a manifestation of God in the present or any future age. The modern era is the "time of the night of the world," defined by the "absence of God"; our age is "already so impoverished that it can no longer recognize the absence of God as an absence" (HW 248). This unwholesomeness (*Unheil*) however, if recognized, can point the way to the wholesome (*das Heile*), "the intactness of being as a whole" (HW 272). The wholesome in turn can point to the holy (*das Heilige*), the holy to the *divine*, the essence of divinity, and the divine finally to the deity himself. Thus, the unwholesome can prepare the way for a new manifestation of God in the age of the night of the world. In the metaphor of the hunt, Heidegger describes the intricate process: "Unwholesomeness as such puts us on the track of the wholesome. The wholesome calls out and beckons the holy. The holy binds up the divine. The divine brings near the deity" (HW 294; cf. HW 272). This process can begin only "if previously and in lengthy preparation, being itself has been illuminated and experienced in its truth" (HB 86), for "only from the truth of being can the holy be thought. Only from the essence of the holy is the essence of divinity thinkable. Only in the light of the essence of divinity is it possible to think and say what the word 'God' means" (HB 102).[10]

C. *Primordial History*

The historicity of being has come to light in the discussion of being as the holy. Historicity, however, is not an attribute of beings which exist in time and change with time, but rather a primordial characteristic of being, according to which being is the ground of all history and may even be called primordial history itself. Since being is the source of history, all history is basically the history of being (*Seinsgeschichte*). Heidegger views the connection between the history of being and that which is customarily called world history in the following way: world history, primarily that of the West, has its roots in the basic metaphysical positions of the leading thinkers. These positions put their stamp upon history by preparing the ground for each new epoch; they are each in turn rooted in someone's original insight into the essence of being as it appears in a particular epoch. Consequently these positions are, on the one hand, "the ground and realm of that which we know as world history, particularly western history" (N II 92; cf. N II 343); on the other hand, they themselves have "their ground in the current essence of truth and the current essential interpretation of the being of beings" (N II 193).

Thus all history is ultimately grounded in the various epochal interpretations of the essence of being. But these interpretations, in view of the definitive primacy of being achieved through the turning in Heidegger's thought, are not to be understood merely as the result of human activity, but principally as self-interpretations afforded by being. Being 'sends itself' to man; it gives itself to be understood in particular ways at different stages of history. By revealing itself to man historically, it is the determining ground and source of all history, it is itself 'history,' the ever-continuing primordial 'event.' All this is implied when Heidegger says: "History is the history of *being*" (N II 28).

The consideration of being's historicity reconfirms the concept of truth as unconcealment found in Heidegger's interpretation of art and poetry. Being sends itself to beings in order to come to unconcealment in them: "It pertains to the essence of truth to establish itself in beings, . . . to be be-ing (*seiend zu sein*) in the midst of beings" (HW 50; cf. 57). Such self-establishing is a happening, and not just any happening, but a primordial one; it is the "event of truth" and thus of being itself (HW 25). Artistic work is an outstanding way in which the truth of being becomes be-ing and historical, since the essence of art is the putting-itself-to-work of the truth of being (HW 25, 64–65).

Poetry is accordingly being's permitting itself to appear in beings, the "self-donation of being in words" (*worthafte Stiftung des Seins*, HD 38). Since such an appearance is the primordial happening which lies at the basis of history, poetry is "the supporting ground of history" (HD 39). The initiative in such a happening is always on the side of being, for history is actualized only when being sends itself to man in a unique way. However, the event of being does not take place without human cooperation, since the source of history is always a banquet feast given by the holy, a wedding feast of gods and men, out of whose union there is born a new mode of truth's putting itself to work, and with it a new epoch of history (HD 98–101).

As primordial history, being is also primordial time. As the holy, it is "older than the ages," "the most ancient time" (HD 57–58). Its temporality, however, does not consist of passing through a succession of past, present, and future, as that of beings ready-at-hand does, but in the fact that it embraces all times. It is the ever-abiding, ever-present "advent of the beginning" (HD 73), which reaches back to the source of the entire past and ahead to the advent of the whole future; it is the source and totality of all times; it is primordial time itself. Thus the word *being* in the title *Being and Time* does not signify something other than that signified by the word *time; time* is rather "the first name of the truth of being, which truth is the essencing of being and thus being itself" (WM 17).[11]

III. Man

In view of the intimate relationship between man and being, Heidegger's effort to think being itself affects his conception of the essence of man.

A. *One Who Dwells Poetically*

Heidegger's interpretation of Hölderlin's line, "Full of merit, man still dwells poetically on this earth," confirms that the essence of man must be defined in terms of his relation to being. Heidegger reads Hölderlin's words in this way: through his conquests and achievements in the realm of beings, man amasses merit for himself in the realization of his destiny as lord of creation. But the essence of life upon earth consists in his dwelling "poetically," i.e., living in the nearness of being where he can cooperate in being's self-communication. This he does by keeping ready a place for being to appear as itself by imparting itself to beings (HD 39, 84–85). Only by dwelling poetically does man achieve his true essence; only by "taking leave of beings [and setting out] on the way to the preservation of the gracious favor of being" (WM 49) does he exist authentically as that which he is: the guardian of being's truth, or the shepherd of being (HB 75, 90).

This is not merely to say that man's essence is characterized by his relation to being; rather his essence *is* this relation. In the existentiell realization of his essential structure, he exists as the protecting, sheltering shepherd of being, keeping himself always ready for the delicate task entrusted to him. Consequently, his essence consists both in 'standing within' the illumination of being as its habitation (*Innestehen*), and in 'standing out' (*Ek-sistenz*) into the self-revealing truth of being (WM 15–16, HB 66–70, HW 55).

Man is thus one who dwells poetically upon the earth. The familiar definition summed up in the words 'rational animal' indeed expresses a truth, but does not attain the uniqueness of the essence of man. Since it considers man from the standpoint of animality and assigns him a designated place in the realm of beings, it does not do justice to his specific humanity, which consists in an ecstatic (in its root etymological meaning of 'standing-out') position within the realm of the truth of being (HB 64–66, 74–75, 89–90, N II 193–94).[12]

B. *Guardian of the House*

The essential relation of man to being reappears in the discussion of language. Heidegger views language as the result of being's communicating itself to beings (cf. US 267, N I 364). It is that wherein the self-revelation of being is received, preserved, and housed; in short, it is "the house of being" (HB 53). The inhabitant of this house is not being, but man, whose commission it is to be the guardian of being through his thought: "Ex-istence inhabits the house of being through thought" (HB 116). Through his dwelling in the realm of language, man lets being break into speech (HB 53); as one endowed with the gift of language, he lives "under the claim of being" (US 90). He is essentially the "bearer of the message" which he receives from being in language (US 136).

Clearly, then, language is not primarily a human instrument by which men communicate, but rather something by which being communicates itself to man, a mode of the self-revelation of being (HW 60–61, VA 212–13, 228–29). In this reversal of the usual conception, speech is not considered psychologically or genetically, but phenomenologically: Heidegger proceeds from the phenomenon of speech and considers everything from the standpoint of the concrete act of speaking. In this view, language (not in the sense of the faculty of speech, but in the sense of the concrete 'mother tongue' through which this faculty expresses itself) is always antecedently given, on the one hand as a structure which belongs essentially to the being of man as a member of a historical people, and, on the other, as the articulability of this people's understanding of reality, and consequently of being itself as it reveals itself to this people. The latter is the primary and most fundamental aspect of the structure of language, just as being is the determining factor in the transcendental relation between man and being.[13]

Thus not only man, but language itself speaks, and its speaking is more primordial, since it claims (*anspricht*) man or addresses itself to him (*sich ihm zuspricht*), and gives him the possibility of speaking himself. Language and man both speak, but each in its own way: language as the primary and primordial speaker, as "the sounding of stillness" (US 30), as the voice of being itself; man as the one who allows language (the truth of being communicating itself historically) to come to audible speech. Human speech is a kind of participation in the speech of language itself, a listening response, an answer to the appeal of language in the form of passing along and concretizing the message sent by language as the voice of being. It is authentic hearing, a *homologein* of the primordial saying of the *logos*, of being itself (US 20, 30–32, 254–55, 260, GL 49, VA 215–20, HH 34).

The relation between the speaking of language and the speaking of man mirrors the often discovered relation between being and man in Heidegger's thought. Language maintains a primacy of power and importance, and yet it is not something separate from man and independent of him. Language both requires and uses man in order to break into concrete speech. Man, in his speaking, is listener and speaker: he is the one addressed by the speaking of language and the one who gives language its determinate form by his own speech (US 30, 135, 155, 255–56, 260, 266, VA 226).[14]

C. The Locus of History

As being is historical in the sense of the primordial originating ground of history, so man is historical as the 'place' where being is recognized as itself and thus is allowed to shine forth in the realm of beings. Man's historicity consists in his being both the receiver and the locus of the reception of each successive self-sending of being. Thus man is historical not primarily because he stands in history as in a stream which rolls along extrinsically to him, but because his existence is intrinsically determined by historicity and can be understood only in terms of his essential relation to being imparting itself historically.

The essence of man, as Heidegger is here concerned with it, is not so much that of an individual man, but that of mankind, in the sense of a historical people: "not man, but the historical essence of man in his origin from the truth of being is at issue" (HB 90–91, cf. N II 380, 482). Through his relation to being man is brought into a community: the emergence of a history-making work of art, for example, "does not reduce men to their own individual experiences, but draws them into a common belonging to the truth occurring in the work, and thus grounds their being-with and being-for each other" (HW 55–56). Similarly poetry, as a mode of truth's putting itself to work, is "the primordial language of a historical people" (HD 40); the poet originates from the wedding feast between gods and men as the one who furnishes the foundations of the history of a people (HD 101).[15]

This point is important for the proper evaluation of Heidegger's understanding of man in the context of his thinking about being. The existential structure of being-with, which was phenomenologically discovered in the analysis of Dasein, now finds its grounding in the self-transmission of being itself. The individualization of man, which came out so strongly in *Sein und Zeit* and seemed to find its starkest expression in man's being-unto-death, is now complemented and balanced by the communal element of belonging to a historical people. It becomes evident that this social aspect is just as much a part of human existence as the capacity to assume sole and individual responsibility for one's own life (*das Sich-selbst-von-sich-selbst-her-übernehmen-können*). Moreover, both characteristics are ultimately grounded in being itself: individualization in Dasein's task of standing forth into the blinding light of being; belonging to a historical people in the particular history-making self-transmission of being.

The complementarity of individualization and belonging to a people yields the answer to a possible objection against the historicity of man as here presented. One might wonder whether the present emphasis on membership in a historical people does not so historicize man that he loses all personal individuality and uniqueness. Is Heidegger now affirming the theory of historical collectivism as opposed to nineteenth-century rugged individualism?

Heidegger clearly stands against any individualism which would hold for an absolute autonomy of man against being, or place man in the position of the absolute ruler of the totality of beings. Since the investigations of Greek thought carried out in *Einführung in die Metaphysik*, this is no longer compatible with Heidegger's thought. However, he just as emphatically rejects any form of collectivism which would attribute absolute dominion over beings to a human community such as a people, tribe, state, or nation. He would say that these are both forms of subjectivism, because they treat man, either individually or collectively, as a subject standing over against beings as objects. As such, they miss the real essence of man, which goes much deeper than a mere subject-object relationship between man and beings, to the transcendental level of man's primordial relation to being. Moreover, it is now clear that man does not hold the position of master, but rather that of protecting servant (HB 89, HW 81, 84–85).

Consequently, the structure of being-with which forms the basis of man's membership in a historical people involves no decision either for collectivism or individualism. Rather, it is the existential structure which lies at the basis of these ontic modes of behavior as their condition of possibility. Neither is it an encroachment upon the personal uniqueness of man, which remains intact. Rather it is a structure which belongs to the essential constitution of man just as primordially as the uniquely individual 'mine-ness' of existence.[16]

IV. *Death*

The conception of death as an existential appears once again in the designation of men as "the mortals" (*die Sterblichen*). Second, another nuance comes to the fore when Heidegger introduces the new concept of the death of the essence of man. Finally, death is explicitly shown to have a relation not only to man, but to being.

A. *"The Mortals"*

From the Hölderlin interpretations on, Heidegger's favorite expression for mankind is "the mortals." Hölderlin writes: "Commoner, more ordinary must the fruit become; then it will be suited to the mortals," and Heidegger understands it as a statement about the self-revelation of being. The essential word, or the fruit of poetry in which being is concretized in order to be understood and so to become the common possession of men, must make itself an ordinary part of everyday life, it must enter into the world of beings (HD 34–35). He similarly explains Hölderlin's idea that the poet must express himself in "mortal thoughts": in order to speak of the holy, the poet must imagine and think of it in the fashion of the mortals, the "sons of earth" (HD 16). He must express it in thoughts which are suited to the mode of thinking and the situation of mortals existing upon the earth. From this we can conclude the following: the mortals are those who cannot receive being directly, but only in particular, concrete beings and in the manner of 'sons of the earth'; they are truly men insofar as they are 'Dasein,' insofar as they exist in the 'in-between' stage, in which they belong to being and yet remain wedded to beings (cf. HW 88).

In another text the mortals are defined more accurately by contrast with other beings. Heidegger writes: "Every individualized reality . . . is possible only when, prior to all else, nature provides the openness (*das Offene*) within which the immortals and the mortals and anything at all can encounter each other" (HD 59). Thus, in the all-encompassing horizon of being, men as the mortals are bounded on the one side by things as beings merely ready-at-hand and, on the other, by "the immortals." These Hölderlin also calls "the heavenly ones," "divine ones," or "gods." The immortals and the mortals belong equally to the holy, or to being (HD 67); neither the one nor the other can relate directly to the holy, but "men require the gods and the heavenly ones require the mortals" in order to accomplish this (HD 66).

In this reciprocal relation the heavenly ones mediate between the holy and the mortals: they convey the greeting of the holy to men. Their proper essence consists in their being messengers. They are "the greeting-bearers, in whom the gladsome one (*die Heitere*) greets"; consequently, their essence is "expressed more properly by the name 'angel' " (HD 19).[17] It is the task of the mortals to receive the message of the holy conveyed by the gods, and give it concrete form among beings through poetry. By accomplishing this task they realize the authenticity of their own existence: for the mortals "the first homecoming consists of poetizing" (HD 24). Again in this context the mortals are men insofar as they belong to being, but can receive the message of being only through the mediation of other beings, which are here conceived of as the gods, or the messengers ('angels') of being.

Once more the character of death as an existential is confirmed, for the term "the mortals" signifies mortality as the proper and essential mode of human being. Mortality, in the full sense intended by Heidegger, marks man off from all other beings—on the one hand, from the immortals and, on the other, from things which are merely ready-at-hand—and at the same time indicates the relation to being which constitutes man's proper essence. Death is thus seen in the fuller perspective of being, for the mortals are those whose task it is to spend themselves in receiving, concretizing, and sheltering the delicate advent of being among beings. Consequently, what may here be called being-mortal is the same existential determination which was earlier encountered as being-unto-death. The difference is that here it is considered as the finite structure of man's existence, insofar as this is essentially determined by the transcendental relation to being itself.[18]

B. *The Death of Man's Essence*

A new trend in Heidegger's thinking about death arises from the problematic of the history of being. In the present age of technology, man stands under an unprecedented threat of death. The atom bomb is generally viewed as the instrument of this new, universal danger. Heidegger, however, finds a more basic, ontological threat of death in the essence of technology itself: "It is not the much discussed atom bomb, as one particular kind of killing-machine, that is so deadly. What has long menaced man with death, even with the death of his essence, is the absolute of pure willing, in the sense of the conscious imposition of man's will upon everything" (HW 271).

The real danger of death in the present age, as Heidegger sees it, comes not from the atom bomb, but from the theory of absolute subjectivity, the doctrinaire assertion of man as the absolute subject, the master of all beings. This is the greater danger, for it means the destruction of man not only in his ontic life, but in his very essence.[19] Here Heidegger overturns everyday modes of thought by reducing them to existential-ontological dimensions. He is not at all interested in a quantitative comparison of two dangers lying on the same level, but in an ontological or 'grounding' relation. The doctrine of man as the subject who is lord of all, who can manipulate the totality of beings, is by far the greater threat because it makes possible technology's claim to absolute power. On the basis of this doctrine, man understands himself as the being which can form, trans-form, manipulate, build, and destroy the whole of creation.

As a result of this doctrine man forgets his vulnerability as part of the totality of beings. As history has shown, the unrestrained struggle of man against beings inexorably turns into the struggle of man against man. Man's desire to dominate other kinds of beings inevitably entails the desire of some men to dominate other men. The violence and wars of the twentieth century offer ample proof of this. The urge to create and dominate entangles man in the evils of slavery and destruction, not as a result of the machinery he invents to carry out his purposes, but because of the underlying conviction of his absolute power. Humanistic subjectivism is the greater menace to mankind.[20]

The essence of man consists in his relation to being; he is essentially the shepherd, the guardian, the steward of being, whose task is to care for the arrival of being among beings. But in technology, which represents the acme of subjectivism, this relation is reversed. Man is seen not as the servant of being, but as the unlimited master of all beings—a reversal which entails a direct denial of the simple, hard fact that being is not the plaything but the supreme benefactor of man. The denial cannot fail to have fatal consequences. Man loses the nearness to being which consti-tutes his true and proper essence: because of technology he is, to all intents and purposes, essentially dead.

But isn't technology a glorification of the might of man and thus really an exaltation of his essence? The glorification is actually illusory, because technology, if allowed to become a doctrinaire 'technologism,' necessarily tends to swallow up man's existence. Everything becomes fair game for the exercise of power; all beings are potential materials of production. Thus "the earth and its atmosphere become raw material. Man becomes human material" (HW 267); he is merely "the most important raw material" (VA 92). There is the frightening prospect "that man will lose his self in unlimited productivity" (HW 270) and become a mere "functionary of technology" (HW 271). Man would then no longer exist as absolutely distinctive Dasein, but only as something ready-at-hand, emptied of his real self, killed in his essence—a 'man' without the essence of man.[21]

The eventual deliverance from this danger must come from the same source as the threat itself, "from there, . . . where the issue turns on the mortals in their very essence" (HW 273). The situation demands a rethinking of the essence of man, a rediscovery of man in his relation to being. To that end, there is a crucial need of men who can perceive and point out the danger, who are strong enough to experience and withstand the full force of the threat, who can peer unshaken into the abyss of the utter destitution of our age (HW 273, 248–49). Heidegger found in Hölderlin such a man. Following Hölderlin's example, Heidegger is endeavoring "to bring man back again into his essence" (HB 61), so that man can "find the way to his abode in the truth of being" (HB 115).

In the face of the threat to man's essence, Heidegger strives for a rethinking of the essence of man, a conversion, a *metanoia*. This is not the intrusion of a religious or theological concern in the traditional sense, because Heidegger is not trying to stimulate a conversion to God, but to being and to a new view of man in his relation to being. Consequently, his interest remains philosophical. It is not, however, without theological consequences, since Heidegger views the needed philosophical conversion as the indispensable prerequisite for a possible return of man to God or a new advent of God to men. First, the horizon must be opened up for such a confrontation; the stage must be set by accomplishing a new understanding, both of man's own self and of being, a new way of thinking in which the dimension of the holy and the realm of mystery are accorded their rightful place. This is the sense in which the following words of Heidegger are to be understood: "The beginning of a new era does not occur merely because a new god bursts in from hiding, or the old god in a new way. Where should he turn on his arrival, if a place has not been previously prepared for him by man? How could there ever be a suitable residence for God unless the splendor of divinity had previously begun to shine in everything that is?" (HW 249)

C. *Death and Being*

To find his way back to his own essence, man must rethink being and his own relation to it. But a new understanding of death is also required. As the determining existential of Dasein, death especially must be seen in its relation to being. In this context, Heidegger discusses death (1) as something positive which belongs to the realm of being, (2) as a place for the breakthrough to being, (3) as the passage to authentic dwelling with being, and (4) in its relationship with language, a relation which is ultimately grounded in being.

In the discussion of the threat to man's essence posed by modern technology, the concept 'death' is obviously used analogously; in the strict sense, death is the extreme and all-embracing possibility of Dasein's individualized existence. Still, these two usages of the term have an intrinsic connection, for the menacing danger of the death of man's essence stems from the misunderstanding or the forgetting of the true essence of man, which is decisively determined by the existential of death in the strict sense. In other words, essential death threatens man because he no longer understands his own essence, and therefore misunderstands death. Thus Heidegger writes: "Our age is destitute not only because God is dead, but because the mortals can scarcely recognize and cope with their own mortality. The mortals are not yet in possession of their essence. Death withdraws and becomes an enigma. The mystery of pain remains veiled. Love is not learned. . . . The age is destitute because the unconcealment of the essence of pain, death, and love is absent" (HW 253).

But it might be objected that man, rather than misunderstanding death, can now dominate and control it as never before. He has become master of the ways and means of inflicting death, even to killing hundreds of thousands instantly. On the other hand, discoveries have also enabled man to prolong life significantly and thus to postpone death more and more; there are some who dream of doing away with death entirely.[22]

The attempt to make death completely manageable by technology is a proof that technological man does not understand his own essence and mortality. In trying to control death, he understands it only as an event occurring at a particular point of time, a biological condition whose intrusion should be put off for as long as possible. To be sure, this death is merely ontic; it is in the category of a thing ready-at-hand which is not yet actual, a future reality which is not yet real. The authentic understanding sees death as an existential, a constant determination of Dasein, the mode of human existence. As such, death does not merely occur at the end of a man's life, but is always and already there. Death in an authentic sense cannot be postponed any more than life itself. It is ever and already present as a positive determination of man.

The technological misunderstanding of death lies in viewing it as purely negative and consequently something to be averted. Technologism tends to consider as positive and real only what it can measure, manipulate, and control. To want to control death is a natural extension of this outlook. If death proves too elusive, intangible, or unpredictable to be grasped and manipulated, then it is considered outside the pale of positive reality, negative and unreal. Accordingly, technology is "the firm negation of death. Through this negation, death itself becomes something negative, something completely inconstant and empty. . . . But what is more real, and that means in the modern idiom, more certain, than death?" (HW 279)

Because of its undeniable and profound reality death must be thought positively and "without negation," as we read in a letter of Rilke cited by Heidegger (HW 279). Similarly in another letter, Rilke calls death "the side of life which is turned away from us, not illuminated by us" (HW 279). Heidegger interprets Rilke as referring to death not as part of Dasein's structure but as belonging to being: "Death and the kingdom of the dead belong to the totality of beings as its other side. This realm is . . . the other side of the whole network (Bezug) of the open" (HW 279). While this region turned away from us might seem to be something negative, it is not so "when we think of everything in the broadest circle of beings" (HW 279). Death is no longer to be explained and understood from the standpoint of Dasein alone, but in relation to, and from the viewpoint of "the whole network of the open," i.e., in and from the standpoint of being.

Thinking death positively means thinking it in relation to being. As an existential of Dasein, death is more real for man than any other reality. It is not ready-at-hand, nor does it belong to the realm of things ready-at-hand, but it is proper to man insofar as he is Dasein and stands in the illumination of being. But what can death, which at first sight appears to be the intrusion of utter darkness, have to do with the illumination of being?

Since death is not controllable by man, it represents a crucial point at which the impassioned effort to reduce all reality to the status of manipulable objects inevitably fails. Consequently, it plays a preeminently central role in man's understanding of himself and of being, since it demonstrates that man is not the absolute master of the totality of beings, nor of himself, but is ultimately naked and defenseless before the overwhelming power of being. Thus, death is the key to the adequate understanding of the essence of man, just as it points categorically to the superiority of being, to which the essence of man is related. "It is death that touches the mortals in their essence and so sets them on the way to the other side of life and thus to the whole of the pure network [of being]" (HW 280).

Since death permits man to experience his subordination to being, it is the locus of a possible breakthrough to being itself. Man can turn the negativity of his own helplessness before the totality of beings into something positive, in that he can understand death not only from the standpoint of his own life, but from the standpoint of being. Death forces man to look beyond the narrow compass of his own life to understand his existence; in this way he can "turn his defenselessness as such toward the open [of being]" (HW 280). Just as, in the earlier phase, death guaranteed the completeness of the analysis of Dasein, and authentic being unto death constituted the authenticity of existence as a whole, so now, in the later Heidegger, death plays a decisive role as the place for man's breakthrough to being itself.

Remarkably enough, death seems to have supplanted anxiety as the privileged avenue of approach to being (cf. SZ 184–91, WM 31–33). But this is not completely new, for death and anxiety were always closely associated. In *Sein und Zeit*, Heidegger demonstrated that only anxiety can sustain the openness of Dasein in the face of the indeterminacy of the 'when' of death. Thus he could assert: "Being-unto-death is essentially anxiety" (SZ 266). This is confirmed again, but now from the other side. Anxiety is essentially being-unto-death, because the anxiety capable of giving Dasein a glimpse into the mystery of nothingness and of being itself, is seen here to be the anxiety in which man experiences the absolute limit of his power over beings and the necessity of his own shattering against the might of being. In anxiety, Dasein gains the realization of its being-unto-death.

A rather remarkable use of the concept of death is found in Heidegger's treatise on Georg Trakl's poetry, "Language in the Poem" (US 35–82). Here death appears as the "downfall" or "destruction" (*Untergang*) to which "the soul," which is "a stranger on the earth," is summoned (US 42). At first sight, this seems quite traditional: death means that the soul of man is called from its pilgrimage on earth to its true homeland in eternity. But Heidegger interprets the passage in an existential-ontological framework and from the standpoint of the problem of being.

The soul, which Heidegger understands as man himself, is a stranger on earth not because its true homeland is elsewhere, but because it must find its true homeland here; to take his proper place among beings on the earth, man must expend much time and energy wandering and searching

(US 41). Consequently the downfall to which the soul is called is "not here conceived . . . as the termination of earthly life" (US 46), "not decay, but the quitting of the decayed form of man" (US 46), i.e., the taking leave of the human form which is not "translucent with blueness" (*durchschienen von der Bläue,* US 47) or which "does not stand in the wind of the holy" (US 47).

As in the Hölderlin interpretations, "the holy" signifies being, which in Trakl is symbolized as "blueness" or "the blue" (*die Bläue,* US 44). The downfall is the perishing of the inauthentic form of man which preoccupies itself exclusively with beings in everyday existence, without asking the meaning of being. The downfall is, at the same time, a passage to the realm of authentic human dwelling upon the earth, i.e., in the blue, in the domain of the holy, in the nearness of being. In order to discover this realm, the stranger must first suffer destruction; he must "lose himself in the spiritual twilight of the blue" (US 51). The one who 'goes under' "is not someone who has passed away in the sense of dying," but rather one who now "looks ahead into the blue of the spiritual night" (US 55).[23] This is a land of night because the authenticity of human dwelling demands that man leave behind the familiar and prosaic surroundings in which he feels at home. In spiritual death there "lies hidden a leave-taking from the former domination of days and seasons"; there is escape from the tyranny of the commonplace (US 52).

What remains after such a radical break with the past is at first nothing, since the soul's everyday world is gone. But beyond this transitional stage there is a 'second death.' The downfall of the soul is not merely "a falling away into emptiness and annihilation" (US 51); it is also the arrival "at a quieter sojourn in the early morning" (US 69); the departed one has passed "into the 'golden showers' of early morning" (US 71; cf. US 54). Through his downfall the stranger comes to reside with being. In stillness, being breaks in upon him like the breaking of a new day and lodges with him. Thus the stranger arrives at the authenticity of his dwelling upon the earth, or "at the beginning of his pilgrimage" (US 52), which is "unto death" (US 23). Through the submergence of his old inauthentic self, he begins to exist as that which he is in the existential-ontological ground of his being: journeying being-unto-death.[24]

The downfall, an analogous death, parallels death in the strict sense as the extreme possibility of Dasein's existence. The destruction of the estranged soul constitutes its passage from inauthentic to authentic dwelling upon the earth; similarly, death in the strict sense plays a decisive role in the authenticity of human existence, for this authenticity consists in the conscious affirmation of one's own being-unto-death. The acceptance of being-unto-death discussed in the existential analysis of Dasein appears here as the metaphorical destruction of the soul which is a stranger upon the earth, or vice versa: the downfall is concretely realized as the assumption of one's own being-unto-death, which constitutes the authentic existence of man. Thus, destruction in the soul's pilgrimage unto death and acceptance of one's own being-unto-death mean the same thing: passing over to the authenticity of existence.[25] Also, the soul's downfall leads beyond the night of departure from everyday beings to the 'early morn' of the abode with being. Similarly, death in the strict sense leads beyond the nothing to being; for it signifies not only the fading away of all beings ordinarily encountered, but also the definitive breakthrough to being itself, insofar as the possibility of death discloses to man his radical defenselessness before beings, and makes him aware of his subordinate position and his essential relatedness to being. The passage of the soul through the dark night of its downfall to the light of early morning is the same occurrence that was previously described as the emergence of the nothing and of being through the illuminative power of the existential of death. In each of these processes, man realizes that he is handed over by death both to the nothing and to being; he understands himself as finite transcendence, as one who dwells on earth and understands being.[26]

Death plays an intimate role even in the structure of human language. As the one who speaks, man dwells in the house of being, where he fulfills the double task of guardian and lighting-up-place for the revelation of being. He lives "under the claim of being" (US 90), for his speaking is a response to the speaking of language, which is the voice of being itself. But this position of service to the speech of language is proper to man not just because he is the one who understands being, but, remarkably enough, because he is mortal: through our dwelling in the world of language, says Heidegger, we are brought into the realm "wherein we, who are employed for the speaking of language, dwell as the mortals" (US 266, cf. US 38). There is thus an interior connection between being one who speaks and being mortal.

At first sight, the association of death and language would seem to be grounded in the essence of man. Heidegger writes: "The mortals are those who can experience death as death. The animal cannot do this. But neither can the animal speak" (US 215).[27] Thus, being-unto-death, in the sense of a conscious knowledge of one's own mortality, and speaking are modes of being proper to man; they are both existentials. "The essential relation between death and language flashes forth," continues Heidegger, "but is still not thought out" (US 215).

To meet Heidegger's challenge, let us start with man as speaker. Human speech bears unmistakable signs of finitude, which is existentially rooted in man's being-unto-death. Man is thrown into language by being immersed in a preexistent language system. He does not invent language in order to associate with other beings; rather, language is given to him as the prior framework within which he can encounter beings. But language, into which man is thrown, is not something eternal, remaining ever stable and immune to change. Language undergoes aging and renewal, introduction of new forms and decaying of old. What is important here is that man cooperates in this process by continually reshaping his language, coining phrases and putting the stamp of his ever-changing experiences upon it. Thus, his relation to language is twofold: he is thrown into it, and he projects it. In respect to language, man is both passive and active; he is the thrown one who projects.

We met this paradoxical pattern in the beginning of Heidegger's search, first in the basic three-dimensional structure constituting man's temporality. Within this structure, precedence was attributed to the element of futurity, since existence meant primarily being-ahead-of-oneself; it was only on the basis of this projectedness toward the future that existence was seen to include the elements of already-being-in and being-with. In other words, man understands himself primarily in terms of the possibilities which are realizable but not yet actual (future); then, on the basis of this, he comes back upon himself as the sum of all experiences which up to the present moment have made him what he is (past); finally, as this future-oriented past, he can authentically address himself to the beings which constitute his present ambiance (present). Since death is the uttermost possibility of man's existence, being-unto-death is the decisive structural element in that temporality which lies at the basis of all human activity, including speech. Accordingly, being-unto-death is the most radical reason for the fact that man speaks as a projecting speaker who is thrown. Being-mortal is thus the ground of man's being-a-speaker; man speaks as the appointed guardian of the house of being because he is mortal.

Can one also say, vice versa, that man is mortal because he is a speaker? To say that man is mortal means that he can experience death as death (US 215), that he can understand it as an existential, as a determination of his own being. Specifically human mortality is thus grounded in man's capacity for understanding being. But this capacity entails the possibility of speaking; for speech, in the existential-ontological analysis, is ultimately grounded in the articulability of the preontological understanding of being (SZ 160–66).[28] Moreover, human speech always speaks of being, always says 'is', it says that something is, how, when, where, and why it is (cf. EM 67–70, N II 246–50). Thus, speaking is inseparably linked with the understanding of being: if someone speaks, he says 'is,' and if he says 'is,' he understands being. The capacity for speech is rooted in the primordial preontological understanding of being.

Being-unto-death and being-a-speaker thus have a common ground in man's understanding of being. Moreover, their relation is such that neither can exist without the other. Man speaks finitely because he exists as being-unto-end; conversely, he knows death as death because he has the capacity for speech—a preontological, articulable understanding of being. Man speaks as he does insofar as he is mortal; likewise, he is mortal insofar as he understands being and so can speak.[29]

But this leads us still farther, even unto being itself. Man speaks because he dwells in language as in the house of being, i.e., he is appointed by being as the guardian of the house. Is this also true of death? Is man also mortal because he lives under the claim and domination of being? Is the connection between death and language ultimately grounded not merely in the essence of man, but in being itself?

The concept of death as a shattering against being points up the essential connection between death and man's position as the lighting-up-place of being. In order that being may come to presence, appear, or be lighted up, man must act as the staging area where being transforms itself into beings, or as the breach through which being breaks into history. But man must break asunder in order to be this breach; he must exist as transitory being-unto-death so that history may occur. He is set in position by being itself to make possible the self-communication of being, precisely by his being shattered in the process. Man's mortal or shatterable being accordingly stands directly in the service of being; he is under the claim of being precisely insofar as he is mortal. Just as man, as speaker, dwells in the house of being, so does he, as mortal, serve in the breach of being. These two determinations are given him by being and are ultimately grounded in being.

Heidegger formulates the complicated relationships between being, language, and death in various ways, all of which basically allude to the fact that man's speaking, his death, and indeed his whole essence are ultimately grounded in the event (*das Ereignis*) of being: "The speaking of language . . . occurs as that which affords . . . the mortals their abode" (US 14); "The event gives the mortals the abode in their essence, so that they are able to be speakers" (US 259); "The event is *the* law, insofar as it gathers the mortals together into the happening, unto their own essence, and maintains them in it" (US 259).

The event is considered as the primordial speaking by which being first expresses itself; it is the original self-revelation through which being emerges into the open and comes into unconcealment (compare the determinations *physis, logos* and *aletheia*, US 256–61, 264–67). The event is not something completely separated from man but takes place through and within him. Moreover, its occurrence brings man into his own essence, which consists precisely in being its natural locus. In order to fulfill this, his essential function, man must be the fragile breach (mortal being-unto-death) through which being can break in, as well as the speaker who can allow being to come to the utterable word. Consequently, the event is that which confers upon man his own proper essence as mortal speaker, or speaking mortal. Being-a-speaker and being-mortal, language and death as existentials of man's being, are thus ultimately grounded in being itself.

V. Summary

In order to think being itself, Heidegger turns to history, art, poetry, and language. In these investigations, being reveals itself in its horizon character as the side of the all-encompassing open which is turned toward man, as the holy which reigns in all beings and approaches man in an ever original way, and as the source of all history. Man dwells poetically in the nearness of being, is the guardian of language which is the house of being, and is the receiver of the current self-communication of being which originates a historical epoch. Man's belonging to a historical people—the concrete expression of the structure of being-with which was disclosed in the existential analysis of Dasein—balances the strongly individualizing tendency of his being-unto-death.

The thought of death is implicit in Hölderlin's use of "the mortals" as a name for man. Heidegger's adoption of the term shows that he continues to consider death as an existential, but now in the perspective of man's relation to being. A further nuance appears in the statements about the threat to man's essence presented by modern technology. The menace derives from a misunderstanding of the essence of man and consequently of death itself. Death must not be considered negatively, but positively, as something belonging to the realm of man's essence and of being. Since death belongs to the realm beyond beings, it is a witness to man's transcendental subordination to being, and as such an extraordinarily appropriate point for the breakthrough to being itself.

This line of thought is extended further in the poetic characterization of death as the downfall of the estranged soul, since the downfall signifies the passage to authentic dwelling in the proximity of being. The relation between death and language is seen to have its roots first in the essence of man, but ultimately in being itself, since it is being which brings man into his essence as both a speaker and a mortal.

6

Death in the
Game of Being

Heidegger's concern in the later writings is the thinking of being. But as a consequence of being's dominant position, secured by the turning of Heidegger's thought, this thinking is no longer to be understood only as an activity of man, but more as a favor accorded man by being. Thus the phrase, "the thinking of being," entails both a subjective and an objective genitive: from the viewpoint of being, it means a self-revelation; from the viewpoint of man, it means being's letting itself come to words in the responsive speaking of man.

In this chapter, we shall consider still another mode of being's self-revelation, in order to define further the role of death: the emergence of being in the essence of 'things.' We shall study the following writings, which fall within the period of the 1950s: four essays which comprise the middle section of the book *Vorträge und Aufsätze* (*Lectures and Essays*, VA): "Das Ding" ("The Thing," 1950), "Bauen Wohnen Denken" ("Building, Dwelling, Thinking," 1951), ". . . dichterisch wohnet der Mensch . . ." (". . . Man Dwells Poetically . . . ," 1951), and "Was heisst Denken?" ("What Summons Thought?" 1952); the article "Die Sprache" ("Language," 1950), published in the book *Unterwegs zur Sprache* (*On the Way to Language*, US); and finally the book *Der Satz*

vom Grund (*The Principle of Ground,* SG, 1957). For a further clarification of what is said in these works, we shall call upon the essay "Gelassenheit" ("Serenity," 1955) which appears in the book of the same title
(GL), and the two brief, though informative publications, *Zur Seinsfrage*
(*On the Question of Being,* SF, 1955) and *Identität und Differenz* (*Identity and Difference,* ID, 1957).

I. *Being and Things*

How does being appear in the things of our experience? Heidegger takes
his point of departure not from being, but from things themselves. He
asks: What is the essence, the thingness of a thing? What makes a thing
what it is? What lets it be and be present as that, as which it is and is
present? Heidegger understands these questions concretely. He inquires
not about the abstract, universal essence of things in general, but about the
thingness of a definite, concrete individual thing; in the essay "Das Ding"
("The Thing") about the thingness or jugness of a jug. Furthermore, he
understands the question phenomenologically—he is looking for the essence of the jug, insofar as this shows itself to man, concerns man, and
"comes near" to him (VA 164–65).

A. *The Essence of Thing as the Gathering of the Quadrate*

Does the jugness of the jug consist in its reality, in the fact that it is a real
object? But what is a real object? It is something independent of a subject,
capable of being presented to, and represented by, a knowing subject.
Objectivity in this sense, however, does not constitute that which the jug
is, does not constitute its being, for the jug is a jug before and independently of its being presented or represented; it is and remains a jug,
whether a knowing subject represents it to himself or not. Thus objectivity, instead of constituting the being of a thing, merely adds a consequent
determination to its already constituted being, namely, the relation to a
knowing subject. Representative, objective thought remains on the level
of the subject-object dichotomy (the ontic level of beings, which are, in
this case, the subject-being and object-being) and does not reach the transcendental, ontological dimension of the being of the thing (VA 165).

If the essence of the jug does not consist in its objectivity, in its
'standing before' and 'across from' a subject as something opposed to it

(*objectum*), in what does it consist? In its independence as something that stands in and by itself? This standing-in-and-by-itself of the jug, however, is not ultimate, but rests on the fact that the jug was brought to this state. It was brought to a 'stand-still' by the operation of producing causes, such as the classical four causes of Aristotle. This having-been-produced, however, is another mode of objectness, for it means the standing of the jug 'before' or 'across from' its producer, either as an antecedent exemplary form or as a subsequent completed product. The concept of the jug as the thing which stands in and by itself thus remains in the framework of the subject-object relation. It defines the jug *ab extra*, from the standpoint of the producer, and therefore does not reach the transcendental dimension of the being of the jug (VA 165–66).

The jug shows itself essentially as a container; its essential feature, that which makes it a jug-thing, is containing. Containing is the unity of taking and holding; this unity, however, does not exist for its own sake, but is oriented toward pouring. Thus pouring determines the containing of the jug, just as the containing, and thereby the jug itself, achieves its true essence as the thing that it is in pouring (VA 170).[1]

The containing of the jug is a gathering of taking and holding. In addition to this gathering, which lies, so to speak, behind the pouring, a second manner of gathering is discoverable in the pouring, a gathering which is pointed forward to the purpose which the pouring serves. There are four moments or elements thus gathered together in the pouring of a drink: the earth, insofar as the drink comes from the earth, e.g., water from a well or wine from a vine; the heavens, which send rain and thaw, sun and warmth to help produce the drink; the mortals, whose thirst is quenched, leisure enlivened, and social living cheered by the drink; and finally the immortals, in whose honor a drink is often poured as a libation (VA 170–71).

These four elements make up the essence of the jug in Heidegger's sense of essence; the particular constellation of the four moments, earth, the heavens, men, and the immortals, constitutes the being of the jug as the particular thing that it is. A thing is thus authentically present in its own thingness insofar as it evokes the 'quadrate,' gathers into unified presence the four moments, brings them to an abiding 'stand-still,' to self-manifestation, to unconcealedness. The essence of a thing thus consists in the gathering of earth, the heavens, the mortals, and the immortals, by which the quadrate comes to pass (VA 172).[2]

149

B. *The "Worlding of World" in the Quadrate*

In formulating the quadrate, Heidegger is saying that a thing appears in its true essence only when it is grasped in the all-embracing horizon of being as a whole. In order to appear as that which it authentically and essentially is, a thing must be understood in its relations to the natural (heaven and earth), human (the mortals), and divine (the immortals) components of the totality of beings.[3] Thus, for example, a jug is not understood in its full essence as a thing when it is seen merely as the product of a technical process, merely as an object to be purchased in a store, or merely as a container of liquids made out of various chemical substances. All these ways of considering the jug overlook some of its essential inner relations; they fail to do justice to the fullness of its possibilities; they do not reach the plenitude of its being.

A thing in its true essence, in its full thingness is much more than a mere fact, more than something 'at hand' (*vorhanden*). It represents in a unique way the full richness of all the 'regions' of being as a whole. It gathers within itself the totality of a world—world being understood here as a horizon of understanding to which the thing gives rise and in which it appears to men. Phenomenologically considered, a world becomes present in the coming-to-presence of each and every thing; thus "a world worlds" in the "thinging of a thing" (VA 178–79). In the gathering process which constitutes the phenomenological essence of a thing, and which allows the quadrate to become present, being itself comes to light in the articulation and structuredness of a particular world, in the definite world of a man, a group of men, or a historical epoch. In the full essence of a thing, being itself draws near to men as a particular world.

To take another example: a rose can be considered purely as an object to be grown and sold. Seen thus, it belongs to the world of the florist, but it is not fully and authentically present as itself, as the thing that it is, because it does not appear in the all-embracing horizon of being as a whole. In order to be present as a thing it must show itself as the gathering of all the elements of the quadrate: the earth in which it has grown, the heavens which have given it sun and rain, the mortals to whom it brings joy and shows beauty, and the immortals in whose honor it appears upon the altar.

Through the gathering of the quadrate, being comes to appear in a particular world. Accordingly, the particular way in which the four elements of the quadrate are present or absent in things is intrinsically connected with the world-picture of the particular men or historical period concerned. For example, the absence of reference to the divine in the things and events of the modern world marks our age as that of the absence of God. Moreover, the understanding of the world and of being which characterizes a particular man or group of men is authentic in the same degree in which the elements of the quadrate are allowed to assert themselves. Seen from the viewpoint of being, this means that being shows itself to men to the degree that the four moments of the quadrate show or hide themselves.

The description of the moments of the quadrate in terms of relations could lead to the misunderstanding that these moments are four types of beings to which everything has a relation, so that the thing and these types of beings are separate from one another. This, however, is not Heidegger's meaning. The four elements are not terms of an ontic relation, but rather moments of the being of the thing. They constitute the thing as a phenomenon, as something which shows itself to men in their knowing, doing, wanting, acting, reacting. The thing is or appears as the collection of these moments themselves. It shows itself fully and authentically only when it is understood as this collection. The four moments must thus be understood not as types of beings, but as an articulation of being itself. Heidegger calls them the "regions of the quadrate" (SF 31), the "four world-regions" (US 214).

In other words, these four elements make up the way in which being, in the structuredness of a world, approaches man in things. In this approaching, being itself becomes present as the nearness which draws near to men according to the degree of manifestation of the four regions of the quadrate. In the self-manifestation of things to men, in the gathering which constitutes the quadrate, being is present as nearness itself: "Nearness holds sway in the drawing-near as the thinging of the thing" (VA 176). The thing as such, insofar as it gathers and brings the quadrate to presence, is thus an appearing of being itself.

The concept of the quadrate, despite its initial strangeness, bears many traits of previous stages of Heidegger's thinking of being. The coming to occurrence of being in the quadrate is a continuation of such earlier themes as the "setting-itself-to-work of truth" in a work of art (cf. "Der Ursprung des Kunstwerkes," HW 28 and *passim*), the notion of being as *physis*, "that which emerges of itself (like the 'emergence' of a rose), and the self-opening unfolding, . . . the emerging and abiding holding sway" (EM 11), the concept of being as *polemos,* the original "setting asunder" (*Auseinandersetzung,* EM 47), and finally the idea of being as *logos,* "the abiding collection, the standing gatheredness of being" (EM 100).

Moreover, the composition of the four regions of the quadrate is prepared by several earlier allusions, such as the contrast between the mortals and the immortals (also called the godly or the heavenly ones) in the interpretations of the poet Hölderlin (e.g., HD 59, 66, 67), the mutual relation of earth and heaven as the place of the bridal feast for men and gods (HW 250), the elements in the analysis of the Van Gogh painting and the Greek temple (HW 22–24, 30–32), the collaboration of heaven and earth in the growth of the oak tree (FW 3), the statement that being as a whole includes "gods and men, world and earth" (N I 476). Thus the concept of the quadrate, as it here appears, is not completely new. Nonetheless it represents a bold attempt to express in a new and comprehensive way the richness of the appearing of being in things.[4]

C. *The Quadrate as the Game of Being*

How is the coming-to-pass of the quadrate to be understood? Is it a case of efficient causality, in which one moment produces the other or all four together produce the quadrate? Or does the thing produce the four moments, or the four the thing? The occurring of the quadrate cannot be explained in any of these ways. It is not a case of cause and effect, but of the breaking-out of being itself in the appearing of a thing in its essence.[5] The coming-to-pass of the quadrate is the essence, in the sense of the coming-to-essential-presence of the thing in its fullness as a phenomenon, insofar as it shows itself in its being, or, expressed another way, insofar as being shows itself to man in the thing. There is here neither a temporal nor an ontological priority of the moments among themselves or of the parts with respect to the whole. The four moments are the quadrate and vice versa; the quadrate is the thing and vice versa. Instead of a categorical relation of causality there is the circular movement of structural moments which mutually refer to each other and mutually constitute each other. This type of motion is the Heideggerian hermeneutic circle, which appears in *Sein und Zeit* as the structure of Dasein (man as existent), and here in the context of the quadrate as the self-expression and self-manifestation of being in things.[6]

Heidegger tries to define this circular movement more precisely by characterizing the coming-to-pass of the quadrate as a "mirroring-game" (*Spiegel-Spiel*). Each of the four moments of the quadrate mirrors the other three and thereby also itself, so that the essence of each moment consists in the mirroring of the other three within the unity of the four. This reciprocal mirroring lights up each of the four and thereby the quadrate itself in a remarkable interweaving and "playing-in-and-to-each-other" (*In-und-Zueinanderspiel*, VA 178).

In *Der Satz vom Grund* Heidegger associates this game with the lighting-up of being. The fact that man stands in the light of being means that he exists in the playing field in which being sends itself into the lighting-up process. In this process man is by no means an unoccupied by-stander. Rather he is caught up by being for the purpose of constituting this playing field as the lighting-place for being. As the lighting-place man is the playing field itself. The playing field is a space and thus it is 'spatial.' It is also 'temporal,' since man exists upon the earth, in history. Thus man is a temporal and spatial playing field of being, a "time-game-space" (*Zeit-Spiel-Raum*). Man is the temporal, finite playing field, upon which being sends itself to man as history; it is the essence of man to be "let in upon" this finite playing field of being. "As those who stand in the lighting of being we are the ones sent, the ones let in upon the time-game-space. This means: we are the ones who are used and needed (*die Gebrauchten*) in this playing field and for it, used and needed to build and form the lighting-up of being, in the broad and many-sided sense of 'keeping' this lighting" (SG 146).

The game that needs man as its playing field is that "in which being as being rests, . . . a sublime and indeed the sublimest game," which we "have scarcely experienced and have not yet thought through in its essence" (SG 186). It seems that this "sublimest game" is considered sublimer than being itself because Heidegger says that we must "think being . . . from the standpoint of the essence of the game" (SG 186).

This observation about the sublimest game corresponds to another remark in Heidegger's book on language, *Unterwegs zur Sprache*. There he writes: "the event (*Ereignis*) is . . . richer than any possible metaphysical determination of being; . . . being with regard to its essential origin can be thought from the standpoint of the event" (US 260, note 1). The sublimest game, from the standpoint of whose essence being itself is to be thought, thus coincides with the Heideggerian 'event.'[7]

Ereignis is a word by which Heidegger attempts to overcome the inhibitions of the language of metaphysics. Thus he explains in *Identität und Differenz* that the root of his thought points "to that region, which the guiding words of metaphysics, being and beings, are no longer adequate to express" (ID 69–70). This region which can no longer be adequately expressed by the word 'being' Heidegger calls "the difference as such" (*die Differenz als solche*, ID 63, cf. 69), from the standpoint of which and in which "beings and being are always already found as being present" (ID 60), i.e., from the viewpoint of which "not only being but also beings appear, each in its own way" (ID 61). This is the "distinction" (*der Unter-Schied*) from which being and beings come forth to presence "as the thus distinguished" (ID 62).

Distinction, difference (Heidegger's famous ontological difference), event, the sublimest game—all of these are names for one and the same thing: that which lies above and beyond and before being and beings (these terms understood in the meaning of traditional metaphysics). This seems to be nothing more nor less than that which Heidegger in his earlier works called being itself.

Heidegger's struggle to find a name for this 'something' is seen in the fact that for a while he called it by the archaic German name for being, *Seyn*; for a time too he used the normal German word for being, *Sein*, with an X superimposed, crossing out the word.[8] By the latter practice he seems to be saying that being, as he understands it, is precisely not that which we normally understand by the word being, but above and beyond this. It is the inexpressible something which holds sway before and in that which is metaphysically called the being of beings. It is being (*das Sein*), whose meaning Heidegger has been interrogating ever since the beginning of his thought. Now, however, it is clear that this being is of a transmetaphysical nature, considered as prescinding from its appearing in beings (although it remains true that it can never come to presence without beings, i.e., it comes to light only in existent man, in Dasein). Heidegger is talking about "being with respect to its own meaning, its own truth (lighting-up)" (US 110). This is being considered in that transmetaphysical region, in which it rests only in itself (SG 186).

Moreover, this is not something that Heidegger is now adding to being as the being of beings, but precisely that from which being comes, in order to come to presence as the being of beings, in other words, in order to come to its lighting-up process in man (Dasein). Thus it is the "place" of the "essential origin" of being as the being of beings (VA 143, cf. US 260, note 1).

Heidegger is here trying mightily to express precisely the moment (not temporally, but phenomenologically understood) of the 'breaking apart' by which being and beings are distinguished as the two poles of the ontological difference. This phenomenological moment is the difference itself which holds the two poles apart and yet at the same time binds them together. It is the distinction, which separates the two elements distinguished and yet at the same time holds them together in the tension of their belonging together. It is the event of simultaneous gathering and breaking apart (cf. *logos* and *polemos*), of shooting up and breaking out of hiddenness into unhiddenness (cf. *physis* and *aletheia*), of the sublimest game which simultaneously plays and rests in itself, the game to which man is admitted as the finite playing field, as the 'time-game-space.'

The sublimest game, in which the quadrate comes to presence and is gathered together in things, is thus the coming-to-pass (event) of the difference. It is being itself "with respect to its own meaning, its truth" (US 110), the moment of the splitting apart, by which being is simultaneously sundered and held together, in order to come into its own truth (unhiddenness). Thus it is not only that "in which the being of beings rests, when it appears as presence" (VA 143), but primarily that "in which being as being rests" (SG 186). But being rests ultimately only in itself, or, as Heidegger writes: "But being—what is being? It is itself" (HB 76). This resting-in-itself is the "sublimest game," for which "there is no example (*Beispiel*) in the realm of beings, presumably because the essence of being is itself the game (*das Spiel*)" (ID 64). The interpretation of the sublimest game as the event of being itself makes it possible to understand the following difficult Heideggerian formulation: "The game has no 'why.' It plays because it plays. It remains only a game: the highest and deepest. But this 'only' is all, the one, unique. . . . Being as grounding has no ground. As the groundless it plays that game, which as destiny plays being and ground to us" (SG 188).

II. *Man in the Quadrate*
A. *The Conditioned Playing Field*

In the previous discussion of the quadrate man appeared as the necessary playing field for the sublimest game, which consisted of the breaking into presence of being in things. The intimate interrelationship of being and human existence in the thought of Heidegger is again apparent. In *Sein und Zeit* it was said that being and truth (being as a phenomenon, manifesting itself, coming to unhiddenness) exist only insofar and so long as there is man (SZ 230). The same thought is expressed in the context of the quadrate. Man is the indispensable "place" for the lighting-up of being in things. Only when "man is appropriated (*vereignet*) to being and being is appropriated (*zugeeignet*) to man" (ID 28), can the event (*Ereignis*) of the quadrate take place in things.

Man himself needs the quadrate in order to exist authentically and essentially. His essence is determined by his belonging to being; being, however, manifests itself to him only in beings, i.e., in things, and things reveal themselves authentically only in the fullness of the quadrate. In order to respond properly to his essential belonging to being, man must thus take his place "among things" (*bei den Dingen*), "in the quadrate" (*im Geviert*, cf. VA 151).

For the authenticity of his existence man needs not only being but things, since it is only in things that being manifests itself to him. Thus Heidegger says, in a play on words impossible to reproduce in English: "We are—in the strict sense of the word—conditioned-by-things" (*die Be-Dingten*, VA 179). This is not a new doctrine for Heidegger, but merely a sharper formulation of the analysis of man's existence in *Sein und Zeit*: one of the essential elements of the existential structure of man (*Dasein*) is "being-among (beings confronting him within the world)" (*das Sein-bei [innerweltlich begegnendem Seienden]*, SZ 192, cf. 175–80).

B. *Dwelling and Sparing*

Heidegger calls man's sojourn in the quadrate "dwelling" (*Wohnen*); men "are in the quadrate, insofar as they dwell" (VA 150). "Dwelling" is understood in an existential sense, and means existence, the essential presence of man on earth and in being. Thus dwelling is not merely one human activity among many nor is it something that man can learn once and for all and then have done with. It is rather *the* human activity, which man must realize and carry out in an ever new and fresh way. He must daily learn it again, just as he must realize his existence anew every instant. Men "must always begin anew to search for the essence of dwelling, they must first learn to dwell" (VA 162).

Dwelling in the quadrate and among things takes place through man's relating himself, in his behavior toward the things he encounters, to each of the four moments of the quadrate. Dwelling occurs by means of a fourfold relation to things, which Heidegger calls "sparing" (*schonen*). Man must "spare" the four elements, help them to attain their own essence, set them free unto their own authentic nature.

Men perform the sparing which constitutes their dwelling in the quadrate insofar as they "save the earth," "receive heaven as heaven," "await the godly as the godly," and "accompany their own essence . . . so that there might be a good death" (VA 149–51). Heidegger describes "the earth" as that which serves and supports man, bears fruits and blossoms, is spread out in stone and waters, and gives rise to growing things and animals. "Saving the earth" means using it in a proper way rather than exploiting it by wastefulness or destruction. "Heaven" includes for Heidegger the course of the sun and moon, the brilliance of the stars, the seasons of the year, weather, clouds, day and night. To receive or accept heaven as heaven is to let all these things be, rather than to interfere with them by attempting, for example, to control the weather or to turn night into day through twenty-four-hour activity. "Awaiting the godly as the godly" means waiting and hoping for "the beckoning messengers of the divinity" in order not to mistake the signs of their presence or absence. "The mortals" are the humans themselves; their attitude within the quadrate consists of "accompanying their own essence to the proper use of this essence, . . . in order that there might be a good death." Men must accept death as an existential structure of their being; they must "go along with" this structure, "accompanying" it to a good end. This they must do not only at the moment of death as the end point of life, but throughout the whole of life. Existentially speaking, dying a good death is the same as living a good life. Both mean existing authentically through accepting death as an existential, as a constitutive structure always with man.

Man, in confronting the beings of his world, should spare these beings, let them be in the full depth of their intrinsic reference to the four regions of being. This sparing letting-be renounces all attempts to force, master, compel, or do violence to things. It is a consequence of man's subordinate position to being and constitutes accordingly the authenticity of his existence as the conserver (*Verwahrer*) and steward (*Verwalter*) of being. The common denominator of all the four ways of sparing the quadrate in things is thus the letting-be. This letting-be is not to be understood as an indifference to or lack of sympathy with things, but rather as a reverent stepping back which acknowledges things to be what they really are: an assembling of the four moments of the quadrate, which allows being itself to become manifest.

Here we approach Heidegger's idea of "serenity (*Gelassenheit*) with regard to things," which can open the way to a new stability (*Bodenständigkeit*) of man in the face of the challenges presented by modern technology (GL 18–26). "Serenity" is admittedly an inadequate translation of Heidegger's *Gelassenheit,* for the German word has a simplicity and at the same time a multitude of overtones which do not appear in its English counterpart. *Gelassenheit* means calmness, self-possession, composure; it also has connotations which accrue to it from its use in the language of German medieval mysticism, where it meant a complete relaxation and letting oneself go before God; moreover the root verb *lassen* (let, leave) connotes the basic idea of letting things be in Heidegger's full sense of allowing them their authentic reality.

Heidegger speaks elsewhere of the loss of man's stability in the technical age as the danger of the essential death of man.[9] Here he seems to show how this danger can be averted. Man must learn to dwell in the midst of things, to understand things, and learn how to let them be as they are. He must to a certain extent deliver himself up to them, without at the same time letting himself be swept away by them and thus losing sight of being, which is somehow above and beyond the things in which it becomes manifest. He must thus give himself over to the trees, without thereby losing sight of the forest. This attitude requires both a 'yes' and a 'no' to things: an affirmation of their own nature insofar as they present the gathering event of being in the quadrate and have an indispensable connection with the existential structure of man as being-among, and also a negation, "insofar as we refuse to let things claim us exclusively and thus distort, confuse, and finally lay waste our essence" (GL 25).

This twofold serenity in the face of things will prevent man, on one hand, from ignoring the beings of his world as irrelevant to his existence and thus forfeiting the being-in-the-world which is an integral part of his existential structure, and, on the other hand, from losing his own identity through a complete preoccupation with the things of his world. This attitude keeps him open to being, which both presents itself and at the same time mysteriously withdraws itself in beings, and whose nearness constitutes man's true homeland, his authentic ground and root soil. Thus serenity with regard to things implies also "openness for the mystery" (GL

26). In other words, letting things be in the fullness of their essence, having respect for all the dimensions or ontological regions which constitute them, involves holding oneself open for being itself. These two elements, which form one unified attitude, "afford us a view of a new type of stability" (GL 26). Serenity with regard to things and openness for the mystery of being "promise us a new ground and root soil, upon which we can stand and withstand the technical world, without succumbing to its dangers" (GL 26). The double nature of serenity points the way to the authentic dwelling of mortal men upon the earth, under heaven, and before the godly.

III. Death and the Quadrate

The previous discussion has begun to indicate what a decisive role death plays in the quadrate. Those who exist in the quadrate as its playing field and, at the same time, constitute one of the regions which make up the game, are "the mortals," those who "are capable of death as death" (*den Tod als Tod vermögen,* VA 150, 177, 196).

A. Mortality as an Existential

The designation of man as the mortal is a confirmation of the previously established fact that death is an existential—indeed, the most decisive existential of man's structure. In his innermost ontological makeup, man exists as being-unto-death. In this existential sense, death is not just man's coming-to-an-end, not pure cessation, but a structure concomitantly given with human existence, a determination according to which man is already dying as soon as he begins to exist.

Heidegger now reaffirms this conception in the perspective of the quadrate. He points out anew that man dies not only at the moment of expiration, but "continuously, so long as he abides upon the earth, under heaven, and before the godly" (VA 150), "so long as he endures upon this earth, so long as he dwells" (VA 196). Consequently then, man's entire life is simultaneously a dying; every existentiell realization (*Vollzug*) of Dasein is at the same time a realization of death, the accomplishment of his essence as being-unto-death. Thus understood, death is not an external event approaching man, but a realization of human existence; it is not something that happens to man, but an act which he actively performs. In

159

the language of *Sein und Zeit* death is a possibility for Dasein, a power to be. Accordingly, Heidegger now writes (in clear contrast to the common idea that men as mortals *must* die) that men are called "mortals" in the quadrate "because they *can* die" (VA 150, 177, 196, emphasis mine).

Is death then an option for man? Surely not in the sense that death is left to the free will of man, as if he could choose whether to die or not. Insofar as being-unto-death is concomitantly given with the structure of human existence, it is an essential necessity. In this ontic sense, man must die, in fact, he must die continually, whether he knows and wishes it or not. But considered existentially, man can either realize his death from within, through the conscious recognition and acceptance of the essentially necessary structure of his mortality, or he can flee from death into inauthenticity. The achieving of his true being-unto-death thus depends upon his own choice. In this sense, death is placed in man's keeping; he not only must die, he can die, authentically and as the ultimate realization of his existence. Existentially speaking, man has the ability to die, the capacity for death.

B. *The Capacity for Death*

Heidegger carries this idea a step further when he writes: "They are called the mortals because they can die. Dying means being capable of death as death" (*den Tod als Tod vermögen*, VA 177). Beyond emphasizing the fact that man can die, Heidegger's statement indicates that man can know and understand death. The reduplicative phrase "death as death" means that man does not die blindly like a beast, but recognizes death as an existential determination of his own being. Death for man is not a flat, blank, one-dimensional wall, against which he unwittingly crashes one day, but it is something he foresees, and thus knows even before he experiences it. Man can see death multidimensionally and in perspective. Whether he develops this knowledge or not, he always takes a position with regard to his death and thus relates it to himself as a power-to-be, an ability or capacity of his own being. Thus he knows death reflexively, he knows it as death.

The reflexive knowledge of death further implies that man encounters death in his capacity as the one who understands being. Knowing death as death means understanding it as it is, within the horizon of being. Without the horizon to provide the perspective within which he knows death, man would not die humanly (*sterben*), but merely come to his end (*verenden*) like an animal. Thus man is not only existentially determined by death; he understands the being of death. Implicit in his being-unto-death is the fact that he is the one who understands being. The designations being-unto-death and the mortal contain two essential determinations of man: heading-toward-death (*Aus-sein auf den Tod*) and the understanding of being.

The German word *vermögen*, which has been translated "being capable of," contains a plurality of meanings difficult to capture in English. The verb means to be able, to have the power or capacity to do something. However, as a noun it connotes not only power, ability, capacity, but also wealth, riches, fortune, means. In the present context the phrase indicates that the ability to die is part of the riches of man, an element of his original natural endowment. As something man is able to do, dying is one of his powers-to-be, one of the means, in fact the outstanding means, of accomplishing his existence.

But even more is hidden in Heidegger's use of *vermögen*, as is evident from another text in which he is speaking not of man's ability to die, but of his ability to think: "To have the capacity for something means to let something draw near to us in its essence, and persistently to protect this admission. Thus we only have a capacity for things that we like" (*Wir vermögen immer nur solches, was wir mögen*, VA 129). Can this idea be applied to the capacity for death? Is it meaningful to say that man has the capacity for death only because he 'likes' death? Heidegger continues: "We genuinely like only something which has previously liked us in our essence, by inclining itself toward us and drawing close to us" (VA 129). Clearly Heidegger is not talking about any psychological phenomenon, any emotion or feeling of love, but rather about something in the ontological sphere. Considered ontologically or existentially, death draws near by giving itself to us as a constitutive element of our existence. It thereby brings us to our own essence as mortals. But this gift is at the same time a claim upon us, since it sets us the task of accepting our mortality in the realization of our existence. In this way death communicates itself to us, draws near, 'likes' us. We can correspondingly 'like' death, insofar as we let it come near us by accepting and affirming it as an existential structure which brings us into our own essence.

Thus, the mortals are capable of death in several ways: they can 'die' authentically in every realization of existence by assuming their proper and distinctive role within the quadrate, and they can positively affirm death as the existential structure which 'lets them in' to their true essence. Moreover, they can recognize death as the outstanding feature of their original natural endowment, as the element which, above all others, confers on them the dignity of their specifically human existence.[10]

C. *Authentic Mortality as Accompanying*

Having the capacity for death as death means letting death draw near to us, letting it be as what it really is, thus sparing it in its true essence. This brings us back to the idea of sparing as an essential component of man's dwelling in the quadrate. Precisely how should man, who dwells in the presence of things and in the presence of being as it appears in the quadrate, spare death? Heidegger writes: "The mortals dwell insofar as they accompany their own essence, namely, having the capacity for death as death, into the use of this capacity, so that there will be a good death" (VA 151).

Man's capacity for death as death is, as we have seen, the mortality or being-unto-death which constitutes his essence as the finite 'there' of being. As such, it is the determining existential structure of Dasein. Accompanying this structure into its proper use thus means transposing existential being-unto-death into its authentic existentiell realization. 'Accompanying' is the conscious and deliberate acceptance of the existential structure of being-unto-death as constituting the essence of man; it is man's being-unto-death authentically realized. Thus it is the same process as that which was earlier called advancing toward death; it is the ultimate determinant of the authenticity of man's being-unto-death and consequently of human existence.

But accompanying occurs within the quadrate, in man's dwelling among the things in which being appears to him. Man does not direct his attention primarily to death, but to things. He does not relate himself first and foremost to his own mortality but to things and to being which shines forth in them; within this context he assumes an attitude to death as an essential moment of the entire process. Consequently, accompanying is "not . . . an empty staring at the end" (VA 151), but the concomitant realization, the sparing, affirming acknowledgment of the structure of being-unto-death in the total process of the serene confrontation with things and with being itself. Man thus exists authentically, or accompanies his essence into its authentic realization, by understanding and accepting himself in confrontation with things as the mortal who dwells upon the earth, under heaven, before the godly, and thus in the nearness of being.

Since accompanying his essence toward death leads man to the authenticity of existence, it entails not a negative attitude, but an affirmative one. It confirms life as what it really is: the dwelling of a mortal in the understanding of being. Accordingly, it is not an option for emptiness and meaninglessness of existence, but a commitment to that which affords Dasein its whole ground and meaning, namely, death, understood fully and positively as the determining constitutive element of human existence, as finite man's standing in the illumination of being. Thus Heidegger asserts: "Accompanying the mortals into the essence of death does not mean setting death as an empty nothing as their goal; neither does it mean dwelling gloomily by an empty staring at the end" (VA 151). It means rather the acceptance of death as a positive structure and an essential moment of existence. This is death in the positive sense; so understood, it is "a good death" (VA 151).

IV. Death and Being

Death is good in the existential sense if it is considered positively, i.e., as Dasein's structure of being-unto-death which equally connotes both aspects of its existence, namely, the capacity for death and the understanding of being. The good death involves both the heading-toward-death which understands being (transcendent finitude), and the forward-looking understanding of being which is heading toward death (finite transcendence). The good death, however, must be seen not only in connection with man's understanding of being, but also in connection with being itself.

A. Death as the Redoubt of Being

In the discussion of Rilke, death was seen as a possible place for a breakthrough to being and as the ultimate frustration of man's striving for absolute domination. By revealing to man his defenselessness against the totality of beings, death discloses to him his subordinate position with regard to being and so points him toward being as "the whole of the pure relation" (HW 280). In the discussion of the quadrate death is the gateway to being, but only indirectly, through the mediation of nonbeing; "Death is the shrine of nonbeing (*der Schrein des Nichts*), that is, of that which is never and in no way a mere being, but which nevertheless is present (*west*), indeed as the mystery of being itself. As the shrine of nonbeing, death conceals within itself the presencing of being (*das Wesende des Seins*). As the shrine of nonbeing, death is the redoubt of being (*das Gebirg des Seins*)" (VA 177).

In death all relations to beings which man confronts within the world are broken, so that the totality of beings is said to disappear. As in anxiety, so in death "the totality of beings collapses" (WM 33). Thus in the present discussion, death takes the place of anxiety as a negative reference to the totality of beings which are slipping away. Death brings man face to face with the negativity of all beings. It is thus "the shrine of nonbeing" (VA 177).

The shrine of nonbeing is not to be understood in an ontic sense, as concerned with the factual end of human life, but ontologically and existentially, as referring to death as the extreme possibility of Dasein, the broadest horizon of self-understanding in the realization of man's existence. In every act man assumes an attitude to himself and understands himself as acting in a certain way. In self-understanding death is always contained as the ultimate horizon overarching everything man does, and as the most definitive and all-embracing act he can perform. Insofar as death is the shrine of nonbeing, it reveals to man the basic instability and negativity of all things, including his own actions and existence.

The concept of death and of man's self-understanding moves quickly beyond the element of negativity to something positive. Nonbeing is not a void or empty nothingness, but that "which is never and in no way a mere being, but which nevertheless is present, indeed as the mystery of being itself" (VA 177). Death lets all beings disappear and exposes the totality of beings as frail and perishable. But in spite of this negativity, beings *are;* they are not nothing in the absolute sense. Thus we are faced with the question of what it means to say that something *is.* What is the being of beings? What does it mean to be?

In this way death forces upon us the question about the meaning of being. The nonbeing revealed by death points out the questionableness of beings, and thus brings being itself to appearance. Here as before, nonbeing reveals itself as a transitory state, a stage on the way to being, a 'veil' of being. Nonbeing can be said to be the mode of appearance of being itself. Earlier it was shown that "the nothing is the negation of beings and is thus being itself, experienced from the vantage point of beings" (WG 5). In the present context, we meet the same idea: "As the shrine of nonbeing, death conceals within itself the presencing of being. As the shrine of nonbeing, death is the redoubt of being" (VA 177).

The expression "the redoubt of being" must be understood according to the original force of the German term Heidegger uses, *"Gebirg des Seins."* The dictionary meaning of *Gebirg* is mountain, mountain-chain, highland. Thus the term indicates a mountain fastness, a secret retreat of being. The prefix *Ge-* in German implies collectivity. Thus, there is the further notion of a locus in which being gathers itself together, suggesting the previously discussed meaning of being as *logos*. In another text Heidegger confirms the connotation of gathering in the term *Gebirg:* "Death thus gathers [us] into the totality of what has already been posited, into the *positum* of the entire network. As this gathering of the positing, it is the original de-posit (*das Ge-setz*) just as a mountain-chain (*das Gebirg*) is the gathering of several mountains into the totality of their network" (HW 280).[11]

There is still another connotation. The word *Berg* is not only a noun meaning mountain, but also the root of the verb *bergen,* meaning several things: to save, secure; salve, recover (ship-wrecked goods, etc.); conceal. The term *Gebirg des Seins* thus indicates that death is the place where being hides in security. Heidegger confirms this interpretation when he completes the expression by an explicit reference to this verb: he says that death is "the highest redoubt (a concealing which gathers together)" (*das höchste Ge-birg [das versammelnde Bergen]*, VA 256).

Retiring to security in its mountain redoubt involves not only a concealing, but also a revealing of being. This is evident from Heidegger's use of word forms built upon the basic verb *bergen.* He speaks of the stronghold both as a place of concealing (*Verbergen*) and of revealing (*Entbergung*). This is a clear reference to the earlier established dual process of concealing and revealing involved in Heidegger's notion of truth as *aletheia* and also, in the present context, to the paradoxical nature of death evidenced as the locus of the supreme veiling and unveiling of being.

Death is first of all the place where being hides itself most thoroughly, because death means the end of existence as being-in-the-world, and thus involves the vanishing of all the beings which make up Dasein's world. All beings disappear, so that only *nothing* seems to be left. Death is thus the shrine of nonbeing, the place of the darkest concealment of being.

But further reflection shows that death is also the place for the greatest self-revelation of being, for it is the outstanding gathering point of the transitoriness and negativity of all beings. Death makes it clear that the meaning of man's being is not to be sought in his contacts with the myriad beings which populate the world of his everyday existence, but in his relation to being itself. Death thus reveals to the mortals not only the meaning of being, but the meaning of their own existence. Death forces them to recognize that they exist "as the mortals which they are, presencing in the redoubt of being. They are the presencing relation to being as being" (VA 177).

The interplay of the two aspects of veiling and unveiling finds further expression in another statement: ". . . the essence of the mortals is called to pay heed to the command which summons them to death. As the extreme possibility of mortal Dasein, death is not the end of the possible, but rather the highest redoubt (the gathering concealment) of the mystery of the revelation calling them" (VA 256). The mortals are "the presencing relation to being as being" (VA 177). As such, they are essentially called to listen to the directives of being. In other words, they are claimed by being as its lighting-up-place in the midst of beings. Being needs and uses the mortals for the sake of its own sublime game. Moreover, it needs and uses them precisely as the mortals because it can only appear in the negativized, finite way proper to it, by both revealing and concealing itself, imparting and withdrawing itself, in a historical and transitory way. In order to do this, being summons finite and mortal man as its time-game-space. Thus the command of being "summons them to death" (VA 256), claims them as its own in their nature as being-unto-death.

Again, death is not understood as the ontic end point of life, but as the ontological-existential structure in virtue of which man experiences the totality of beings as disappearing into the nothing, and thus gathers himself together in his essential orientation toward being as the force which calls him and gives meaning to his existence. In this sense, death is not the cessation of life nor "the end of the possible" for man, but the culmination of the self-revelation of being, which withdraws and conceals itself at the same time, thus appearing as mystery.

The interpretation of the twofold self-securing of being in death (the simultaneous veiling and unveiling of being in its mystery) is confirmed by two other Heideggerian texts. In the one, death amounts to the greatest concealment of being: "in death being collects in its greatest concealment"

(US 23); in the other, however, "death as the extreme possibility of Dasein is capable of the greatest lighting-up of being and of its truth" (SG 186–87). Thus death shows most conclusively that being reveals itself only by concealing itself, for death represents the supreme synthesis of these two movements. Death is the self-withdrawing communication of being, the supreme rallying point of the double movement of truth as *aletheia,* by which being both manifests and enshrouds itself. It is the outstanding example of the hiddenness of being; death is "as the shrine of nonbeing, the redoubt of being" (VA 177).

B. *Death as the Measure of the Immeasurable*

Death as the place of man's breakthrough to the truth of being is expressed by still another metaphorical formulation. Here we are concerned with the sublime game spoken of before, in which being is thought of as the ungrounded ground of all beings, to which man finds access in virtue of his mortal essence. We are brought as mortals into this game, but we are mortals "only . . . insofar as we dwell in the nearness of death" (SG 186). Death makes possible man's participation in the process of the self-imparting and self-illumination of being, since it is death "which, as the extreme possibility of Dasein, is capable of the greatest lighting-up of being and its truth. . . . Death is the still unconsidered measure of the immeasurable, i.e., of the sublimest game in which man is involved on earth" (SG 186–87).

Death is the extreme possibility of Dasein. This means that it is not merely the last in a series of possibilities, all of which fall essentially into the same category, but rather that it is the all-embracing possibility which constitutes the horizon or backdrop for all the other possibilities of Dasein. It is precisely *the* possibility which gathers all others into itself and thus brings the totality of existence into one complete unity. Death is the extreme possibility not just because it is the last, but more importantly because it is the definitive one for man.

Thus death is that wherein man "receives the measure for the breadth of his essence" (VA 196). But man's essence consists in his relation to being, indeed man *is* "the essential relation to being as being" (VA 177). Therefore, death is not only the measure of man's essence, but also the measure of being, the declaration of the bounds of the 'immeasurable,' as this comes to light in the authentic realization of human existence.

But death is the measure of the immeasurable not only in a passive, but in an active sense as well. It is not merely the appointed measure wherein being appears as the determining correlative of the breadth of man's essence, but it itself sets the limits. It performs an active measuring function by leading man through the stage of detachment from all beings, beyond the stage of nonbeing to being itself. Obviously, this does not mean that man can adequately measure the immeasurable (which would be a contradiction in terms), but rather that death can lead man to recognize being precisely as the immeasurable, as ultimately enigmatic and inexhaustible. Being is ever 'mystery' (cf. HD 124, VA 177, 256). Accordingly, the only appropriate mode of knowing being for what it really is consists in allowing it to preserve its ultimately unfathomable character.

Up to now, the phrase "of the immeasurable" has been understood grammatically as an objective genitive, indicating that being, under the title of the immeasurable, is the object which is measured through death. But it can also meaningfully be considered as a subjective genitive. In this case, it is the immeasurable itself (being) which measures: that which sends death as the measure of being and of the essence of man is precisely the immeasurable, or being itself. In this reading, the measure does not stem ultimately from death, but from being, which assigns death to man or "summons him to death" (VA 256) and thus imparts itself to man in death. For it is in death that being leads man to recognize that his essence is constituted not by his relations to beings, but rather by his transcendental orientation to being. Thus death is the revelation of the authentic essence of man and of being itself.[12]

Through death (understood as Dasein's existential of totality) man is involved in the sublime game of being, which is the coming-to-pass of the event of being, "the sublimest game in which man is involved on earth" (SG 187). Heidegger specifies "on earth" (irdisch) because man is admitted to the game of the self-communication of being precisely as the mortal, i.e., as the temporal-finite playing field on which the game takes place. Thus Heidegger says: "As the ones standing in the clearing of being, we are the ones sent, the ones admitted to the time-game-space. This means: we are the ones needed and used in and for this playing field, needed and used to work and build upon the clearing of being" (SG 146).

Heidegger explains that this metaphor of the game refers to what he previously called transcendence or the understanding of being. "In the as yet rather awkward and provisional language of the treatise *Sein und Zeit* this means: the basic character of Dasein, which is man, is determined by the understanding of being" (SG 146). Man is brought to his essence as the one who understands being precisely by death, his finite mortality. He understands being, he relates to being in the finite manner proper to him, insofar as he exists as being-unto-death, just as, vice versa, he exists as being-unto-death, and relates properly to his own death, insofar as he is the one who understands being. Both these determinations are united in his essence. In the newer manner of speaking, he is involved in the sublime game precisely as the mortal.

But the mortal is not only "brought" into the game; he is also "placed" in it (SG 187). He is never a mere spectator, but essentially a participant. Moreover, he cannot participate externally without interior involvement, for the outcome of the game is of vital importance to him. His own existence is at stake, for his essence is constituted by his very participation in the game. If the game is 'lost,' he loses his own essence; he lives inauthentically in the preoccupation with mere beings and never comes to the realization of the mystery of being. This game is accordingly a matter of life and death, in the deep ontological sense that man's very essence is at stake. Thus everything hinges upon man's playing properly and whole-heartedly. His participation in this game is, in fact, the authenticity of his existence.

We can summarize this analysis as follows:

a. As the extreme, all-embracing possibility of Dasein, death is both actively and passively the measure of man's essence, as it is of being itself, since it gathers man together in a totality and in his orientation to being, even though man is not capable of adequately measuring being, which is precisely the immeasurable.

b. Death is the measure of the immeasurable in the double sense of objective and subjective genitive. Being as the immeasurable is both the 'object' which is measured by death and the 'agent' which sends death to man as the measure of his being. Death is thus the messenger of being, which mediates to man his own essence and the presencing of being itself.

c. Through death, i.e., through his own essential mortality, man is involved in the sublimest game of the truth of being. His own existence is thereby at stake, for participation in this game constitutes the authenticity of his being.

C. *Significance of These Images*

Death as an existential of Dasein is the redoubt and the measure of being, for it lifts man out of the totality of beings and gathers him together in his orientation toward being, which conceals itself in death or, to put it another way, communicates itself to man in death as the measure of man's essence and of being itself. Several conclusions follow which are of vital importance for the relationship between being, man, and death in Heidegger's thought.

First, death as the redoubt and measure of being contains the ultimate meaning of human existence. Death lets all beings sink away into nothingness; thus it teaches that the authentic meaning of Dasein does not lie in the realm of beings, neither in any single individual being, nor in Dasein itself as an individual being, nor in the totality of beings. The meaning of man thus lies higher than beings, even higher than being itself, if this is considered solely as the being of beings. It lies rather in the sublime game of being itself, which transcends the presencing of being as the ground of beings.

Put in another way: the meaning of man's existence consists precisely in his playing along in the game of the event of being, in his specific role as the finite-mortal time-game-space of this game. It lies in his cooperation in the self-illumination of being, which takes place in the double mode of communicating and withdrawing, of revealing and concealing itself. Man's participation in this process is his ex-istence, his standing-forth into the twofold motion of truth as *aletheia,* and his collaboration in the work of producing the distinction between being and beings.

The second consequence of this new aspect of Heidegger's thought about death is that being takes on a much more explicitly historical character. It sends itself epochally, and forms the all-comprehensive horizon of the total world view, the understanding of being, and the self-understanding of each particular historical era. Being appears as the "spirit of the age" (GL 18). Since death is the redoubt and the measure of being, it becomes now the key to this comprehensive horizon of understanding. Death reveals the manner in which being shows itself to the men of a particular age. In order to determine how the men of a certain epoch understand their own existence, their world, and being in general, one must investigate their concept of death. In order to answer the question: what is the world view of a particular age, how does being appear to a particular historical people, one must first know how they feel about death.

Furthermore, death is the key to the understanding of being not only for the outsider who is observing or studying a particular group of men, but also for the men of that age themselves. Thus we can say quite generally that the understanding of being, in the sense of one's total world view, must ultimately hinge upon one's understanding of death. How one looks upon the world as a whole derives necessarily from the manner in which one looks upon himself as mortal. It is man's understanding of death that determines his total understanding of the world, of being, and of himself because death, on the one hand, is the determining, all-embracing existential of Dasein, and is thereby the central element of man's understanding of himself, and, on the other hand, is the redoubt of being and thus the outstanding locus of the self-interpretation or the self-revelation of being itself.

Seen from the viewpoint of the finitude of man, and of being as it reveals itself, death is the existential basis and the profoundest sign of the essential finitude of man. Consequently, one authentically understands man's existence to the extent that one understands death. Similarly, death is the place in Dasein in which the finite presencing of being finds its sharpest expression, for it is in death that being shows itself in its greatest negativity, by revealing itself precisely through the complete concealing of itself. Accordingly, one authentically understands being to the extent that one understands death, which is the structural element of Dasein in which the finite negativized presencing of being appears in a unique and most distinctive way.

Heidegger gives expression to the decisive significance of death for the revealing, concealing, and measuring of being in the following formulation: "as the extreme possibility of Dasein, death is capable of the greatest lighting-up of being and its truth" (SG 186–87). This can now be understood as follows: the understanding of death is capable of liberating man from his inauthentic relationships to beings and thus freeing his gaze to look upon being, which constitutes the authentic meaning of his existence. Moreover, the understanding of death is the key to, and therefore the origin and ground of, man's total understanding of himself, the world, and being; this is true not only of individual men, but also of all the epochs of human history.

V. *The Question of Being-in-Death*

In the analysis of Dasein carried out in *Sein und Zeit* Heidegger briefly touched upon the question of man's immortality, the possibility of life after death. He concluded that this is a purely ontic question, which can neither be properly raised nor settled in the existential analysis of Dasein. Certain passages in the later works deal with this matter, putting it in the new perspective acquired through the turning.

A. *Death as a Transition*

In the analysis of Heidegger's interpretation of the poetry of Georg Trakl, mention was made of the "downfall of the pilgrim soul upon the earth." It was observed that the downfall did not lead to annihilation, but to the possibility of the full and authentic unfolding of human life; thus it meant the transition from inauthentic to authentic dwelling upon the earth. Could it be argued that the downfall brought about by the ontic end of a man's life is also a transition to a fuller and more authentic life? Does the downfall idea point to a new type of life after death?

Certainly Heidegger says nothing explicitly in his Trakl interpretation about what was previously called the problem of 'being-in-death.' In fact he treats the entire question of the downfall within the context of existence in this world. The soul is a pilgrim precisely because it has not yet found its true home on earth. Just as death in *Sein und Zeit* is incorporated into the being of Dasein as an existential structure, so here the downfall in question is entirely contained within the earthly life of man. Thus there is no more explicit reference here than in *Sein und Zeit* to the question of life in death.

But the concept of death as a transition occurs again in the context of the quadrate, in the discussion of a bridge as a thing which gathers together the four elements of the quadrate: "Always and ever in distinctive ways, the bridge accompanies the hesitating and the hasty steps of men back and forth, as they cross over to other shores, and finally, as the mortals, cross over to the other side" (VA 153). Heidegger further points out that the mortals, "always underway to the last bridge, are basically striving to get beyond their ordinariness and unwholeness, in order to bring themselves before the wholeness of the godly" (VA 153); does this mean that the mortals enter through death into a new, 'whole' life 'on the other side'? The statement easily lends itself to such an interpretation, but the context shows that Heidegger is again speaking of man's dwelling upon the earth—about the existence of the mortals among things, in which being appears to them according to the fourfold structuring of the quadrate. Heidegger is concerned with the bridge only as such a 'thing,' a phenomenon through which being reveals itself to man in his earthly existence. Thus he remains within the methodological boundaries set in *Sein und Zeit,* namely the explanation and interpretation of phenomena. In the later works as well as the earlier ones, the fundamental principle of his thought remains: "ontology is possible only as phenomenology" (SZ 35).[13]

These references to death as transition do not mean that Heidegger is taking a position with regard to the problem of an afterlife, but must be evaluated solely as his interpretation of a fairly common literary expression. At the most, the image of the bridge, as well as that of the downfall of the pilgrim soul upon earth, offers a stimulating and possibly instructive metaphor for the discussion of the problem of being-in-death. But Heidegger himself remains scrupulously neutral with regard to this problem.[14]

The strictly phenomenological orientation which Heidegger announced as a program in *Sein und Zeit* is confirmed again throughout the later works, especially in the study of Nietzsche. In Heidegger's view, Nietzsche hoped to overcome the nihilism of his age by a programmatic reaffirmation of the sensible world, in opposition to the doctrine of Platonism which held the sensible world to be merely the reflection of the true suprasensible world (N I 87–88, 539–43). Heidegger too, although he does not speak in Nietzsche's metaphysical categories and does not support Nietzsche's violent attacks upon the suprasensible world, embraces the view that *this* world, the phenomenal world of human existence must be taken with full seriousness. Because of this, Heidegger directs his philosophical gaze exclusively to existence as men know and experience it in this world.

This desire is the origin of Heidegger's interest in locating the authentic essence of man in his relation to phenomenal being as it appears in history and in beings, as well as in the authentic dwelling of man upon the earth. This concern is clearly expressed in the considerations of the quadrate. Again and again we read: "To be a man means to be as a mortal on the earth" (VA 147); "Even when the mortals 'enter into themselves,' they do not leave behind their belonging to the quadrate" (VA 158); "The rational animals must first *become* mortals" (VA 177); "We are, in the strict sense of the word, conditioned-by-things (*die Be-Dingten*). We have left behind the presumption of anything unconditioned" (VA 179); "After all, dwelling means sojourn of man upon 'this' earth, to which every mortal knows himself to be entrusted and exposed" (VA 192).[15]

B. *Finitude and the Later Heidegger's Image of Man*

Heidegger's later writings are a renewed profession of the finitude of Dasein. Man is the mortal; he must learn to dwell upon the earth as the mortal. Is this a pure immanentism, a gloomy finitism? By ignoring the possibility of life beyond death, does Heidegger make death a horror, and existence a hopeless affair? Is his thought, after all, basically pessimistic?

Such reflections treat existence and death in the ontic-existentiell perspective. They see existence as the stretched-out extent of life, and death as the point where this course reaches its end. On this level, one could perhaps challenge Heidegger's neutral position with regard to the problem of being-in-death, arguing that the question is of such vital importance that it must absolutely be answered, one way or the other. But to make this reasonable, one must be able to show how man's being or not-being after his ontic death could be a phenomenon in the Heideggerian sense. Since this is impossible, it is philosophically rash to demand such an answer of Heidegger.

As has been pointed out, Heidegger is not concerned with man's ontic life and death. Without denying this side—indeed as a phenomenologist he must necessarily always start from it—he nevertheless aims primarily at the existential-ontological dimension, at the being-structures which make the ontic dimension of existence possible, intelligible, and meaningful. Heidegger's concern is being and therefore also man's understanding of being and of himself as the 'there' of being. Man has the ontological structure of being-unto-death and the understanding of being; he is the mortal 'understander' of being or the being-understanding mortal. He exists as being-unto-death, which is at the same time openness to being. This dual structure has been phenomenologically demonstrated, and thus remains true whether man is oriented toward a new life in his ontic death, or not.

In Heidegger's ontological perspective, death is not an occurrence at the end of life, but a structural element which is present in every action by which Dasein fulfills its existence. Moreover, it is not simply another structure like many others, but it is *the* structure which primarily determines man's essence and renders existence possible. Being-unto-death is the essential ground of man's finite understanding of being. In other words, being-mortal is the origin of man's ability to participate in the sublime game of the self-illumination of being. Man plays as the required finite game-space of the time-game of being: he can only play insofar as he is the finite-temporal mortal. It is important to note that death is thereby given a very positive function in Heidegger's existential thought. It is precisely the structure which allows man to enter into his essence, and thereby lies at the basis of his relation to being.

Furthermore, death is the redoubt and the measure of being. Accordingly, far from being that which definitively seals off the horizon of man, death is that which definitively opens his view toward being itself. Death is considered not as something which closes the door, but as the key which unlocks it. It is the place of being's greatest illumination, the locus of the concealing-revealing event of truth, the most highly concentrated gathering of the mystery of being itself (cf. SG 186–87, VA 256, US 23).

This positive view, which sees death and finitude in the light of being, explains why Heidegger's later image of man is no longer heroic-tragic, but bears the traits of reverence, readiness for service, and serenity. As the mortal, man belongs to the quadrate; his task is to 'spare' or nurture the four regions and thus to take care of being, which comes to its self-manifestation by means of the mirroring game of the four elements (VA 150–51, 178). He is the participating and cooperating playing field of the sublime game of being (SG 146). As such, man belongs to being: "man's essence as such is attentive, because he belongs to the calling command, to the presencing [of being]" (SF 28). He is present for the sake of being: "We are ourselves only . . . insofar as we point to that which withdraws itself. This pointing (*Weisen*) is our essence (*Wesen*)" (VA 135).

Man's essential assignment is to wait upon the "advent of the favor" of being; as long as this continues, he dwells humanly on the earth (VA 204). He can in no way force being, but only hold himself ready for its arrival (US 32, 154, WP 46) and prepare the way for it through his thought (VA foreword, SF 42, US 197–98, 361). Everything therefore depends on "whether we are waiting and watching, watchers who see to it that . . . the stillness of the appeal contained in the word of being triumphs" (SG 209). The essential role of the mortals is to wait; "thus

175

there remains only one thing, to wait until that which is to-be-thought addresses itself to us" (VA 139, cf. GL 15, 37, 50, 52, 59, 66, 73). This task requires two things: serenity toward things and openness for the mystery of being, which conceals and reveals itself in them (GL 25–28).

Thus the finitude of the mortals now expresses itself not through resolute advancing toward death, as in *Sein und Zeit*, but in attentive, waiting serenity. As the mortal, man dwells expectantly and sparingly upon the earth, under heaven, and before the godly, listening to the command, ready for the arrival, and open to the mystery of being.

VI. *Summary*

The essence of things shows itself to be the event which assembles the four moments constituting a single quadrate, i.e., a fourfold structure in which being reveals itself to man. The event of the quadrate as the bursting forth of being is the 'sublime game' in which man and being come to their essential presence and from which being takes its origin as the being of beings.

Man is the participating playing field for the sublime game of being and belongs to being in the sense that he is both needed and used for the game. His authenticity consists in his dwelling among things, in which the being-game takes place and approaches him. Dwelling demands that he spare or nurture the four elements of the quadrate; this means a preserving of the four regions of being and thus constitutes his service of being, which appears in its fullness in things.

Since the good death, death considered positively, brings man to his authentic essence, it unites him with being. Death is the shrine of nonbeing, insofar as it lets all beings vanish, but as such it is also the redoubt of being, the place in which the deepest hiddenness and the broadest revelation of the mystery of being are gathered together. As the extreme possibility of Dasein, death is further the measure of the immeasurable, the limiting measure of man's essence and of being; being itself sends death to man as his measure, in order to manifest itself therein. The designation of death as the redoubt and measure of being also means that death contains the meaning of existence and determines man's entire understanding of being, the world, and himself.

Although Heidegger alludes to death as a transition, he takes no philosophical position with regard to the problem of being-in-death. The neutral attitude which he originally announced in *Sein und Zeit* derives from his existential-phenomenological method. First, he never considers death ontically, but only existentially and ontologically as a structure of Dasein's realization of existence, while the question of a life after ontic death is an ontic-existentiell problem. Second, he investigates and interprets only phenomena, and man's possible being-in-death is not a phenomenon.

The problem of human existence is for Heidegger the problem of authentic dwelling upon the earth or, in the perspective of the quadrate, the sojourn of the mortals upon the earth, under heaven, and before the godly—among things in the nearness of being. Thus, the finitude of man, which has been so sharply defined before, receives here a new confirmation. However, this finitude now has a new look: it finds its authentic expression in the attitudes of reverence, readiness to serve, serenity with respect to things, and openness to the mystery of being.

7

Conclusion:
Death & Heidegger's
Way

In *Sein und Zeit* Heidegger sees death as the extreme possibility of Dasein, as the possibility of the impossibility of existence (SZ 250, 262). But after the turning, death is the shrine of nonbeing and the redoubt of being (VA 177). Is this the same death? In *Sein und Zeit* authentic existence consists in the resolute advancing of individualized Dasein toward death, which brings Dasein to the possibility of "being itself in impassioned freedom-unto-death, liberated from popular illusion, facticious, sure of itself, and anxious" (SZ 266). But after the turning, the mortals dwell authentically "insofar as they accompany their own essence, which consists in the fact that they are capable of death as death, into the use of this capacity, so that there will be a good death" (VA 151). Passionate advancing and relaxed accompanying: is this the same Heidegger?

The fact that there is a difference between the early and the later Heidegger is nothing new; the contrasts have been pointed out by many of his commentators. The difference is especially noticeable in the conception of death, and yet there is a line of continuity in Heidegger's thought, a continuity which lies deeper than, and indeed provides the basis for, the differences. The key to the continuity is Heidegger's original intention of appropriately asking the being-question. The feature which ties together all the writings of Heidegger, which provides the unity to his entire seemingly meandering thought-way, is his dogged and unswerving pursuit of the meaning of being. If death seems to present a different face in different works, it is because Heidegger's thought is not static, but is continually moving; it accordingly sees death from different perspectives at different stages of the journey.

I. *The Being of Dasein: Finite Understanding of Being*

It was pointed out at the beginning of our interpretation of *Sein und Zeit* that the themes of being, man, and death approximate three concentric circles. The analysis of death forms a part of the existential analysis of Dasein, which in turn serves to prepare the way for the working out of the question of being. Being itself is not thematically handled in *Sein und Zeit*, for the published section of the work treats only the being of Dasein, the being who poses the question of being. The being of Dasein turns out to be concern, the meaning of which consists in the three-dimensional structure of temporality. The concrete expressions of the three time dimensions are death (future), guilt (past), and situation (present), all of which are to be understood existentially and ontologically. Death as the existential of totality, the extreme and all-embracing power-to-be of Dasein, represents the fullness of the entire structure, so that it contains the full implications of the finitude of Dasein.

But being-unto-death, even considered in its broadest sense as the sum total of death, guilt, and situation, does not exhaust the definition of Dasein, for Dasein is precisely the being-unto-death which asks the question of being and therefore understands being. In the works in which Heidegger's turning takes place, especially in *Kant und das Problem der Metaphysik*, it becomes clear that Dasein is characterized by both the understanding of being and being-unto-death, by transcendence and finitude. These are not merely two coexisting determinations of Dasein, but are intimately associated and intertwined; they form an inseparable unity in the essence of Dasein. Man, who understands being and therefore asks the question of being, is finite being-unto-death, even to the extent that his finitude is precisely the ground of his questioning about the meaning of being. On the other hand, man, who is being-unto-death, is primordially the same man who understands and questions the meaning of being, to the extent that his questioning understanding of being is precisely the deepest root of his finitude.

The interlocking nature of man's being-unto-death and his understanding of being, which is often so puzzling in the earlier writings, receives both new confirmation and a certain clarification in the later works. Thus, for example, the idea of man's shattering against being, namely the fact that man himself must be breakable in order to fulfill his role as the locus of history or the breach through which being breaks into history, explains from a new viewpoint why he must exist as finite being-unto-death. Likewise, the poetry interpretations show that man must be the mortal, in order to receive the historically conditioned message of the holy and transmit this message to other mortals. The discussion of language points to the same relationship, for it is precisely man's being-mortal which enables him to respond to the address of being, to concretize the speech of being by speaking in human language. Similarly, the contemplation of the quadrate in connection with the essence of things demonstrates that being, in order to appear in its fourfold fullness in things, both needs and uses finite mortal man as the time-game-space of its own sublime game.

These later laborious attempts to define more carefully the relation between being and Dasein show that the essential constitution and role of man as Dasein remain the same both before and after the turning. Man is the combination of death and 'standing in the clearing of being.' Whether this complex structure be called being-unto-death and the understanding of being, finitude and transcendence, being-unto-shattering and being-the-breach, being-mortal and receiver of the message of the holy, mortality and speech, or being the mortal and the time-game-space for the sublime game of being, the duality remains ever the same. The two aspects of man's being described in so many different terms are the expressions of Heidegger's basic insight into man as temporality, the unified center of the complementary and interlocked tendencies which constitute the dynamic tension of his existence.

II. Being: The Finite Phenomenon

The twofold being-structure of Dasein means that being, as it appears to man, i.e., self-revealing, phenomenal being, which is Heidegger's constant and exclusive concern, appears in a finite way.

In the Heideggerian writings in which the turning takes place, the finite presencing of being is evidenced in at least three ways. First, being "presences" (*west*) as the horizon of man's transcendence; as such, it appears as a nothing, the negation of all beings, because it itself is no particular being. Second, it manifests itself in the structuredness of a world, which is always a definite, determined, and limited world, a particular world of a particular Dasein. Third, it appears as the open in which everything man encounters opens itself to his confrontation, as the unconcealedness which allows everything man experiences to become revealed to him, as the truth which illumines everything true while remaining hidden itself. Being manifests itself by simultaneously unveiling beings and veiling itself. Since it can reveal itself only by refusing to unveil itself, only by concealing itself, it is penetrated by a 'not' or a negativity. It is negativized in its very appearance, and comes to presence as finite. In all these modes of its presencing, being appears to finite man as finite.

The trait of limitation in the appearing of being remains in all the later variations of the theme of being revealing itself to man. As *physis* and *ousia* in the thinking of the Greeks, being is the emerging and abiding holding sway which rules over man by surrendering itself to his power-activity, while still remaining the unconquerable, overpowering force. As *logos* or gathering, it is according to Heraclitus also *polemos*, the primordial strife, the original sundering by which being splits itself up into beings while nevertheless remaining gathered within itself. As the combination of *einai* and *noein* in the thought of Parmenides, it is the primordial unity of the emerging and abiding holding sway (a unity which antecedes the dichotomy of subject and object) into which man is incorporated as the perceiver who brings the ever moving process of being to successive halts in beings. As the origin of all history, being is the self-communicating originator of each succeeding epoch, which, however, withdraws itself in the very act of self-communication. In art, being puts itself to work, again in a historical way, so that it always bears a definite historical stamp. Being in poetry is the holy which sends its message to man, but shows itself precisely in this message as incomprehensibly elevated, as the fullness overflowing its own bounds, as the ever constant new beginning, as what is nearest to man and yet farthest removed from him, in short, as absolute mystery. In language, being itself speaks, but in such a way that it needs human speaking in order to make itself heard. In the essence of things, being is present as world, as the particular historical structuredness of the four regions of being which constitute the quadrate; in revealing the essence of things, however, it remains concealed.

The finitude of being is quite different from the finitude of Dasein. Dasein is finite because it exists as being-unto-death. Being, on the other hand, is finite insofar as it appears only in finite Dasein and in finite beings for the sake of Dasein. The finitude of being thus connotes two things: (1) dependence upon man, who understands being in a questioning way and therefore is capable of letting being appear; (2) the necessity of being to appear in something other than itself, in some particular being —whether this be a particular being as such or the totality of beings, or history or art or poetry or language or the essence of things—in which being must conceal itself in order to appear at all. The finitude of being therefore arises from its character as a phenomenon, as something manifesting itself to man. To distinguish this finitude from the *existential* finitude of man, which has its roots in the existential structure of being-unto-death, we could call the finitude of being, which is grounded in its character as a phenomenon, *phenomenal* finitude.

Even though the finitude of man and the finitude of being are quite different from each other, still they are inseparable. Being shows itself as a phenomenon only insofar as it appears in and through Dasein. Likewise man is man only insofar as he primordially understands and questions being in his character as being-unto-death, or, in other words, insofar as he dwells in the nearness of being as the mortal. But this mutual dependence of being and man does not mean a relationship between two elements of the same nature and equal value. The relationship is marked by a single definite direction, which corresponds to the ontological priority of being over Dasein. Heidegger's early investigations, especially in *Sein und Zeit,* seem to indicate that the initiative and priority are on the side of Dasein, but after the turning being clearly dominates. This is the most profound meaning of the turning which we have interpreted as the central movement of Heidegger's thought. The subordinate position of man and the primacy of being, established through the turning, are abundantly corroborated in the later discussions of history, poetry, art, language, and things.

III. *Heidegger's Image of Man*

In the early phase of Heidegger's thought, in *Sein und Zeit,* man appears as a heroic-tragic figure. Completely reduced to his own individual resources by his being-unto-death, Dasein must seek authenticity in the existentiell acceptance of his own existential structure of finitude. At the middle stage of the journey, in the consolidation of the turning through the analyses of *Einführung in die Metaphysik,* this image is still predominant. Nevertheless, one can sense the beginning of a change in the appearance of a certain reverence for being as the overpowering force, which finite, 'breakable' man is deputed to serve and administer.

At the end of the investigation, the attitude of reverence has fully supplanted the heroic-tragic characteristics of *Sein und Zeit.* Man is still finite, but his finitude no longer finds expression in a seemingly stubborn and rebellious acceptance of his own nature, but in a relaxed acknowledgment of the task of living upon the earth in the nearness of being for the sake of the self-illumination of being. Finite man is the servant of being, serene in his relation to things and open to the mystery of being.

A. *The First Stage*

Before the turning Heidegger's thought proceeds from Dasein toward being. In *Sein und Zeit* Dasein occupies center stage, both as the starting point and the object of the inquiry. Dasein is to be investigated as a phenomenon. It is to show itself, and is to be understood only from itself. To be sure, this total investigation is to serve as a preparation for the interrogation of the meaning of being. But this means two things:

1. Dasein is to be understood from the viewpoint of Dasein alone. This leads to the appearance of complete autonomy on the part of Dasein. There is only one way for Dasein to achieve authenticity: it must accept itself and everything else as an element of its own phenomenological investigation. In this sense, Dasein, purely from the method of questioning employed, is reduced completely to its own resources and closed up within itself. The totality of this attempt to understand itself only from itself is guaranteed precisely by man's being-unto-death, for every man has only his own death to die. Moreover, he must die this death alone, for any help which might possibly come to him from others remains something external to the dying man himself.

2. The self-understanding of Dasein points beyond itself to the question of being. The existential analysis serves to work out only one element of the being-question, namely, the structure of the questioner, and is thus undertaken only with a view toward the subsequent investigation of the other moment of the question, the meaning of being itself. This means

that Dasein is not completely reduced to itself, not entirely closed within itself, but open toward being.

In this stage of the investigation the openness is only preliminary, hypothetical, and postulated, for it remains to be seen whether the openness is real or theoretical. In other words, at the end of *Sein und Zeit* we know much about the interrogator of the meaning of being, but practically nothing about that which is being interrogated, the meaning of being itself. Whether Dasein is really and ontologically open toward being as something other than itself, or whether being should turn out to be nothing more than a constitutive element of Dasein's own questioning, is still an unresolved question.

To put it another way: at this point of Heidegger's analysis, the question is unanswered whether being is anything more than a projection of man, the mere objective correlate of the question Dasein necessarily poses. Since the sole preoccupation of *Sein und Zeit* is Dasein, and since Dasein is investigated only from its own viewpoint, the book gives the impression that being is *de facto* nothing more than the object of Dasein's questioning. If such should turn out to be the case, then Dasein really stands completely alone. His exclusive role and his only authentic existence is the empty, reflexive acceptance of himself. Standing alone and self-assertive, existing only for the sake of his own structure, Dasein gives the unmistakable appearance of a heroic-tragic figure.

B. *The Middle Stage*

The works following *Sein und Zeit* investigate the other element of the being-question, the 'objective' moment of being itself. The discovery of the mysterious character of being as the hidden origin of all truth in the important essay, *Vom Wesen der Wahrheit*, leads Heidegger to the view that being is more than a human projection. For if being were completely dependent upon man, there would be no reason why it should not be completely under the control of man, no reason why it should be able to conceal itself from him. The self-concealment of being which lies at the basis of the revealing of beings is the surest possible guarantee of the fact that being is something beyond the control of man.

This state of affairs becomes even clearer in *Einführung in die Metaphysik*. Man is the most uncanny of all beings, who necessarily uses his might against being and yet is simply incapable of conquering being.

As the most powerful among all beings he is a mighty warrior, a titanic hero, who paradoxically must be shattered in the very performance of his assigned task.

Since this task is assigned to him by being itself, his essential role is to serve being. By accepting his own breakable and mortal Dasein, he is accordingly speaking his most profound 'yes' to the overpowering force of being. He can still be looked upon as a heroic-tragic figure, because he still has a titanic task as the most uncanny and most powerful of all beings. But now his existence has a meaning which goes beyond himself, namely his service of being. Although he himself must be shattered in the performance of the task, still his existence has nobility and meaning because of the master he serves. This new trait in Heidegger's image of man springs from the fact that being has now won a position of superiority over man, in other words, from the fact that the turning has taken place.

C. *The Final Stage*

In the later works being is the determining factor, that which communicates itself, puts itself to work; it is the holy and the sublime, the self-expressing speaker, the ever new beginning, that which comes to presence in things and emerges in the quadrate. The authentically dwelling man sees himself being carried along by being, spoken to by being in all beings, and living under the claim of being. He no longer confronts his own finite existence alone and anxious, but dwells serenely and securely in the hiddenness of being.

Being is the unchallenged superior power which shows man the favor of needing and using him. Man is still the most uncannily powerful of all beings, but his power-activity consists in his administering and preserving the power of being among beings and in history. Insofar as he dwells authentically, he sojourns serenely among things. By his sparing and nurturing attitude toward things, he preserves his openness to being, which communicates itself to him in death and yet remains hidden as the ultimate mystery. In the face of the universal priority of being, man is the expectant and respectful shepherd of being. His authenticity is his relaxed serenity toward beings and his openness to mystery.

Thus, the transformation in the image of man stands in direct relationship to the transformation in the relation between man and being which we have called Heidegger's turning. The image of man changes according to the varying perspectives of the different stages of Heidegger's way, so that the three sketches we have drawn correspond to Heidegger's thought before, in, and after the turning. The turning thus shows itself to be the key to the unity of Heidegger's entire thought.

IV. *Heidegger's View of Death*

It remains to explicitate the significance of the turning for Heidegger's conception of death. In *Sein und Zeit* death appears as the extreme possibility of Dasein; at the end of the way it is the redoubt of being. Is this the same view of death?

A. *Death as the Extreme Possibility of Dasein*

As the extreme possibility of Dasein, death is the existential of totality which completes the self-understanding of Dasein. Existentially considered, death is Dasein's being in relation to its end and the ultimate horizon of its power-to-be and ability to understand itself. As this horizon, death is present implicitly in every realization of existence. It tells Dasein that the last and most all-embracing and most comprehensive thing which Dasein can do and be is being-unto-death. Since being-unto-death offers the possibility of understanding Dasein in its totality, it is at the same time the necessary condition for the authenticity of Dasein. Speaking concretely, the authenticity of Dasein consists in its conscious and willing acceptance of its own being-unto-death, for authentic existence and authentic being-unto-death are one and the same.

The preceding refers, of course, to the self-understanding of Dasein before the turning, in the context of the attempt to understand Dasein only in and through itself and from the viewpoint of its own structures. But immediately after the turning death appears in *Einführung in die Metaphysik* as the shattering against being. The significance of this title is that death is no longer seen merely from the viewpoint of Dasein in its own structures, but from the viewpoint of Dasein precisely in its relation to being. Shattering against being connotes that there is an inner relationship between Dasein's being-toward-death and Dasein's essential task of being the breach through which being breaks into history. In this new perspective, Dasein is being-toward-death precisely because it is the breach of being.

This new view of death is developed more fully in the later writings.

Man is no longer called Dasein, but 'the mortal.' Accordingly his being is still primarily determined from the viewpoint of death; he is still being-to-ward-death; death remains the extreme possibility of existence. But this affirmation receives a completely new accent, since death is now the extreme possibility of man's being precisely because it is the outstanding locus of being's self-revelation in Dasein. In other words, death is the place in Dasein where being gathers itself together and draws man's attention to itself, so that it can reveal itself to man. Death is sent to man by being as the mountain fastness in which being both conceals and reveals itself most profoundly, or as the measure by which being gives itself to man as the measuring rod for the extent of his own essence.

Death has become the extreme possibility of Dasein, not because it exposes man as hopelessly reduced to his own solitary resources, but rather because it reveals being and man's position of service in relation to being. Death is the last and supreme thing which man can do, not because every man must die some day, but because death makes clear that man, who from the very beginning of his existence has in some way had an under-standing of being, is essentially one who is 'there' in the clearing of be-ing and for the sake of the illumination of being.

Looking back to the very beginning of Heidegger's thought, one can perhaps surmise that he has always implicitly thought of death in this way. Even in *Sein und Zeit,* he was analyzing the structures of Dasein as the one being in all creation which understood being, and he was discussing death as a means of the self-understanding of Dasein, all in regard to the question of being. Thus man has always appeared, implicitly at least, in his relation to being. To be sure, this has become clear only in the perspective created by the turning. Heidegger had to undergo the pro-found transformation we have described, before even he could see the full implications of his initial insight. The turning has meant not merely negotiating an ordinary curve in the road, but opening up a whole new panorama, gaining a broader view of a hitherto unsuspectedly lush and variegated landscape.

The fundamental unity which lies at the basis of this gradual trans-formation is indicated by the fact that Heidegger uses different spellings for the same words before and after the turning: Dasein begins to be written Da-sein, existence (*Existenz*) becomes ek-sistence (*Ek-sistenz*). When Heidegger says in *Sein und Zeit* that death is the extreme possibil-ity of Dasein's existence, the emphasis is on man. Death is the outstanding power-to-be of man—who must understand himself from his own viewpoint and with reference to himself, who stands alone as he asks himself about the meaning of being, and who exists authentically by accepting the finitude of his own structure. But after the turning, the emphasis changes. Death is the extreme possibility of ek-sisting Da-sein. This means that death is now the primary and definitive power-to-be of man who understands himself from the viewpoint of his relation to being, who is claimed and summoned by being precisely by means of the being-question, and who reaches his authenticity by ek-sisting, by standing outside of himself and forgetting his own interests, in order to accept willingly his task as the historical place of the illumination of being.

The difference between these two views of death arises from the difference of perspective in each case. Man is first judged on his own terms, from the viewpoint of his own existence; later he is seen from the viewpoint of being. But this change of perspective is not a total reversal or a radical dropping of one road of inquiry to embark upon a completely different one. The transformation is made possible by the persistent following of one path, the interrogation of the meaning of being. Within the context of this constant pursuit, Heidegger investigates first the element of the questioner, Dasein, and then the element of that-which-is-questioned, being itself. Some critics have seen the differences between the earlier and later Heidegger as so great that they must deny all unity to his thought. But it seems more commensurate with the facts to interpret the differences as a tribute to its richness, and the continuity as proof of its rigor.

B. Death and the Finitude of Dasein

When one considers the transformation in Heidegger's concept of death under the aspect of man's finitude, one discovers a similar sameness and difference. This is manifest from a study of two formulations of authentic finitude in man—"advancing toward death" and "accompanying one's essence to a good death."

In *Sein und Zeit* man is finite because he is being-unto-end. His authenticity consists in advancing toward death, withstanding or enduring death as his most proper, distinctive, and extreme possibility-to-be. Advancing brings Dasein to its only authentic freedom, the freedom to be being-unto-death. This "freedom unto death" is the authenticity of Dasein who understands himself only on his own terms, from his own viewpoint, and with reference only to himself, liberated from all entangling relations to other beings and all illusions of the "people-self," sure of himself and only of himself because he sees and understands everything in relation to himself, feeling anxiety in the face of death because death is nothing more than the possibility of the impossibility of existence, "the shrine of nonbeing."

But the turning brings to man's finitude a new dimension and new depth. Man remains finite, because he remains being-unto-death, now called "the mortal." But seen in the context of the questioning of being itself, this now means that he is the mortal in order that he can be of service to being in its simultaneous self-revelation and self-concealment, in the historical event of its self-concealing revelation. The existential finitude of man receives its meaning from the phenomenal finitude of being, from being as the phenomenon *par excellence* which shows itself precisely by withdrawing itself.

Man's authentic finitude thus consists of a new kind of freedom. Instead of a freedom based upon a stubbornly self-assertive advancing against death, we find a relaxed accompanying of one's own nature toward its highest self-fulfillment in death, a calm acceptance and affirmation of one's own capacity for death which lets one's own self and all other beings be what they are, and thereby acknowledges Dasein's position of service with regard to being. This acceptance is a new kind of withstanding or enduring of death as Dasein's most proper and extreme possibility, but this now means an enduring of finitude in the service of being. This attitude is no longer marked by anxiety, but by calm self-composure and attentiveness, for death is no longer merely the shrine of nonbeing, but "as the shrine of nonbeing, the redoubt of being."

Accordingly the authentic dwelling of the mortals after the turning is no longer described as a passionate advancing toward death, but rather as a relaxed accompanying of one's own capacity to die up to the accomplishment of a good death. Each of these formulations bespeaks an acceptance of death as that which renders possible authentic finitude. Before the turning, however, the death which is accepted is understood merely as a structure of Dasein, whereas after the turning it is both an endowment and an assignment of Dasein given it by being itself. The ontological individuation of Dasein standing alone in its finitude, which could not help but suggest an attitude of stubborn resistance or, at best, disgruntled resignation before the turning, yields now to the ontological security of finite Dasein who is admitted into the favoring shelter of being itself, a security which gives rise to the attitude of relaxed acquiescence to the task imposed by the all-powerful and all-pervasive influence of being itself.

C. Death and the Openness of Dasein

We have attempted to show that the unity of Heidegger's conception of death can be appreciated only by a proper understanding of the turning. The turning is thus the key to the understanding of Heidegger's philosophy of death, as it is for his entire philosophy. However, the converse is also true; death is the key to Heidegger's turning.

At the end of our analysis of *Sein und Zeit* it was pointed out that it is precisely death which is capable of keeping Dasein open, rather than completely closed in upon itself in total self-understanding and complete self-grounding. It is only death which makes it impossible to close the circle of Dasein's existence in complete self-containment. Death will simply not allow itself to be completely 'ontologized,' considered purely as an existential-ontological structure of Dasein, but stubbornly maintains its ontic-existentiell character.

The tension between the ontic and the ontological is found in all characteristics of Dasein's existence. The analysis of Dasein is basically nothing more than the working out of the existential-ontological structures which lie at the bottom of the ontic-existentiell realization of existence. The ontological analysis thus presupposes the ontic appreciation of human existence as its point of departure. But this tension is especially true of the structure of death, for death is Dasein's existential of totality; as the extreme power-to-be it embraces and epitomizes all the other possibilities of Dasein. Thus death is the point of departure not only for a part, but in a certain sense for the whole of the analysis of Dasein. It is the point from which Dasein can be observed and analyzed as a totality.

In this sense one can say that the entire ontological analysis of Dasein depends upon the analysis of death, and, insofar as the ontology of death presupposes the ontic-existentiell reality of death as its point of departure, the existential analysis of death is ultimately anchored in ontic-existentiell death. When Heidegger writes: "the existential analytic . . . is ultimately existentielly, i.e., ontically rooted" (SZ 13), he is equivalently saying that it is ultimately rooted in the onticity of death, which provides the unshakable guarantee of the totality of the ontological analysis, because it embraces the totality of existence.

This function of ontic-existentiell death as the last root of the existential-ontological analysis explains its special significance in *Sein und Zeit*. Death is unique and distinctive precisely because it is a border-line phenomenon, which can be only partially incorporated into the analysis. As a power-to-be, or an avenue of self-understanding, it can legitimately be listed among the various possibilities of Dasein, but, on the other hand, it is radically and essentially different from all the other possibilities since it is the only extreme, all-embracing, 'transcendental' power-to-be of Dasein. Insofar as it is such a distinctive possibility, it remains irreducibly outside the list of normal possibilities which enable Dasein to understand itself, necessarily unique and *sui generis*. It remains finally 'un-ontological' or 'un-intelligible.'

Thus death furnishes the ultimate convincing proof that Dasein cannot be fully understood on the basis of its own structures. In death as the existential of totality or the ultimate and all-embracing possibility of self-understanding, Dasein is brought up short against something impervious to understanding. It is confronted with an 'other,' which it is unable to incorporate fully into its own existential structure and which it cannot simply reduce to a function of its own understanding and willing. This negative trait of man's self-understanding—the realization that he understands himself most fully when he sees that he does *not* understand himself fully—corresponds to the mystery-character of being which we have discovered in the analysis of Heidegger's later works. We understand being most profoundly when we realize that we do *not* adequately grasp it in itself, that being shows itself most plainly and clearly when it withdraws into the darkness of its own hiddenness.

This pointing-beyond-itself, this openness of Dasein toward something other than itself is the most profound and significant result of the analysis of death. Moreover, this result is attributable precisely to the stubbornly irreducible ontic-existentiell character of death. If we must say of death, as we do of Dasein in general, that its ontic uniqueness lies precisely in the fact that it is also ontological, then we must also say the opposite, for it is equally true and undeniable that its ontological uniqueness, i.e., its special significance for the existential analysis of Dasein, must be sought in the fact that it is and always remains ontic.

Since death is the ultimate guarantee of the openness of Dasein, it keeps the problematic of *Sein und Zeit* open for a further evolution of the question of being. Since death cannot be fully incorporated into the structure of Dasein in its questioning of the meaning of being, or, in other words, since death cannot be understood solely on the basis of the structure of Dasein itself, the ultimate ground of death, and thereby the ground of Dasein as a whole, must be sought in some 'other.' In the writings in which the turning takes place, the 'other' proves to be being itself, which is simply superior to Dasein and beyond Dasein's control or disposition. Death is thus the element which makes it possible for Heidegger to make the transition from the element of the questioner (Dasein) to the element of that-which-is-questioned (being) within the total context of the being-question. Death enables him to continue his journey from the analysis of Dasein to the turning toward being itself.

The later writings further confirm the fact that death represents the point of Dasein's openness to being itself. Death as the "redoubt of being" and the "measure of the immeasurable" is the preeminent locus of being's hiddenness and self-revelation. As such, it is the point where Dasein is precisely not closed within itself but rather open to something other—to being itself. Death plays a dual role in the structure of Dasein. On one hand, it is the epitome of the finitude of Dasein, while on the other, it reveals the deepest ground and meaning of this finitude: Dasein's openness to being.

V. *The Phenomenon of Death*

The previous presentation has often emphasized the distinction between ontic-existentiell and ontological-existential death. It has also shown that Heidegger is primarily, and indeed exclusively, concerned with existential death, death as an ontological structure of existing Dasein. But it has also made manifest the somewhat untidy fact that these two aspects of death cannot be completely separated. Death can play its distinctive and all-important ontological role in Heidegger's thought only because it retains its ontic-existentiell reality. The uniqueness of death lies precisely in the fact that it is both ontic and ontological.

While the ontological side of death, according to Heidegger's central insight and prime intention, receives extensive treatment, the ontic aspect remains almost completely ignored. To be sure, this is dictated by Heidegger's methodology, for the entire analysis takes place within the context of his questioning of the meaning of being, and ontic death is not an intrinsic element of this questioning. It is not death as an event which is not yet real for Dasein, but death as an ever-present structure of existence, which is of interest and value for the existential analysis.

Thus the fact that the ontic phenomenon of death receives little or no attention in Heidegger's works does not necessarily connote a deficiency in his philosophy. However, it does mean that there is no such thing as a fully developed philosophy of death in Heidegger. Such a philosophy would consider death from both sides, the ontic and the ontological. It would investigate the ontic-existentiell phenomenon of death, as it is ordinarily encountered in everyday life, i.e., in the dying of other men. In this phenomenon death shows itself from the outside. It is a phenomenon not for the one undergoing death, but for the one left behind.

Heidegger discusses this phenomenon only briefly (SZ 237–41), and then merely to show that it contributes nothing to the existential-ontological analysis, or in other words, that it is not suitable as "a substitute theme for the anslysis of the totality [of Dasein]" (SZ 240). Nevertheless he points out certain characteristics of this phenomenon: (1) that the death of others represents at first sight the remarkable change of a being from the mode of Dasein or life to "not-being-there-any-more in the sense of no-longer-being-in-the-world," or from the state of Dasein to "being-merely-present-at-hand" (SZ 238); (2) that the being which remains after the change is phenomenally something more than a lifeless material thing; it is "a nonliving thing, which has lost its life," which even in the purely scientific area—e.g., for anatomy—can be of significance for those left behind (SZ 238); (3) that the relationship of those remaining behind to the dead person is not a taking care of something merely present-at-hand, but a real care or concern, which finds expression in ritual celebration, in caring for the grave, etc.; (4) that those remaining behind, in their relationship of care and concern, in their grief and recollection, are still in a certain way with or in the presence of the deceased (SZ 238).

Although this analysis of the dying of others reaches the phenomenon of death only 'from the outside' and is not capable of "experiencing this transition and understanding it as something experienced" (SZ 237), still it raises certain questions which seem to require further consideration; for example, how is the 'change-over' of dying to be understood? Does it not touch the totality of Dasein, transposing Dasein as a whole into a different dimension? And if so, does one do justice to the phenomenon by characterizing it as a "change-over from Dasein to merely-being-present-at-hand"?

Moreover, what is the 'being-with' which still unites those remaining behind with the deceased? Can it be understood merely unilaterally or is there any ground for a mutual or reciprocal relationship? In the first case, how is a unilateral relationship possible? In the latter case, how is the 'being-with' to be understood from the side of the deceased? What does the cult of the dead, a phenomenon to be found in the most widely dispersed and diverse peoples and cultures, tell us about the attitude of man to death and to his dead? Does it witness to a dim awareness or an implicit assumption of a life for the deceased? What is the basis of this? Why do men tend to imagine a 'beyond' in which the dead have a certain type of existence? What truth is concealed in the many deeply rooted myths about the dead?[1]

These are all questions which Heidegger does not pose, because they do not immediately concern the ontological problematic. Still he never seems to lose sight of the phenomenon of ontic death, even in the later writings. In the interpretation of the poet Hebel he calls human dwelling upon the earth "a wandering from birth to death," a sojourn "between earth and heaven, between birth and death" (HH 17). In his book on language there are two further allusions to ontic death, each of which occurs in a context of great seriousness and a very definite sense of reverence. On the first occasion, in his conversation with a Japanese professor, he expresses his joy over the fact that he possesses pictures of the grave of a former Japanese student who died at an early age, and of the sacred grove in which the grave is located (US 85). In the other text, he hints at the mysterious relationship between death and language by recounting the fact that Wilhelm von Humboldt worked on his last essay "Über die Verschiedenheit des menschlichen Sprachbaues" ("On the Diversity of Human Language-Structure"), "as his brother writes in the foreword, 'alone in the vicinity of a grave' up to the time of his death" (US 267).

These references, sketchy and undeveloped as they are, testify to the very provocative fact that ontic death almost universally arouses feelings of awe and reverence. This reverence embraces a large host of elements, such as wonderment, surprise, shyness, embarrassment, confusion, sadness, resignation, compliance, meekness, acknowledgment of some greater power.

These subjective elements seem to point to certain structures of an objective correlate in the phenomenon of death which produce such reverence —impenetrability, darkness, power, inevitability, universality, greatness, majesty, mystery. In its ability to awaken and even to command reverence, death even seems to be something numinous, like Rudolf Otto's *mysterium tremendum et fascinosum,* indeed as something 'holy' like being itself.[2]

But how are we to understand the 'holiness' of death? If death is a *mysterium tremendum et fascinosum,* a mystery which not only awakens fear but at the same time promises peace and security, does it not follow that man must not only fear death but also love it? No one will dispute the fact that man fears death, but does it make sense to say that he can love it?

It may be illuminating in this connection to cite one of Heidegger's assertions about death as an existential structure. He says that mortal man "is capable of death" insofar as he "likes" it, because death first "likes" man, i.e., allows man to enter into his essence and be that which he is, thus making it possible for him to exist authentically and to understand his existence in its totality. Applying this to the phenomenon of ontic death we could say that death is 'lovable' because it is the limiting boundary of man's time-line, which allows him to enter into the totality of his existence and thus lets him be finally and definitively what he has become throughout the entire course of his existence. Thus, ontic death is that which makes man 'whole.' It is not merely an end but a completion, not a final emptying but definitive fulfillment. As a point of transition, it marks the change-over from inauthentic to authentic existence, from preliminary, derivative, temporal, negativized to ultimate, definitive, totally positive existence.[3]

If this be so, can we not call death 'holy' because it lets man be whole? And is not death, understood now in a sense quite different from Socrates' conception of it, something to be desired with fondest yearning? Is not ontic death the crown of life, the final peak of self-fulfillment?

But what does fulfillment or completion mean here? What is the definitiveness wrought by death? What is man's ultimate mode of being? Is man's being-in-death a kind of being or nonbeing? Or is it a combination of both? Must we say of ontic death what Heidegger says of death as an existential, that it is not only the shrine of nonbeing but the redoubt of being, indeed that it is precisely as the shrine of nonbeing that it is also the redoubt of being? But then what does 'being' mean in the phenomenon of death? And what is the 'nonbeing' involved here? How are we to understand this combination of being and nonbeing? What is it that is both concealed and revealed in the redoubt of death? What is it that is both feared and revered in this shrine?

Heidegger's thought provides us with no answers to these questions. But it does make us aware of their profundity and, in so doing, renders an important service to man in the age of technology. Death may seem the farthest thing from technological man's mind, and yet it is constantly with him, ever near him as he tries not only to master the universe, but to understand who he is and what he is doing.

To find workable answers, man needs first to learn the attitudes of questioning and waiting, for death is the one power whose secret he cannot extort by his own efforts alone. Prometheus can steal fire from the gods, but mortal man can only dwell serenely on the earth, under heaven, and before the godly, open to the mystery of his own existence and of being.

> *Could perhaps wonderment open the locked door?*
> *In the manner of waiting . . .*
> *if this is relaxed . . .*
> *and man's being stays pointed there . . .*
> *from where we are called.* (GL 73)[4]

Notes

1. Introduction: Perspectives on Death

1. Søren Kierkegaard, *Concluding Unscientific Postscript to the Philosophical Fragments*, trans. David F. Swenson and Walter Lowrie (Princeton: Princeton University Press, 1941), p. 148.

2. Cf. Max Müller's distinction between three kinds of "difference" operative in Heidegger's thought: *transzendentale, transzendenzhafte* and *transzendente*, in *Existenzphilosophie im geistigen Leben der Gegenwart*, 2d enl. ed. (Heidelberg: Kerle Verlag, 1958), p. 73. In the present connection, the *transcendent* ground of phenomenal beings would be a ground beyond or outside such beings, while the *transcendental* ground sought by Heidegger is within or immanent to them. Thus, his direction is not 'up' and 'outward' but rather 'into' or 'within.' For a discussion of his posing of the problem of God as experienced by modern man, see chapter 5 of this study.

3. The *Phaedo* is cited according to the standard Greek text of Plato by Henricus Stephanus (Geneva: excudebat Henr. Stephanus, 1578) and also the English translation by W. H. D. Rouse, in *Great Dialogues of Plato* (New York: New American Library, Mentor Books, 1956).

4. One of the most thorough and enlightening studies of phenomenology available is Herbert Spiegelberg's *The Phenomenological Movement: A Historical Introduction*, Phaenomenologica, nos. 5 and 6, 2 vols. (The Hague: Nijhoff, 1960).

5. M. A. H. Stomps, "Heideggers verhandeling over den dood en de Theologie," *Vox Theologica* 9 (1938): 63–73; S. U. Zuidema, "De dood bij Heidegger," *Philosophia reformata* 12 (1947): 49–66; Janis Cedrins, "Gedanken über den Tod in der Existenzphilosophie" (Ph.D. diss., University of Bonn, 1949); Wolfgang Kroug, "Das Sein zum Tode bei Heidegger und die Probleme des Könnens und der Liebe," *Zeitschrift für philosophische Forschung* 7 (1953): 392–415.

6. Joachim Wach, *Das Problem des Todes in der Philosophie unserer Zeit* (Tübingen, 1934); Karl Lehmann, *Der Tod bei Heidegger und Jaspers* (Heidelberg, 1938); R. F. Beerling, *Moderne doodsproblematiek, een vergelijkende studie over Simmel, Heidegger en Jaspers* (Delft, 1945); Régis Jolivet, *Le problème de la mort chez M. Heidegger et J.-P. Sartre* (Abbaye S. Wandrille, 1950); J. Glenn Gray, "The Idea of Death in Existentialism," *Journal of Philosophy* 48 (1951): 113–27.

7. The first to point out and exploit the significance of the distinction

between the order of appearance and the order of composition of Heidegger's works was William J. Richardson, S.J., in his uniquely authoritative study, *Heidegger: Through Phenomenology to Thought*, Phaenomenologica, no. 13 (The Hague: Nijhoff, 1963).

2. *Death in the Analysis of Dasein*

1. Thus Heidegger's thought from the very beginning rests upon the thesis of the forgottenness of being in the history of western philosophy, a conviction which has provoked sharp and widespread disagreement among his critics.

2. *Sein und Zeit*, 7th ed. (Tübingen: Niemeyer, 1957). My translations follow generally, but not exactly, the English version by John Macquarrie and Edward Robinson, *Being and Time* (New York and Evanston: Harper and Row, 1962); these are easily locatable in *Being and Time*, thanks to the translators' thoughtfulness in indicating the *Sein und Zeit* pagination in the margins of their work. An illuminating study of *Sein und Zeit* which stresses the importance of understanding Heidegger's being-question is Magda King's *Heidegger's Philosophy: A Guide to His Basic Thought* (New York: Dell, 1964). Another helpful introduction to Heidegger, concentrating mainly on themes from *Sein und Zeit* and containing an interesting biographical account of Heidegger's life (pp. 1–10) is Joseph J. Kockelmans' *Martin Heidegger: A First Introduction to His Philosophy* (Pittsburgh: Duquesne University Press, 1965).

3. Evidences along the way: pp. 14, 17, 23, 37, 39, 52, 131, 183, 196, 200, 213, 230, 231, 268, 290, 301, 372.

4. For the relations between Husserlian and Heideggerian phenomenology, see the article by Walter Biemel, "Husserls Encyclopedia Britannica Artikel und Heideggers Anmerkungen dazu," *Tijdschrift voor Philosophie* 12 (1950): 246–80, and Herbert Spiegelberg, *The Phenomenological Movement: A Historical Introduction*, Phaenomenologica, nos. 5 and 6, 2 vols. (The Hague: Nijhoff, 1960), 1:275–83.

5. Heidegger points out the deceptiveness of the substantive use of the word 'being,' in *Einführung in die Metaphysik*, 52–53. Eugen Fink illustrates the constant danger of mistaking being for *a* being by a clever variation on the Midas legend: "Man's mind is like Midas of the legend: everything he touched turned into gold; even food and drink turned into hard metal for him. Likewise, everything we think turns into the hard and solid form of 'being,' of something that is. And even the 'is' which we apply to a being, even the *being* of a being, as soon as we try to think it explicitly, is transformed into a 'higher' kind of a being. We then speak of 'being' as if it were a being." *Sein, Wahrheit, Welt: Vor-Fragen zum Problem des Phänomen-Begriffs*, Phaenomenologica, no. 1 (The Hague: Nijhoff, 1958), pp. 144–45.

6. This is my brief explanation of the Heideggerian concept of man as "Dasein," a term which I have chosen to leave in the original German, as have

many commentators in English, including the translators of *Sein und Zeit,* John Macquarrie and Edward Robinson.

7. The title of a very able commentary on *Sein und Zeit* is *L'ontologie phénoménologique de Heidegger, un commentaire de "Sein und Zeit,"* by Albert Chapelle (Paris: Editions universitaires, 1962).

8. The overlooking of this strictly ontological function of the existential analysis led most of Heidegger's early critics to interpret *Sein und Zeit* as a gloomy view of human existence, a kind of existentialism in the pejorative sense. By now, however, the realization is widespread that the question of being is Heidegger's primary concern, even at the beginning of his way in *Sein und Zeit.* This transformation of opinion has been brought about largely by the efforts of Max Müller, author of *Existenzphilosophie im geistigen Leben der Gegenwart* (Heidelberg: Kerle, 1949; 2d ed. 1958), who has called the earlier interpretation an *"anthropologisch-existentialistische Missverständnis,"* and W. J. Richardson, whose *Heidegger: Through Phenomenology to Thought* doggedly traces Heidegger's pursuit of the question of being from the beginning to the end of his thought.

9. Some linguists see an etymological link between the Greek words *phaino,* "appear," and *phos* (earlier *phaos*), "light." Heidegger does not mention this, but develops the relationship between *phaino* and *physis* in *Einführung in die Metaphysik* (pp. 54 and 77).

10. The importance of the phenomenological aspect of Heidegger's thought is underlined by Bernhard Welte, "Remarques sur l'ontologie de Heidegger," *Revue des sciences philosophiques et théologiques,* 31 (1947): 379–93.

11. Aristotle *Metaphysics,* 4. 1. 1003a.

12. Thomas Aquinas' distinction between "first act" and "second act" may shed light on the Heideggerian use of *ontological* and *existential* on the one hand, *ontic* and *existentiell* on the other: "Act . . . is twofold; first, and second. The first act is the form and integrity of a thing; the second act is its operation" (*Summa Theologica,* 1. 48. 5); "there is a double effect of grace, even as of every other form; the first of which is *being,* and the second, *operation*" (*Summa Theologica,* 1–2. 111. 2). Citations are from *St. Thomas Aquinas, Summa Theologica,* translated by Fathers of the English Dominican Province, 3 vols. (New York: Benziger, 1947).

13. Explanations of the hermeneutic circle are to be found in Hans-Georg Gadamer, "Vom Zirkel des Verstehens," *Martin Heidegger zum 70. Geburtstag* (Pfullingen: Neske, 1959), pp. 24–34, and in Heinrich Ott, *Denken und Sein: Der Weg Martin Heideggers und der Weg der Theologie* (Zollikon: Evangelischer Verlag, 1959), pp. 50–52.

14. "This, the most horrifying of evils, means nothing to us, . . . because so long as we are existent death is not present and whenever it is present we are nonexistent," Letter to Monoeceus, L26, cited in George K. Strodach, *The Philosophy of Epicurus* (Evanston, Ill.: Northwestern University Press, 1963), p. 180.

15. A Japanese philosopher, Hajime Tanabe, carries this idea a step further by pointing out that man not only 'lives dying' but also 'dies living,' that is, during the whole of life he is constantly forced to give things up, deny himself, do without things, offer himself; Tanabe sees this as related to the Japanese Zen concept of 'dying as resurrection.' "Todesdialektik," in *Martin Heidegger zum 70. Geburtstag*, pp. 93–133. Karl Rahner writes similarly in the tradition of Christian theology: "Because we die our death in this life, because we are continually taking leave, continually parting, looking towards the end, continually disappointed, ceaselessly piercing through realities into their nothingness, continually narrowing the possibilities of free life through our actual decisions and actual life, . . . we die throughout life, and what we call death is really the end of death, the death of death." *On the Theology of Death*, 2d English ed. (New York: Herder and Herder, 1965), p. 85.

16. Alphonse de Waelhens explains the intensely personal and individual character of death: "La mort est la possibilité . . . la plus personelle, parce que la moins commutable, qui soit en nous . . . (puisque la mort me rejette vers le plus pur moi-meme)." *La Philosophie de Martin Heidegger* (Louvain, 1942), pp. 143–44. On death as the first fully personal decision of man, see the excellent book of Ladislaus Boros, *The Mystery of Death* (New York: Herder and Herder, 1965), esp. pp. 73–81, 84. The heavy emphasis in this part of Heidegger's work on the individualizing effect of death is balanced in the later works by the idea of man's belonging to a historical people and the concept of relaxed dwelling of the mortals upon the earth and their 'accompanying' of their own nature to a 'good death.'

17. On the certainty of death Rudolph Berlinger writes: "The knowledge of death is not knowledge from experience, but natural knowledge of which every man is capable from the fact that he is what he is, how he is, and who he is." *Das Nichts und der Tod* (Frankfurt am Main: Klostermann, c. 1953), p. 149, translation my own. F. W. von Herrmann points out that death does not first have to be discovered, because it is included in the very self-awareness of man's existence, as the end of that existence; thus, the knowledge of death as the end of Dasein "is given not *a posteriori*, but *a priori* in the actualization of one's self-transparency" (*im Vollzug des Erschlossen-seins*). *Die Selbstinterpretation Martin Heideggers* (Ph.D. diss., University of Freiburg im Breisgau, 1961), p. 130.

18. Heidegger's sharpest early critic, Adolf Sternberger, points out this contrast in *Der Verstandene Tod: Eine Untersuchung zu Martin Heideggers Existenzial-Ontologie* (Leipzig, 1934), p. 91.

19. Cf. Thomas Aquinas, *De Ente et Essentia*, Caput 5: "Omnis autem essentia vel quidditas potest intelligi sine hoc quod aliquid intelligatur de esse suo: possum enim intelligere quid est homo vel phoenix, et tamen ignorare an esse habeat in rerum natura" ("But every essence or quiddity can be understood without anything being understood about its 'to be': for I can understand what a man or a phoenix is, and still not know whether it has 'to be' in nature").

Divi Thomae Aquinatis Opuscula Philosophica, ed. R. M. Spiazzi (Turin-Rome: Marietti, 1954). Translation my own.

20. Otto Pöggeler explains that inauthenticity is not simply something which can be conquered once and for all, but rather that Dasein must live in a continual tension, exerting constant effort to pull himself out of the throes of inauthentic everydayness. "Sein als Ereignis—Martin Heidegger zum 26. Sept. 1959," *Zeitschrift für philosophische Forschung,* 13(1959): 597–632, esp. 613. In the same vein Sternberger calls everydayness the "springboard" for authenticity in Heidegger's thought. *Der verstandene Tod,* p. 97.

21. Cf. Joseph de Finance, *Ethica Generalis* (Rome: Gregorian University Press, 1959), p. 247.

22. *Summa Theologica,* 1. 48. 5 (translation mine).

23. Cf. the classical presentation of the mystery of time in St. Augustine's *Confessions,* Book 11.

24. Peter Fürstenau says that the continual repetition of the two-phased rhythm of movement between the two dimensions of existence within the hermeneutic circle leads to a steady deepening of our understanding of the constitution of Dasein. *Heidegger, Das Gefüge seines Denkens* (Frankfurt am Main: Klostermann, 1958), p. 16. Another very perceptive critic, Fridolin Wiplinger, speaks of this reciprocal relationship as the "Einheit von existenzial-ontologischer Konstruktion und existenziell-ontischer Konkretion." *Wahrheit und Geschichtlichkeit* (Freiburg and Munich: Alber, 1961), p. 281.

25. Here we need to be reminded that, just as Heidegger primarily understands the word 'being' in a verbal sense, so also he conceives of Dasein not substantively, but verbally, dynamically, as something continually happening, coming-to-be, becoming itself.

26. In stressing this transcendental character of the possibility of death, Fürstenau calls it "the universal horizon of all possible individual possibilities of authentic Dasein. . . . The particular possibilities are possibilities of authentic Dasein only to the extent that they are co-constitutive in their relationship to the extreme possibility. Authentic Dasein is at one and the same time being toward the current possibility and being toward the extreme possibility of death." *Heidegger, das Gefüge seines Denkens,* p. 57. Translation mine.

27. The German word for "moment" or "instant" is *Augenblick,* literally "eye's-look"; it conveys the notion of seeing in a way which is absent in the corresponding English terms.

28. *Moderne doodsproblematiek: een vergelijkende studie over Simmel, Heidegger en Jaspers* (Delft, 1945), p. 119.

29. Ibid., p. 122.

30. Ibid., p. 200.

31. Ibid., p. 223 (translations in this and the preceding three citations are mine). Other critics who have shared this general opinion of *Sein und Zeit* are Alfred Delp, who calls Heidegger's thought a "heroism of finitude," "permeated by a final great inner pessimism" (*Tragische Existenz: Zur Philosophie Martin*

Heideggers [Freiburg: Herder, 1935], pp. 83, 94); S. U. Zuidema: "nihilistic" and "irrationalistic existentialism" ("De dood bij Heidegger," *Philosophia reformata* 12[1947]: 59, 62); Karl Löwith: Heidegger is a "godless theologian" (*Gesammelte Abhandlungen* [Stuttgart: Kohlhammer, 1960], pp. 82, 116–17; cf. also his *Heidegger: Denker in dürftiger Zeit*, 2d enl. ed. [Göttingen: Vandenhoeck, 1960]); Helmut Thielicke: Heidegger's philosophy of death is a kind of "secularism" and "heroic nihilism" (*Tod und Leben: Studien zur Christlichen Anthropologie* [Tübingen, 1946], pp. 82, 91). Marjorie Grene, while acknowledging that there are two sides to Heidegger, sees "the incisive, devastating insight into the ultimate loneliness of individual existence, the philosophical formulation of the place of death in life" as that which is "noteworthy in Heidegger" (*Martin Heidegger* [New York: Hillary House, 1957], p. 14); she sums up the impression created by *Sein und Zeit*: "the emphasis, the living centre of the whole picture, lies . . . in this very act of assimilation, in the death-facing, birth-absorbing, destiny-making resolve by which human being rises, in isolation from the gossiping crowd, to its proper stature, and in which it finds itself, in the face of its dissolution, unutterably and irremediably alone" (p. 41). Laszlo Versenyi thinks that even the later Heidegger still bears the same traits: "in spite of Heidegger's claim that his thinking is neither theistic nor atheistic . . . he has overcome humanistic metaphysics—as well as philosophy—only by becoming a mystic poet and godless theologian." *Heidegger, Being, and Truth* (New Haven and London: Yale University Press, 1965), p. 164.

32. Cf. the projected outline of the *total* work on pp. 39 and 40 of *Sein und Zeit*, plus the list of questions to be handled in the never completed third section of part I, which would have been entitled "Time and Being," on p. 100. Magda King provides a helpful "Attempt to Outline Heidegger's Answer to the Question Asked at the Beginning of *Sein und Zeit*" at the conclusion of her book, *Heidegger's Philosophy: A Guide to His Basic Thought* (New York: Dell, 1964), pp. 175–81.

33. *Existenzphilosophie im geistigen Leben der Gegenwart*, pp. 53–54.

34. HB 72. The "turning" in Heidegger's thought will come up for full discussion in succeeding chapters of this study.

35. "Über den philosophiegeschichtlichen Ort Martin Heideggers," *Philosophische Rundschau* 1 (1953–54): 65. Eugen Fink remarks that the great majority of Heidegger's readers "get stuck" in the interpretation of the concrete phenomena of existence and thereby misunderstand his thought as a kind of existentialism or anthropology, overlooking the fundamental connection of these interpretations with the question of being. "Philosophie als Überwindung der 'Naivität,'" *Lexis* 1 (1948): 124. Marjorie Grene sees the two aspects of Heidegger's early thought: "In fairness to the man who denies his existentialist affiliation, we must . . . view him as an ontologist. Yet in fairness to his decisive role in the history of existentialism, and to the decisive role of existentialism in contemporary thought, we must discount his ontology in order

to evaluate, distinctly from it, the analysis of personal existence." *Martin Heidegger,* p. 14.

36. *Der verstandene Tod,* pp. 113–24.

37. *Heidegger: Das Gefüge seines Denkens,* p. 157.

38. Thus Beerling, *Moderne doodsproblematiek,* pp. 190–231, and De Waelhens, *La Philosophie de Martin Heidegger,* pp. 330–52.

39. "Über den philosophiegeschichtlichen Ort Martin Heideggers," p. 65.

40. On the influence of 'environment' on philosophical writing Heidegger himself states: "Since even the greatest, i.e., at the same time the loneliest thinkers do not live in some extraterrestrial space or some other world from this, they are always surrounded and touched and, as people say, 'influenced' by what is contemporary and traditional around them" (N I 497). Translation mine.

41. This roughly sums up the objections of Sternberger, *Der verstandene Tod,* pp. 30–31, 66–67, 133; Beerling, *Moderne doodsproblematiek,* pp. 230–31; Delp, *Tragische Existenz,* p. 94; and Erdmann Schott, *Die Endlichkeit des Deseins nach Martin Heidegger* (Berlin, 1930), p. 8.

42. *Möglichkeit und Wirklichkeit bei Martin Heidegger,* pp. 39–43, 48–51.

43. Death pertains exclusively to Dasein because, in Heidegger's view, only Dasein can really die (*sterben*) or experience death (*Tod*). Thus, death is to be distinguished from the mere ending or passing-away of other living beings (*verenden*) and from a purely physiological-biological, and therefore ontic, conception of man's ceasing-to-be (*ableben*); cf. *Sein und Zeit,* pp. 240–41, 246–47. Somewhat related to this view is Jose Ferrater Mora's interesting concept of *analogia mortis,* according to which the phenomenon of ceasing-to-be is both the same and different on various levels of reality: in inorganic nature, organic nature, and man. *Being and Death* (Los Angeles: University of California Press, 1965).

44. *Das Nichts und der Tod,* p. 142; cf. also p. 149.

45. *Der verstandene Tod,* p. 145. The phrase *"schlechthinnige Nichtigkeit"* is Heidegger's own (*Sein und Zeit,* p. 306). The French critic, Régis Jolivet, also thinks that Heidegger is denying the possibility of an after-life (*Le problème de la mort chez M. Heidegger et J.-P. Sartre* [Abbaye S. Wandrille, 1950]); however, he misses the point of Heidegger's whole attempt to pursue the question of being, and sees him as little more than a German version of Sartre. Thus he calls both men without distinction "nihilists," "materialists," and "philosophers of the absurd" (pp. 11, 12, 17), for whom death is a "plunge into nothingness," a "definitive and total annihilation of man's reality" (pp. 19, 37). Jolivet mistakenly identifies *das Nichts* of *Sein und Zeit* with absolute nothingness, the *nihil absolutum* of classical metaphysics, as Sartre himself does (*L'être et le néant,* pp. 613–29). Max Müller gives a more nuanced and accurate explanation: "The 'Nichts' is for Heidegger neither a *nihil negativum* nor *nihil absolutum* as it is for Sartre; rather it is 'nothing' in

the sense of a 'not' with regard to beings (*das 'nicht zum Seienden'*)" (*Existenzphilosophie im geistigen Leben der Gegenwart*, p. 64). He explains the difference in approach as follows: "The realm of Sartre remains the phenomenal and thereby ontic realm of the approach of traditional ontology; the philosophy of Heidegger, on the other hand, attempts to penetrate to the . . . foundations of the ontological" (p. 68). Jean Beaufret writes in like vein of the difference between Heidegger and Sartre: "The analysis of Sartre may be very valuable on the level of psychology . . . [but] I should like to emphasize that the level on which he is working is by no means the same as the level on which Heidegger works." "Martin Heidegger et le problème de la vérité," *Fontaine* 11 (1947): 772.

46. Alwin Diemer emphasizes that death in *Sein und Zeit* is an element of the self-understanding of Dasein in its temporality, and thus says nothing pro or con about the possibility of an after-life. "Grundzüge Heideggerschen Philosophierens," *Zeitschrift für philosophische Forschung* 5 (1950–1951): 562–63. Albert Chapelle also stresses the ontological nature of the analysis of death in *Sein und Zeit*. *L'ontologie phénoménologique de Heidegger*, pp. 105–18.

47. The German theologian Karl Rahner points out that the notion of man's survival requires a revision of our ordinary concept of time: "We do not mean that 'things go on' after death, as though we only changed horses, as Feuerbach puts it, and rode on. It is not a continuation of the peculiar distraction and vagueness of temporal existence, which is an openness always in need of new determinations and hence basically empty. . . . To think of time as simply lasting beyond the death of man and of the soul in this time, so that time is renewed instead of being absorbed into the definitive, is to cause oneself insuperable difficulties, with regard to the concept and the existential achievement of the Christian thought." *Theological Investigations* 4 (Baltimore: Helicon Press, 1966), p. 347. Cf. also Robert Gleason, "Toward a Theology of Death," *Thought* 32 (1957): 39–68.

48. Ladislaus Boros expresses clearly the meaning of death as finitude in Heidegger: "According to him, death is *a fundamental modality of living, concrete existence*. Our existence carries death within itself, and not only—or, at least, not primarily—because we can in reality die at any moment. Any given existence may be defined as a dedication to, an immersion in death, not only because it is on its way to meet death, but more truly essentially because it constantly realizes in itself the 'situation' of death. This presence of death is so fundamental to existence that not one of its stirrings can be understood otherwise than in the light of a constitutive ordering toward death. In every act of existence death is present from the beginning. Its own end belongs of right to every existent being as an outstanding debt, a *perfectio debita*." *The Mystery of Death*, pp. 8–9.

49. On the interesting notion of being-in-death as the condition of man's no longer being distinct from his own possibilities but definitively identical with them, see Rudolf Berlinger, *Das Nichts und der Tod*, p. 135.

50. The German word for "finite" is *"endlich,"* which lends itself admirably to Heidegger's interpretation of finitude as being-unto-end. This is not to say that all the definitions of finitude found in traditional metaphysics are hereby denied or discarded, but merely that in Heidegger's phenomenological view, they are seen as secondary, because they are derived from the primordial existential meaning of finitude as man's being-unto-end.

3. Broadening the Horizon

1. *Critique of Pure Reason,* B 19. The translation is mine, from the German text of the *Kritik der reinen Vernunft* published as volume 37a of the *Philosophische Bibliothek* (Hamburg: Felix Meiner Verlag, 1956).

2. *Critique of Pure Reason,* A 145, B 184; cf. KM 117–56.

3. Regarding Heidegger's interpretation of Kant it must be noted that *Kant und das Problem der Metaphysik* limits itself to the *Critique of Pure Reason,* so that neither the ethician Kant, of the *Foundation of the Metaphysics of Morals,* the *Critique of Practical Reason* and the *Metaphysics of Morals,* nor the rationalist believer Kant, of the *Critique of Practical Reason* and *Religion within the Limits of Mere Reason,* come in for consideration. By presenting Kant only in the light of his first great work, Heidegger exposes himself to the same danger of one-sided criticism to which many of his (Heidegger's) own critics have fallen prey by interpreting him solely on the basis of *Sein und Zeit.* Moreover, the Kant interpretation covers only about half the transcendental analytic in the *Critique of Pure Reason;* this allows Heidegger to lay principal stress on the section on schematism, and thus to emphasize the nature of the schemata as time determinations. He thereby ignores the transcendental dialectic, which Kant seems to have considered the most important part of the book.

Heidegger acknowledges the limitations of *Kant und das Problem der Metaphysik* in his foreword to the second edition; he also mentions explicitly that the transcendental dialectic contains a further problematic (KM 221). Two later publications supplement Heidegger's interpretation of Kant: *Die Frage nach dem Ding (The Question of the Thing,* 1962), containing the text of a lecture course given in 1935–1936, in which Heidegger sees the system of the principles of the pure understanding as the "center" of the *Critique of Pure Reason* (p. 97), and *Kants These über das Sein (Kant's Thesis on Being,* 1962), which explains the Kantian determination of being as "not a real predicate," but "merely the positing of a thing" (*Critique of Pure Reason,* A 598, B 626).

4. Heidegger will often later emphasize that "the nothing" discussed in *Was Ist Metaphysik?* is not to be understood in the sense of purely negative or empty or absolute nonbeing, but rather as something totally other than beings (SF 37–40). As such, it is "the sharpest counterpart of the purely negative. The nothing is never 'nothing'; it is also by no means 'something' in the sense

of an object; it is rather being itself, to whose truth man is committed only when he has overcome himself as a subject, i.e., when he no longer regards beings as objects" (HW 104).

Heidegger has earlier met 'the nothing' as a kind of 'something,' in his study of the medieval thought of Duns Scotus. Thus in his *Die Kategorien- und Bedeutungslehre des Duns Scotus* (Tübingen, 1916) he writes: "[for Duns Scotus] *non ens* is still an object of knowledge, is an element in judgments, is grasped in meanings and signified by words. Because judgments are possible about *non ens*, there must be a universal concept of *non ens*, a category which does not fall under the ten categories of reality" (pp. 105 106).

5. In his conversation with a Japanese professor about the emptiness signified by the absence of all scenery in a certain type of Japanese drama, Heidegger later writes: "Emptiness is thus the same as the nothing, namely that presence which we are attempting to think as the opposite of everything which is present or absent"; to which his interlocutor replies: "Certainly. That is why we in Japan have immediately been able to understand your essay *Was Ist Metaphysik?* . . . We are still amazed that the Europeans could make the mistake of interpreting the nothing discussed in that essay in a nihilistic way. For us emptiness is the most sublime name for what you are trying to say through the word 'being' " (US 108–109).

6. J. B. Lotz thus calls Heidegger's 'nothing' a "transition stage on the way to being" (*Durchgangsphase zum Sein*) or the "opposite pole to beings, but at the same time . . . [a] preliminary form of being" (*Gegenpol zum Seienden, aber zugleich . . . [eine] Vorform des Seins*). *Existenzphilosophie und Christentum* (München, 1958) p. 20. Likewise Rudolph Berlinger sees the nothing as a "vehicle" by which thought can "interrogate the meaning of being," or as "the threshold of being." *Das Nichts und der Tod* (Frankfurt am Main: Klostermann, c. 1953) pp. 14, 152.

7. On the existential-ontological meaning of world, cf. Bernhard Welte, "Das Heilige in der Welt," *Kosmos, Tier und Mensch: Freiburger Dies Universitatis 1948–1949* (Freiburg im Breisgau: Alber, 1949), pp. 145–48, and Walter Biemel, *Le concept du monde chez Heidegger* (Louvain-Paris, 1950).

8. Heidegger later explains his concept of world: "The concept of world, as it is developed in *Sein und Zeit,* can only be understood in the context of the question of 'Da-sein,' which in turn remains bound up with the basic question of the meaning of being (not of beings)" (HW 92). Cf. also HB 100: "In that definition 'world' means . . . the openness of being"; and VA 92: " 'World' . . . means the nonobjective presencing of the truth of being for man, insofar as man is essentially committed to being." Cf. also Max Müller, *Existenzphilosophie im geistigen Leben der Gegenwart,* 2d enl. ed. (Heidelberg: Kerle Verlag, 1958), p. 124, and "Klassische und moderne Metaphysik oder Sein als Sinn," *Sinn und Sein: Ein philosopisches Symposion* (Tübingen: Niemeyer, 1960), p. 328.

9. Cf. Heidegger's remark in *Einführung in die Metaphysik*: "Insofar as a being is as such, it puts itself into and stands in unconcealedness, *aletheia.*

206

We unthinkingly translate, and that means we misinterpret this word as 'truth.' But now finally we are beginning to translate literally the Greek word *aletheia*" (EM 77).

10. De Waelhens and Biemel elucidate on this peculiar use of *Un-*: "In Heidegger the *Un-* has by no means a negative meaning in the ordinary sense. It is rather intensifying, strengthening. . . . This Heideggerian intensification must not be understood as a quantitative swelling, but rather as a pointing to that which is primordial, original. The *Un-* points out the relation to the origin, and thus corresponds to *Ur*. This origin, or the original as such, is that which is prior to all the well-known and ordinary aspects of a thing, but which is as such precisely that which is not seen. The *Un-* thus retains the meaning of 'not,' but not in the sense of a deprecatory or negativing 'not'; rather it is a negation of the ordinary, signifying the bursting of the bounds of the familiar and well-known. This bursting is inevitable, because the original is always at first buried under debris and encrustations, and is thus inaccessible." "Heideggers Schrift 'Vom Wesen der Wahrheit,' " *Symposion* III (1952): 497–98. Else Buddeberg adds in the same connection: "This primordial 'Un-' . . . does not mean the opposite of truth, or un-truth, but rather the pre-essence of truth, in the sense of truth which has not yet been unfolded." *Heidegger und die Dichtung* (Stuttgart: Metzler, 1953), p. 16, note 1.

11. Heidegger uses various terms to express the ineffability, and thus to a certain extent the illimitability or infinity of being: *"das Unberechenbare und Ungreifbare . . . alles stimmend . . . doch das Unbestimmte, Unbestimmbare"* (WW 19); *"das Unumgängliche"* (WW 23); *"das sich verbergende Einzige"* (WW 25).

12. No matter what terms we may use in speaking of the *sui generis* character of being, our language must suffer from the fact that all our words stem from experience with the realm of beings. Thus all discourse in the realm of ontology retains traces of its origin in the world of the ontic. This points to the need for a doctrine of analogy in language, for an inner flexibility and variability in the meanings of words, so that they can serve to describe phenomena in different areas of reality, and even, by a particularly long stretching, be applied to being itself. Adolf Sternberger points out Heidegger's extensive use of analogical terms from the area of building: structure, foundation, sketch, projection, ground. *Der verstandene Tod: Eine Untersuchung zu Martin Heideggers Existenzial-Ontologie* (Leipzig, 1934), p. 82.

13. "Foundational thought" is William Richardson's translation of the Heideggerian terms *"das wesentliche Denken," "Seinsdenken,"* and *"Denken des Seins." Heidegger: Through Phenomenology to Thought* (The Hague: Nijhoff, 1963). By it Heidegger signifies the direct focusing of thought on being itself which he attempts in many of the later works, and which turns out to be not so much an activity of man, but rather a self-communication of being. The genitive "of being" in the phrase "thinking of being" thus turns from an objective to a subjective genitive, and "being" becomes a complex process whose fullness comprises both meanings.

14. De Waelhens and Biemel see the essay *Vom Wesen der Wahrheit* as the decisive turning-point in Heidegger's thought: "In definite contrast to *Sein und Zeit,* the starting point here is not Dasein, in order to arrive at being, but rather Dasein itself is understood from the viewpoint of being. This appears to be the decisive step in the development of Heidegger's thought." "Heideggers Schrift 'Vom Wesen der Wahrheit,' " p. 477.

4. *Being, Man, & Death in the New Position*

1. *Einführung in die Metaphysik* was not published until 1953, eighteen years after its ideas were first delivered as a university course. Likewise, *Vom Wesen der Wahrheit* had to wait thirteen years—originated 1930, published 1943—and *Nietzsche* 15 years—originated in courses given 1936–1946, published 1961—before appearing in print. All are key writings for the development of Heidegger's thought. Thus, whatever the explanation may be, the delay in publication of these works meant that the earlier Heidegger commentators and critics had incomplete written evidence to work with.

2. Concerning Heidegger's thesis on the forgottenness of being cf. chapter two, note 1. Alfredo Guzzoni explains the difference between traditional metaphysics and Heidegger's thinking-of-being by pointing out that metaphysics moves in the area of the difference between being and beings without experiencing and interrogating this difference itself, as Heidegger does. "Ontologische Differenz und Nichts," *Martin Heidegger zum 70. Geburtstag* (Pfullingen: Neske, 1959), pp. 35–39. Max Müller too affirms the forgottenness in classical metaphysics; he sees its greatness in the fact that it "for the first time really asked about the being of beings," but its limitation in the fact that it cannot "develop the questions of the essence of essence, the being of being, or the godliness of God." "Klassische und moderne Metaphysik oder Sein als Sinn," *Sinn und Sein: Ein philosophisches Symposion* (Tübingen: Niemeyer, 1960), p. 318.

3. A thorough study of Heidegger's interpretations of the pre-Socratics is contained in George J. Seidel, *Martin Heidegger and the Pre-Socratics* (Lincoln: University of Nebraska Press, 1964).

4. In a later writing Heidegger elaborates on what he understands by "the same" (*das Selbe*). It is not mere equality or pure identity, but rather the unity of different elements, which are both held apart and kept together by the difference itself, and are thus gathered together into a primordial oneness: "Das selbe ist . . . das Zusammengehören des Verschiedenen aus der Versammlung durch den Unterschied. Das selbe lässt sich nur sagen, wenn der Unterschied gedacht wird. . . . Das selbe versammelt das Unterschiedene in eine ursprüngliche Einigkeit" (VA 193; cf. also ID 18–19).

5. Heidegger later contends that the early Greek thinkers did not regard things as objects in the context of the subject-object schema, but rather perceived beings as something standing-over-against or confronting man

(*Gegenüber* rather than *Gegenstand*, SG 139–40). The question of subjectivism will come up again later in this chapter, in the interpretation of Heidegger's turning.

6. On the ontological difference between being and beings, Max Müller writes: "In the first draft of section III of the first part of *Sein und Zeit*, Heidegger tried—as he told me personally—to distinguish a threefold difference: (a) the '*transcendental*' or ontological difference in the narrower sense: the distinction of a being from its own being-ness; (b) the '*transcendentist*' (*transzendenzhafte*) or ontological difference in the broader sense: the distinction of a being and its being-ness from being itself; (c) the '*transcendent*' or theological difference in the strict sense: the distinction of God from beings, from being-ness, and from being. But since it was not known through experience but only set up speculatively, this attempt was given up as being itself still 'onto-theological,' because it ventured a statement about God which is not immediately based on the experience of 'essential' (foundational) thought." *Existenzphilosophie im geistigen Leben der Gegenwart*, 2d enl. ed. (Heidelberg: Kerle Verlag, 1958), pp. 73–74.

7. Heidegger has already announced in *Was Ist Metaphysik?* that he intends to drop the term 'transcendence,' since it belongs to the terminology of the metaphysics or ontology of beings, whereas he is attempting to reach the level of being itself (WM 21).

8. At this point Heidegger begins to write both 'there-being' and 'existence' differently; the earlier *Dasein* becomes *Da-sein*, while *Existenz* becomes *Ek-sistenz*. These changes indicate a new emphasis on the fact that man's essence is to stand out into the openness of being, that he is the 'there' of being and exists for the sake of being. On the significance of these changes cf. Werner Brock, *Existence and Being by Martin Heidegger* (London: Vision Press, 1949), pp. 161–64.

9. Cf. Aristotle's *Politica*, 7, 1332b.

10. Heidegger rejects the charge of subjectivism in *Vom Wesen des Grundes*, 38, 42, and 15 note 14. J. B. Lotz elaborates on this point: "Certainly [being] does not appear in Heidegger as idealistic-subjectivistic. It is not something simply posited by man but antecedes man and forms the basis for his existence. All beings, including man, are rooted in being; it is broader than any being, overreaches all beings and is thus somehow transcendent." *Existenzphilosophie und Christentum* (Munich, 1958), p. 21. Cf. also Jean Beaufret, "Martin Heidegger et le problème de la vérité," *Fontaine* 11 (1947): 770.

11. "Sein als Ereignis—Martin Heidegger zum 26. Sept. 1959," *Zeitschrift für philosophische Forschung* 13 (1959): 621.

12. "Über den philosophiegeschichtlichen Ort Martin Heideggers," *Philosophische Rundschau* 1 (1953–1954): 86; cf. also Schulz's *Der Gott der neuzeitlichen Metaphysik* (Pfullingen: Neske, 1957), p. 54.

13. *Der Gott der neuzeitlichen Metaphysik*, p. 54.

14. Cf. HB 71–72, where Heidegger mentions the elements involved

in the turning. He does not speak of being and nonbeing, but rather of "the eksistent essence of man" and man's "ekstatic relation to the lighting-up of being."

15. *Denken und Sein: Der Weg Martin Heideggers und der Weg der Theologie* (Zollikon: Evangelischer Verlag, 1959), pp. 73–84.

16. *Denken und Sein*, p. 83 (emphasis Ott's).

17. *Denken und Sein*, p. 159, note 20; cf. also pp. 56–57. Magda King expresses the difference before and after the turning as follows: "What changes in Heidegger's later works is his way of 'getting into the circle': being is no longer approached through man's understanding, but rather it is man's understanding which is approached through the manifestness of being." *Heidegger's Philosophy: A Guide to His Basic Thought* (New York: Dell, 1964), p. 33.

18. Emerich Coreth expresses the similarity and the difference between Kant's and Heidegger's transcendental positions: "Kant's transcendental question is so essentially basic to Heidegger's thought, that it can only be properly understood . . . from this viewpoint. At the same time, however, the transcendental problematic is developed beyond Kant in such a way that a profound dialogue with Kant . . . and with the whole 'metaphysics of subjectivity' of western thought takes place." "Heidegger und Kant," *Kant und die Scholastik heute* (Pullach bei München: Berchmanskolleg, 1955), p. 225; cf. also Coreth's *Metaphysik* (Innsbruck-Wien-München: Tyrolia, 1961), p. 48. Max Müller points out the historical continuity and the differences between Kant's "transcendental," Husserl's "phenomenological," and Heidegger's "existential" transformation of metaphysics (*Klassische und moderne Metaphysik*, pp. 311–32). On the distinction between what Kant wanted to say and actually did, or could, say, cf. *Kant und das Problem der Metaphysik*, p. 183.

19. Thus Walter Schulz writes: "Heidegger's thought is pointed to the turning from the very beginning"; he took this step "because he remained true to the direction of his first great work." "Über den philosophiegeschichtlichen Ort Martin Heideggers," pp. 88, 86.

20. Ott points out in this connection: "*Sein und Zeit* was open to misunderstanding and people have actually misunderstood it by making Heidegger an existentialist"; "the misunderstanding was in fact almost suggested by *Sein und Zeit* itself." *Denken und Sein*, p. 98; cf. also pp. 138–39, 159, 194. Heidegger said that he could not foresee exactly where his thought would lead, precisely because it was a *way*: "Meanwhile the attempt was stirring to walk a particular path, although I didn't know where it would lead. Only its closest views were known to me because they unceasingly attracted me, even though the field of vision often shifted and dimmed" (US 91).

21. Thus the concept of authenticity has taken on new meaning through the turning. Whereas authentic existence in *Sein und Zeit* consisted in the acceptance of one's own structure as guilty being-unto-death, this

acceptance is now seen as something imposed upon man by being, indeed as part of his service to being.

5. Death in History, Poetry, & Language

1. When Heidegger asks, "What is being?" he is using the copula 'is' in a broad or analogical sense, since it is used properly only of beings, and not of being itself; this is the whole point of the ontological difference. In other texts, Heidegger writes more carefully, for example, putting 'is' in quotes when he uses it in reference to being (N II 206, 462). He makes explicit mention of this difficulty in "Überwindung der Metaphysik": "What 'is' being? Can we even ask about 'being,' what it is?" (VA 84).

2. Thus Heidegger is not attempting a simple return to the pre-Socratics: "it is not a question of some kind of Renaissance of pre-Socratic thought; such a project would be idle and senseless" (WM 11, cf. HW 39–40, US 133). Heidegger's dialogues with the great western philosophers are contained in the following works: the pre-Socratics in EM; Heraclitus in "Aletheia" and "Logos" in VA; Parmenides in "Moira" in VA, and in WD 106–49; Anaximander in "Der Spruch des Anaximander" in HW; Plato in PW; Aristotle's concept of *physis* in AP; Duns Scotus in DS; Kant in KM, FD and KS; Hegel in "Hegels Begriff der Erfahrung" in HW, "Hegel und die Griechen" in HG, and "Die Onto-Theo-Logische Verfassung der Metaphysik" in ID; Nietzsche in N I and N II, "Nietzsches Wort, 'Gott ist tot' " in HW, "Wer Ist Nietzsches Zarathustra?" in VA, and in WD 19–47. There are also brief discussions of Leibniz and others in SG, and sketches of the history of western philosophy as the history of being in "Überwindung der Metaphysik" in VA, and in N II.

3. His earlier interpretation of the choral ode of the *Antigone* (EM 112–26) is an example of Heidegger's appreciation of poetry as a source of knowledge about the world view, self-understanding, and understanding of being prevalent in a particular historical age and culture.

4. On the primacy of being cf. HD 51, 56, 61, 62, 66, 94, 110, 138, 142; HW 49, 59; HB 53, 58, 74, 83, 84, 90; WM 47, 49, 50; ED 11; GL 37, 44, 50, 52, 59, 66, 73. On the interdependence of man and being cf. HD 38, 40, 68–69, 128; HW 59, 60; HB 69, 75, 77, 94; WM 50; FW 4.

5. Echoes of the *physis* character of being are to be found in HD 55, 138. The gathering function of being as *logos* appears in GL 41–42, VA 207–29. Being is seen as *polemos*, the inner struggle or interior differentiation which both distinguishes and holds together, in HD 58, 61, 70; HW 43; HB 112; VA 77–78; N II 209, 240–46. The notion of being as difference, which seems to proceed from the *polemos* insight, will become more and more important in Heidegger, eventually uniting in itself the full panoply of meaning signified by the terms *polemos, physis, logos,* and *aletheia,* and constituting the process or event (*Ereignis*) which will be being's most meaning-

ful name in the later Heidegger. Max Müller writes that being "is itself this history of its own differentiation, of laying itself out in the two poles of being and beings. It thus stands above these two different poles and is at the same time prior to them as their difference." *Existenzphilosophie im geistigen Leben der Gegenwart,* 2d enl. ed. (Heidelberg: Kerle, 1958), p. 45. Ott similarly calls being as difference "the historical agitation (i.e., motion) of being" (*Denken und Sein,* p. 156).

6. The self-concealing revealing appears in several forms: being can never be grasped as an object (HD 51, 55, 65, 109, 138; HW 42, 104; HB 70, 87; WH 14–15); it is nearest to us and is still overlooked (HD 16, HB 76, WM 48), manifests the mystery of reserved nearness (HD 14, 24, 25), springs up as the pure primordial and yet remains in its origin (HD 143), and is the place of nearness, the homeland which the poet can only find by leaving it and wandering abroad (HD 21, 23, 79, 83, 90–91, 123, 131–32, 134).

7. Source (*Ursprung*): HD 21, 23, 124, 125, 138, 139; the open (*das Offene*): HD 59–60, 97, 98, 114, 139; HW 41, 43, 49; GL 39, 40, 41, 44, 50; illumination or clearing (*Lichtung*): HD 16, 18, 98, 112, 114; HW 41, 42, 49, 55; HB 67, 77; ED 7.

8. The holy (*das Heilige*): HD 18, 26, 56–58, 61–74, 82, 98, 99, 118, 139; HW 250, 272, 294; HB 85, 102.

9. The elements of the concept of the holy are taken from the classical analysis of Rudolf Otto, *Das Heilige,* 7th ed. (Breslau, 1922), published in English under the title, *The Idea of the Holy* (New York: Oxford University Press, 1958).

10. The theme of preparing the way for a new revelation of God precisely by taking seriously the values of 'this' world occurs again in Heidegger's interpretation of Nietzsche; moreover, Heidegger sees the 'absence of God' as grounded in the forgottenness of being which began with Plato and has become acute in modern times (cf. N I 352–53, N II 396). Seemingly convinced that 'the old gods are dead' and the God of Judaeo-Christianity is not recognized by modern man, Heidegger requires a new attitude on the part of man to the world, in order to prepare the way for God to become again meaningful to man. Cf. his provocative statement about the 'God of philosophy' in *Indentität und Differenz:* "To this God man can neither pray nor offer up sacrifice. Before the *causa sui* man can neither fall on his knees in reverence, nor can he make music and dance before this God. Accordingly god-less thought, which must abandon the God of philosophy, may well be closer to the godly God. This means only that it is more free for him than onto-theo-logy [the traditional metaphysics – ed.] would like to believe" (ID 71). On the question of God in Heidegger's thought cf. Max Müller, *Existenzphilosophie im geistigen Leben der Gegenwart,* pp. 48–49; Heinrich Ott, *Denken und Sein: Der Weg Martin Heideggers und der Weg der Theologie* (Zollikon: Evangelischer Verlag, 1959), pp. 138–52; Joseph Möller, *Existenzialphilosophie und katholische Theologie* (Baden-Baden,

1962), pp. 132–44, 190–93; Walter Schulz, *Der Gott der neuzeitlichen Metaphysik* (Pfullingen: Neske, 1957), pp. 27–30, 43–56; Gustav Siewerth, *Das Schicksal der Metaphysik: von Thomas zu Heidegger* (Einsiedeln: Johannes Verlag, 1959), pp. 52–62, 361–519; Henri Birault, "De l'être, du divin et des dieux chez Heidegger," *L'existence de Dieu* (Tournai: Castermann, 1961), pp. 49–76; William J. Richardson, "Heidegger and God, and Professor Jonas," *Thought* 40 (1965): 13–40. A fascinating presentation of the relevance for theology of the early Heidegger of *Sein und Zeit* is John Macquarrie's *An Existentialist Theology: A Comparison of Heidegger and Bultmann* (London: SCM Press, 1955). For the significance of Heidegger's later works for theology, see *The Later Heidegger and Theology*, ed. James M. Robinson and John B. Cobb, Jr. (New York: Harper and Row, 1963).

11. Here is another effect of the turning: in *Sein und Zeit* primordial time is the meaning of Dasein, here it is the first name of being. But there is a continuity in the thought: time is the meaning of Dasein; but the meaning of Dasein, i.e., of man as the there of being, is being itself, since the essence of man consists in his functioning as the clearing where being becomes 'lighted up'; thus the meaning of Dasein is not purely temporality in itself, but temporal existence 'filled with' being, or being appearing in a temporal way. In Dasein, time and being meet and belong together; thus, time is not only the meaning of man, but also the 'first name' of being.

12. We have already pointed out the change in spelling of the terms *Da-sein* and *Ek-sistenz* in the later Heidegger. Other existential determinations of Dasein undergo a similar transformation. Being-in-the-world is now "dwelling in the truth of being" (HB 111); concern is the acceptance of the task of being the lighting-up-place of being (HB 71, cf. HB 77, WM 15); resoluteness is "the opening-up of Dasein from imprisonment among beings to the openness of being" (HW 55, cf. GL 61), which later becomes "serenity with regard to beings and . . . openness to the mystery [of being]" (GL 26).

13. Cf. HH 34: "Man speaks that language [literally: from out of that language] to which his being is assigned [literally: addressed, *zugesprochen*]. We call this language the mother-tongue."

14. On the significance of language and the particular role of the word in Heidegger's thought cf. Beda Allemann, *Hölderlin und Heidegger* (Zurich: Atlantis, 1954), pp. 108–19. A helpful study of Heidegger's own use of language is the book by Erasmus Schöfer, *Die Sprache Heideggers* (Pfullingen: Neske, 1962).

15. Heidegger frequently speaks of a "people" (*Volk*) or "humanity" (*Menschentum*) in the later writings, e.g., HD 29, 43, 64, 74, 84, 86, 101, 104, 141; N II 257–58, 483, 489.

16. In *Vom Wesen des Grundes* Heidegger has already spoken of the problem of individuality and community. There he pointed out that Dasein has an ontological orientation or structure of existing "for its own sake" (*umwillen seiner*), which however is not egotistic or solipsistic, but rather forms the ontological basis for subsequent attitudes of egotism or altruism. As

the underlying condition of possibility for these attitudes, it is itself neutral with regard to them (WG 38).

17. The mediating or messenger role of angels in the Graeco-Judaeo-Christian tradition is confirmed in Gerhard Kittel, *Theological Dictionary of the New Testament* (Grand Rapids, Michigan: Eerdmans, 1964), vol. 1: 74–87. Thus among the Greeks since the time of Homer, "the *angelos* is 'one who brings a message,' a 'messenger.' . . . And in the time of Homer the role of the messenger is sacral. He stands under the special protection of the gods" (p. 74). The Judaeo-Christian conception exhibits a remarkable continuity with this idea. "The Old Testament Jewish view of angels as representatives of the heavenly world and messengers of God is taken over quite naturally by the men of the New Testament" (p. 83).

18. That Heidegger thinks of "the mortals" in terms of their relationship to being is confirmed in the essay "Logos": cf. VA 215, 216, 217, 218, 225, 226.

19. What is here translated "essence" is the German word *Wesen*, which can also be rendered being, existence, reality, creature, substance, and thing. "Essence" has been chosen because Heidgger is talking of the possibility of destroying that which specifies man, gives him his dignity and particular role in the universe, makes him basically and essentially what he is, i.e., his 'essence.'

20. Heidegger develops his ideas on technology further in the essays "Die Frage nach der Technik" ("The Question of Technology," VA 13–44) and "Überwindung der Metaphysik" (VA 71–99), the lecture "Gelassenheit" (GL 11–28), and the book *Der Satz vom Grund* (SG 52–61, 137–38, 196–203).

21. Heidegger also calls this condition the "homelessness" (*Heimatlosigkeit*), the "loss of roots or rootedness" (*Verlust der Bodenständigkeit*) of contemporary man; cf. HB 87, N II 395, GL 18, HH 31–32.

22. For a forceful presentation of the problems involved here, cf. the masterful fantasy-for-adults by C. S. Lewis, *That Hideous Strength* (New York: Macmillan, 1946).

23. The idea of a downfall as a new beginning appears also in Heidegger's book on Nietzsche: "Zarathustra *begins* by *going under*. Zarathustra's beginning is his downfall; Nietzsche never thought of any other kind of Zarathustra" (N I 323).

24. The concept of death as a transition to authenticity is similar to the concept of "dying as resurrection" which is important in Japanese Zen-Buddhism. Hajime Tanabe in his essay "Todesdialektik" develops this thought in dialectical style: death appears as the process of self-denial which must occur over and over in life, but which always leads to an elevation to a higher plane of existence; it is a descent from self and an ascent to new life in love of the communality of existence (pp. 104, 126, 132); the dying of the "old man" is simultaneously the resurrection of the "new man" (p. 113); one should strive "to become dead in the midst of life" (p. 106), just as the

Apostle Paul admonished the Christians "to live as if they were not living" (p. 129).

25. Heidegger mentions three elements of authentic dwelling which remind one of the triad which formed man's authenticity in *Sein und Zeit*: "wandering in solitude, looking at the visions of the invisible, and consummate sorrow" (*die Wanderung in der Abgeschiedenheit, das Schauen der Anblicke des Unsichtbaren und der vollendete Schmerz*, US 73). With a little imagination, these three elements can be seen to correspond to those enumerated in the introduction to *Was Ist Metaphysik?* as constituting *"das volle Wesen der Existenz"* (WM 15); (1) "standing-in the openness of being," here poetically called "looking at the visions of the invisible"; (2) "the enduring of this standing-in (concern)," called here "consummate sorrow"; and (3) "endurance in the extremity (being-unto-death)," here seen as "wandering in solitude" or "the pilgrimage unto death" (US 23) which is the lot of the mortals.

26. In reference to Nietzsche, Heidegger again confirms the intimate association of being and nothing in the structure of Dasein as the finite lighting-up-place of being: "Where he treats of nothing and of death, there he is thinking of being, and only this, most profoundly" (N I 471).

27. The difference between man's knowledge of death and the phenomenon of a premonition of death observed in some animals is discussed by Janis Cedrins, "Gedanken über den Tod in der Existenzphilosophie" (Ph.D. diss., University of Bonn, 1949), p. 6 and by R. Virasoro, "Presencia de la muerte en la filosofia de nuestro tiempo," *Actes du XIe Congres international de philosophie* 13 (Amsterdam, 1953): 239.

28. In *Sein und Zeit* Heidegger speaks of the existential structure of *Rede* (speech), which represents the articulability or intelligibility of what is revealed to man through the other two structures of his self-knowledge— understanding and disposition (*Verstehen* and *Befindlichkeit*). *Rede* is the ground of possibility for the interpretation and assimilation of what is disclosed by understanding and disposition about man's being-in-the-world, and is thus the ontological ground of human speaking (SZ 160–62).

29. Vincent Vycinas mentions the close relationship of mortality and the understanding of being in man: "Death . . . indicates man's transcendentality, i.e., his capability to stand beyond himself and beyond everything which is." *Earth and Gods; An Introduction to the Philosophy of Heidegger* (The Hague: Nijhoff, 1961), p. 228.

6. Death in the Game of Being

1. The determining of the jugness of the jug in terms of pouring, i.e., in terms of its utilizability or 'purpose,' comes near to the fourth of Aristotle's four causes, the *telos*. In this connection compare Heidegger's analysis of the four causes of Aristotle in the essay, "Die Frage nach der Technik" (VA 16–17). Moreover, this way of determining the essence of a thing seems to be a logical development of Heidegger's discussion of the "tool" (*Zeug*) character or "readi-

ness-to-hand" (*Zuhandenheit*) character of beings within-the-world in *Sein und Zeit* (SZ 68–69).

2. The concept of the 'immortals' here is an extension of the same notion encountered in the interpretations of Hölderlin, in which the 'immortals' (*die Unsterblichen,* also called *die Himmlischen, die Göttlichen, die Götter*) were seen primarily as messengers from being to man. The concept is here enlarged by the addition of a second element. The 'immortals' are part of the phenomenological essence of things, an element in the constitution of beings as we experience them. They function as signs of divinity, of the presence of the holy in the things of daily existence. There is thus a striking similarity between Heidegger's (and Hölderlin's) notion and the biblical-theological conception of angels either as heavenly beings which act as messengers from God to men or as personifications of divine actions. Cf. the explanation by the biblical theologian John L. McKenzie: "The belief in heavenly beings . . . runs through the entire Bible and exhibits consistency. . . . In some instances . . . the influence of apocalyptic literature can be traced and mythological allusions appear in their description; but the biblical conception of these heavenly beings is in general remarkably restrained compared to Jewish literature. In the New Testament as in the Old Testament the angel is sometimes no more than another word for a divine communication or a divine operation personified." *Dictionary of the Bible* (Milwaukee: Bruce, 1965), p. 32.

3. This interpretation is based on W. J. Richardson's penetrating and very plausible explanation of why Heidegger arrived at precisely *four* moments of the quadrate: *Heidegger: Through Phenomenology to Thought,* Phaenomenologica, no. 13 (The Hague: Nijhoff, 1963), p. 572.

4. Other examples of the four moments of the quadrate in Heidegger's works are the analysis of the bridge (VA 152–53), the description of the Black Forest farmhouse (VA 161), the characterizing of the "poetic dwelling" of the mortals (VA 195–97), the interpretation of the opening stanza of Georg Trakl's poem *"Ein Winterabend"* (US 21–22), and the remarks about human dwelling in the essay on the poet Johann Peter Hebel: *Hebel—der Hausfreund* (Pfullingen: Neske, 1967), pp. 17–18.

5. Cf. Vincent Vycinas, *Earth and Gods; An Introduction to the Philosophy of Martin Heidegger* (The Hague: Nijhoff, 1961), p. 231: "Any attempt to explain, to ground, or to causally relate one of the four to the other three is impossible, because any grounding or causing presupposes the world and thus is posterior to the foursome. The interplay of the foursome is the ground on which any grounding, any explanation, or any cause-effect relation can take place. The four of the foursome are transcendent, i.e., they are beyond the realm of mere beings; they are held or implied in the worldness of world."

6. For an explanation of the "hermeneutic circle" see Heinrich Ott, *Denken und Sein: Der Weg Martin Heideggers und der Weg der Theologie* (Zollikon: Evangelischer Verlag, 1959), pp. 50–52, and the article of Hans-

Georg Gadamer, "Vom Zirkel des Verstehens," *Martin Heidegger zum 70. Geburtstag* (Pfullingen: Neske, 1959), pp. 23–34.

7. For the importance of the notion of event (*Ereignis*) in Heidegger's thought, see the incisive article by Otto Pöggeler, "Sein als Ereignis—Martin Heidegger zum 26. Sept. 1959," *Zeitschrift für philosophische Forschung* 13 (1959): 597–632.

8. Being is called "Seyn" in HD 127, ED 7, WW 26, VA 92, 96, 97. Being is "crossed out" in the essay, *Zur Seinsfrage:* SF 5, 30, 31, 41, 43.

9. See HW 271–73.

10. The linguistic associations of the words *mögen* (like), *vermögen* (be capable of), and *möglich* (possible) are briefly discussed also in HB 57.

11. The word "network" is my translation of both the German words *Bezug* and *Ge-züge* in the quoted passage; the latter word is of Heideggerian coinage. "De-posit" is my version of Heidegger's word-play *Ge-setz,* since law (the customary meaning of *Gesetz*) is that which has been laid down as part of the original endowment of man's existence; death is seen here as the supreme law or the deepest deposit.

12. The double character of the genitive, both subjective and objective, is a testimony to the fact that the fullness of meaning intended in this formulation includes *both* poles of the subject-object schema, i.e., it goes beyond, or is prior to, each of them. Being as the immeasurable is thus transcendental; as such it is the ultimate ground and condition of possibility of the distinction between subject and object.

13. Thomas Langan writes of Heidegger's methodology: "Phenomenologist? Yes, but he gives a new cast to what phenomenology means, one that is strongly opposed to some basic Husserlian principles. . . . Heidegger's phenomenology is indeed so personal that it forms the very epicenter of this thought." *The Meaning of Heidegger: A Critical Study of an Existentialist Phenomenology* (London: Routledge and Kegan Paul, 1959), p. 7. On Heidegger's phenomenology see "Phänomenologie" by Alwin Diemer in *Philosophie, Das Fischer Lexikon* 11: 258–69, and Herbert Spiegelberg, *The Phenomenological Movement: A Historical Introduction,* Phaenomenologica, nos. 5 and 6, 2 vols. (The Hague: Nijhoff, 1960), pp. 318–26, 346–52.

14. Joseph Möller also sees the reason for Heidegger's neutral attitude in the strictness of his method: "The question of the after-life remains completely bracketed . . . according to the phenomenological method." *Existenzialphilosophie und katholische Theologie* (Baden-Baden, 1962), p. 137.

15. Similar statements are found in VA 149, 161–62, 181, 202–204; US 32–33; SG 209–11; HH 17–18.

7. *Conclusion: Death & Heidegger's Way*

1. Walter F. Otto discusses the views of death of various peoples as reflected in their culture and customs, in the essay "Die Zeit und das Sein"

published in the *Festschrift* for Heidegger's 60th birthday, *Anteile: Martin Heidegger zum 60. Geburtstag* (Frankfurt am Main: Klostermann, 1950), pp. 7–28. Here he points out that "death and the past evoke devotion"; the experience of all peoples for thousands of years "sees in death a greater, consecrated [kind of] being" and indicates the "incomparably higher rank" "of one who has passed through [the gates of] death" (p. 15).

2. Bernhard Welte gives beautiful expression to the majesty of death: "Death is . . . a peak of reality, ranging far beyond all controls and manipulations of man into the realm of mystery, . . . something that embraces and transforms us and our whole world, that goes beyond everything, whose import is limitless. We see—in thought—the character of something absolutely untouchable, commanding silence, a nameless majesty enfolding the dead. . . . And we see that the mystery which itself comes near with the nearness of death, touches us in the imperishable innermost region of our being. . . . Never is a beloved face loved more intimately, never is it more incomparable, never is the beloved preciousness of being and of the world more plain, never does everything touch our heart so deeply as at the moment when death signs the face of someone we love. Holy is death." "Das Heilige in der Welt," *Kosmos, Tier und Mensch: Freiburger Dies Universitatis 1948/49* (Freiburg im Breisgau: Alber, 1949), p. 166.

3. Rudolf Berlinger sees death as a leap into the realm of authentic freedom: "Because the transition both ends something and opens something up, i.e., being, because . . . dying is no natural process but a historical event of man, therefore . . . the transition is at the same time a leap, a lifting-up in the act of crossing over. . . . This step is not a step on the same level, like crossing a stream, but a step into [a region] where there is no level at all, no ground or flooring: [the region of] freedom. This is the *anabasis* that takes place in dying." *Das Nichts und der Tod* (Frankfurt am Main: Klostermann, c. 1953), pp. 139–40.

4. *So könnte denn das Staunen das Verschlossene öffnen?*
   Nach der Art des Wartens . . .
   wenn dies ein gelassenes ist . . .
   und das Menschenwesen dorthin ge-eignet bleibt . . .
   woher wir gerufen sind. (GL 73)

Bibliography

A. *Works by Martin Heidegger*

Heidegger's works are listed in chronological order of their publication. Where English versions have appeared, full publication data of the translation is given; otherwise the English titles are my own translation.

DS   Die Kategorien- und Bedeutungslehre des Duns Scotus, Habilitation dissertation, Freiburg im Breisgau: University of Freiburg, 1915 (Duns Scotus' Theory of Categories and Meaning)

SZ   Sein und Zeit, in Jahrbuch für Philosophie und phänomenologische Forschung, VIII, pp. 1–438, Halle, 1927 (Being and Time, tr. by John Macquarrie and Edward Robinson, New York: Harper and Row, 1962)

KM   Kant und das Problem der Metaphysik, Bonn: Cohen, 1929 (Kant and the Problem of Metaphysics, tr. by James S. Churchill, Bloomington: Indiana University Press, 1962)

WG   Vom Wesen des Grundes, Halle: Niemeyer, 1929 (The Essence of Reasons, tr. by Terence Malick, Evanston, Ill.: Northwestern University Press, 1969)

WM   Was Ist Metaphysik?, Bonn: Cohen, 1930 (What Is Metaphysics?, tr. by R. F. C. Hull and Alan Crick, in Existence and Being, ed. Werner Brock, Chicago: Regnery, 1949)

WW   Vom Wesen der Wahrheit, Frankfurt am Main: Klostermann, 1943 (On the Essence of Truth, tr. by R. F. C. Hull and Alan Crick, in Existence and Being, ed. Werner Brock, Chicago: Regnery, 1949)

HD   Erläuterungen zu Hölderlins Dichtung, Frankfurt am Main: Klostermann, 1944 (Explanations of Hölderlin's Poetry)

PW
HB   Platons Lehre von der Wahrheit, mit einem Brief über den "Humanismus," Bern: Francke, 1947 (Plato's Doctrine of Truth, with a Letter on "Humanism")

HW   Holzwege, Frankfurt am Main: Klostermann, 1950 (Woodland Trails)

FW   Der Feldweg, Frankfurt am Main: Klostermann, 1953 (The Country Lane)

EM   Einführung in die Metaphysik, Tübingen: Niemeyer, 1953 (Introduction to Metaphysics, tr. by Ralph Manheim, New Haven: Yale University Press, 1959)

WD   Was Heisst Denken?, Tübingen: Niemeyer, 1954 (What Is Called Thinking? with an introduction by J. Glenn Gray, New York: Harper and Row, 1968)

ED   Aus der Erfahrung des Denkens, Pfullingen: Neske, 1954 (From the Experience of Thought)

VA   Vorträge und Aufsätze, Pfullingen: Neske, 1954 (Lectures and Essays)

WP   Was Ist das—die Philosophie?, Pfullingen: Neske, 1956 (What Is Philosophy?, tr. by William Kluback and Jean T. Wilde, New York: Twayne, 1958)

SF   Zur Seinsfrage, Frankfurt am Main: Klostermann, 1956 (On the Question of Being, tr. by William Kluback and Jean T. Wilde, New York: Twayne, 1958)

SG   Der Satz vom Grund, Pfullingen: Neske, 1957 (The Principle of Ground)

HH   Hebel—der Hausfreund, Pfullingen: Neske, 1957 (Hebel, the Family Friend)

ID   Identität und Differenz, Pfullingen: Neske, 1957 (Essays in Metaphysics: Identity and Difference, tr. by Kurt F. Leidecker, New York: Philosophical Library, 1960; also Identity and Difference, tr. by Joan Stambaugh, New York: Harper and Row, 1969)

AP   Vom Wesen und Begriff der *physis*, Aristoteles Physik B I, in Il Pensiero, III, pp. 131–56, 265–89, Milano-Varese, 1958 (On the Nature and Concept of *physis* in Aristotle's Physics, B I)

US   Unterwegs zur Sprache, Pfullingen: Neske, 1959 (On the Way to Language)

GL   Gelassenheit, Pfullingen: Neske, 1959 (Discourse on Thinking: A Translation of Gelassenheit, tr. by John M. Anderson and E. Hans Freund, New York: Harper and Row, 1966)

HG   Hegel und die Griechen, in Die Gegenwart der Griechen im neueren Denken, Tübingen: Mohr (Siebeck), 1960, pp. 43–57 (Hegel and the Greeks)

N   Nietzsche, 2 vols., Pfullingen: Neske, 1961 (Nietzsche)

FD   Die Frage nach dem Ding, Tübingen: Niemeyer, 1962 (What Is a

Thing? tr. by W. B. Barton and Vera Deutsch, Chicago: Regnery, 1968)

KS   Kants These über das Sein, Frankfurt am Main: Klostermann, 1962 (Kant's Thesis on Being)

B. *Other Works Cited*

Allemann, Beda, *Hölderlin und Heidegger,* Zürich: Atlantis, 1954

Aquinas, Thomas, *De ente et essentia,* in *Opuscula Philosophica,* ed. R. M. Spiazzi, Turin-Rome: Marietti, 1954

———, *Summa Theologica,* translated by Fathers of the English Dominican Province, 3 vols., New York: Benzinger, 1947

Aristotle, *Metaphysics,* tr. H. Tredennick, in The Loeb Classical Library, Cambridge: Harvard University Press, 1956

———, *Politica,* Vol. X, Works of Aristotle, tr. Benjamin Jowett, Oxford: Clarendon Press, 1921

Augustine, *Confessions,* tr. Vernon J. Bourke, New York: Fathers of the Church, Inc., 1953

Beaufret, Jean, "Martin Heidegger et le problème de la vérité," *Fontaine* 11 (Paris, 1947): 758–85

Beerling, R. F., *Moderne doodsproblematiek: een vergelijkende studie over Simmel, Heidegger en Jaspers,* Delft, 1945

Berlinger, Rudolph, *Das Nichts und der Tod,* Frankfurt am Main: Klostermann, c. 1953

Biemel, Walter, "Husserls Encyclopedia Britannica Artikel und Heideggers Anmerkungen dazu," *Tijdschrift voor Philosophie* 12 (Louvain, 1950): 246–80

———, *Le concept du monde chez Heidegger,* Louvain-Paris, 1950

———, "Heideggers Begriff des Daseins," *Studia Catholica* 24 (Nijmegen, 1949): 113–29

——— and De Waelhens, Alphonse, "Heideggers Schrift 'Vom Wesen der Wahrheit,' " *Symposion* III (Freiburg-München, 1952): 473–508

Birault, Henri, "De l'être, du divin et des dieux chez Heidegger," *L'existence de Dieu,* Tournai: Castermann, 1961, pp. 49–76

Boros, Ladislaus, *The Mystery of Death,* New York: Herder and Herder, 1965

Brock, Werner, "Introduction," *Existence and Being by Martin Heidegger,* London: Vision Press, 1949

Buddeberg, Else, *Heidegger und die Dichtung,* Stuttgart: Metzler, 1953

Cedrins, Janis, *Gedanken über den Tod in der Existenzphilosophie,* Dissertation, University of Bonn, 1949

Chapelle, Albert, *L'ontologie phénoménologique de Heidegger: un commentaire de "Sein und Zeit,"* Paris: Editions universitaires, 1962

Cobb, John B., Jr. and Robinson, James M., eds., *The Later Heidegger and Theology,* New York, Evanston & London: Harper & Row, 1963

Coreth, Emerich, "Heidegger und Kant," *Kant und die Scholastik heute,* Pullach bei München: Berchmanskolleg, 1955, pp. 207–55
――――, *Metaphysik,* Innsbruck-Wien-München: Tyrolia, 1961
De Finance, Joseph, *Ethica Generalis,* Rome: Gregorian University Press, 1959
Delp, Alfred, *Tragische Existenz: Zur Philosophie Martin Heideggers,* Freiburg im Breisgau: Herder, 1935
De Waelhens, Alphonse, *La philosophie de Martin Heidegger,* Louvain, 1942
―――― and Biemel, Walter, "Heideggers Schrift 'Vom Wesen der Wahrheit,' " *Symposion* III (Freiburg München, 1952): 473–508
Diemer, Alwin, "Grundzuge Heideggerschen Philosophierens," *Zeitschrift für philosophische Forschung* 5 (Meisenheim/Glan, 1950–1951): 547–67
――――, "Phänomenologie," *Philosophie,* Fischer Lexikon No. 11, Frankfurt am Main: Fischer, 1958
Fink, Eugen, "Philosophie als Überwindung der 'Naivität,' " *Lexis* 1 (Lahr, 1948): 107–27
――――, *Sein, Wahrheit, Welt: Vor-Fragen zum Problem des Phänomen-Begriffs,* Phaenomenologica, no. 1, The Hague: Nijhoff, 1958
Fürstenau, Peter, *Heidegger: Das Gefüge seines Denkens,* Frankfurt am Main: Klostermann, 1958
Gadamer, Hans-Georg, "Vom Zirkel des Verstehens," *Martin Heidegger zum 70. Geburtstag,* Pfullingen: Neske, 1959, pp. 24–34
Gleason, Robert, "Toward a Theology of Death," *Thought* 32 (New York, 1957): 39–68
Gray, J. Glenn, "The Idea of Death in Existentialism," *Journal of Philosophy* 48 (New York, 1951): 113–27
Grene, Marjorie, *Martin Heidegger,* New York: Hillary House, 1957
Guzzoni, Alfredo, "Ontologische Differenz und Nichts," *Martin Heidegger zum 70. Geburtstag,* Pfullingen: Neske, 1959, pp. 35–48
Jolivet, Régis, *Le problème de la mort chez M. Heidegger et J.-P. Sartre,* Abbaye S. Wandrille, 1950
Kant, Immanuel, *Kritik der reinen Vernunft,* Philosophische Bibliothek Band 37a, Hamburg: Meiner, 1956
Kierkegaard, Søren, *Concluding Unscientific Postscript to the Philosophical Fragments,* tr. David F. Swenson and Walter Lowrie, Princeton: Princeton University Press, 1941
King, Magda, *Heidegger's Philosophy: A Guide to His Basic Thought,* New York: Dell, 1964
Kittel, Gerhard, *Theological Dictionary of the New Testament,* Vol. I, Grand Rapids: Eerdmans, 1964
Kockelmans, Joseph J., *Martin Heidegger: A First Introduction to His Philosophy,* Pittsburgh: Duquesne University Press, 1965
Kroug, Wolfgang, "Das Sein zum Tode bei Heidegger und die Probleme des

Könnens und der Liebe," *Zeitschrift für philosophische Forschung* 7 (Meisenheim/Glan, 1953): 392–415

Langan, Thomas, *The Meaning of Heidegger: A Critical Study of an Existentialist Phenomenology,* London: Routledge and Kegan Paul, 1959

Lehmann, Karl, *Der Tod bei Heidegger und Jaspers,* Dissertation, University of Heidelberg, 1938

Lewis, C. S., *That Hideous Strength,* New York: Macmillan, 1946

Lotz, Johannes B., *Existenzphilosophie und Christentum,* München, 1958

Löwith, Karl, *Gesammelte Abhandlungen,* Stuttgart: Kohlhammer, 1960

———, *Heidegger: Denker in dürftiger Zeit,* Frankfurt am Main: Fischer, 1953; 2nd enlarged edition, Göttingen: Vandenhoeck, 1960

Macquarrie, John, *An Existentialist Theology: A Comparison of Heidegger and Bultmann,* London: S.C.M. Press, 1955; New York and Evanston: Harper and Row, 1965

———, *Martin Heidegger,* Richmond, Va.: John Knox Press, 1968

McKenzie, John L., *Dictionary of the Bible,* Milwaukee: Bruce, 1965

Möller, Joseph, *Existenzialphilosophie und katholische Theologie,* Baden-Baden, 1952

Mora, José Ferrater, *Being and Death,* Los Angeles: University of California Press, 1965

Müller, Max, *Existenzphilosophie im geistigen Leben der Gegenwart,* Heidelberg: Kerle, 1949, 2nd enlarged edition, 1958

———, "Klassische und moderne Metaphysik oder Sein als Sinn," *Sinn und Sein: Ein philosophisches Symposion,* Tübingen: Niemeyer, 1960, pp. 311–32

Müller-Lauter, Wolfgang, *Möglichkeit und Wirklichkeit bei Martin Heidegger,* Berlin: De Gruyter, 1960

Ott, Heinrich, *Denken und Sein: Der Weg Martin Heideggers und der Weg der Theologie,* Zollikon: Evangelischer Verlag, 1959

Otto, Rudolf, *Das Heilige: Über das Irrationale in der Idee des Göttlichen und sein Verhältnis zum Rationalen,* Breslau, 1922; English trans., *The Idea of the Holy,* tr. John W. Harvey, New York: Oxford U. Press, 1958

Otto, Walter F., "Die Zeit und das Sein," *Anteile: Martin Heidegger zum 60. Geburtstag,* Frankfurt am Main: Klostermann, 1950, pp. 7–28

Plato, "Phaedo," *Great Dialogues of Plato,* tr. W. H. D. Rouse, New York: New American Library, 1956 (Mentor Books MT 302)

Pöggeler, Otto, "Sein als Ereignis—Martin Heidegger zum 26. Sept. 1959," *Zeitschrift für philosophische Forschung* 13 (Meisenheim/Glan, 1959): 597–632

———, "Metaphysik und Seinstopik bei Heidegger," *Philosophisches Jahrbuch* 70 (Freiburg im Breisgau-München, 1962): 118–37

Rahner, Karl, *Theological Investigations,* 5 vols., Baltimore: Helicon, 1961–1966

————, *On the Theology of Death*, New York: Herder and Herder, 1961, 2d ed., 1965

Richardson, William J., *Heidegger: Through Phenomenology to Thought*, Phaenomenologica, no. 13, The Hague: Nijhoff, 1963

————, "Heidegger and God, and Professor Jonas," *Thought* 40 (New York, 1965): 13–40

————, "Heidegger and Theology," *Theological Studies* 26 (Woodstock, 1965): 86–100

Robinson, James M. and Cobb, John B., Jr., eds., *The Later Heidegger and Theology*, New York, Evanston and London: Harper and Row, 1963

Schöfer, Erasmus, *Die Sprache Heideggers*, Pfullingen: Neske, 1962

Schott, Erdmann, *Die Endlichkeit des Daseins nach Martin Heidegger*, Berlin, 1930

Schulz, Walter, *Der Gott der neuzeitlichen Metaphysik*, Pfullingen: Neske, 1957

————, "Über den philosophiegeschichtlichen Ort Martin Heideggers," *Philosophische Rundschau* 1 (Tübingen, 1953–1954): 65–92, 211–31

Seidel, George J., *Martin Heidegger and the Pre-Socratics*, Lincoln: University of Nebraska Press, 1964

Siewerth, Gustav, *Das Schicksal der Metaphysik: Von Thomas zu Heidegger*, Einsiedeln: Johannes Verlag, 1959

Spiegelberg, Herbert, *The Phenomenological Movement: A Historical Introduction*, 2 vols., Phaenomenologica, nos. 5 and 6, The Hague: Nijhoff, 1960

Sternberger, Adolf, *Der verstandene Tod: Eine Untersuchung zu Martin Heideggers Existenzial-Ontologie*, Leipzig, 1934

Stomps, M. A. H., "Heideggers verhandeling over den dood en de Theologie," *Vox Theologica* 9 (Assen, Holland, 1938): 63–73

Strodach, George K., *The Philosophy of Epicurus*, Evanston, Ill.: Northwestern University Press, 1963

Tanabe, Hajime, "Todesdialektik," *Martin Heidegger zum 70. Geburtstag*, Pfullingen: Neske, 1959, pp. 93–133

Thielicke, Helmut, *Tod und Leben: Studien zur Christlichen Anthropologie*, Tübingen, 1946

Versenyi, Laszlo, *Heidegger, Being, and Truth*, New Haven and London: Yale University Press, 1965

Virasoro, R., "Presencia de la muerte en la filosofia de nuestro tiempo," *Actes du XIe Congres international de philosophie* 13 (Amsterdam-Louvain, 1953): 237–42

Von Herrmann, Friedrich-Wilhelm, *Die Selbstinterpretation Martin Heideggers*, Dissertation, University of Freiburg im Breisgau, 1961

Vycinas, Vincent, *Earth and Gods: An Introduction to the Philosophy of Martin Heidegger*, The Hague: Nijhoff, 1961

Wach, Joachim, *Das Problem des Todes in der Philosophie unserer Zeit*, Tübingen, 1934

Welte, Bernhard, "Das Heilige in der Welt," *Kosmos, Tier und Mensch: Freiburger Dies Universitatis 1948/49*, Freiburg im Breisgau: Alber, 1949, pp. 139–83

————, "Remarques sur l'ontologie de Heidegger," *Revue des sciences philosophiques et théologiques* 31 (Paris, 1947): 379–93

Wiplinger, Fridolin, *Wahrheit und Geschichtlichkeit: Eine Untersuchung über die Frage nach dem Wesen der Wahrheit im Denken Martin Heideggers*, Freiburg im Breisgau: Alber, 1961

Zuidema, S. U., "De dood bij Heidegger," *Philosophia reformata* 12 (Kampen, Holland, 1947): 49 66

Index

Death (*Continued*)
and finitude, 4, 72, 103, 171,
174–76, 179–80, 188–90
and freedom, 218 n.3. *See also*
Death, freedom unto
and the image of man, 57–58,
62–66, 113–16, 174–76, 182–
86
and language, 142–45, 194
and the openness of Dasein, 3–4,
65, 190–92
and the turning, 4, 72–73, 115–
16, 178–79, 186–92
as before-standing, 24
as breakthrough to being, 140,
163, 167
as concealment of being, 164–67,
175
as death, 160
as downfall of the soul, 140–42,
172
as existential, 24–26, 110, 135,
145, 159–60, 186–88, 200 n.15
as existential of totality, 23, 46–
47, 186–88, 195
as extreme possibility, 26, 186–88
as holy, 195, 218 n.2
as limit of man's power-activity,
102
as measure of the immeasurable,
167–69, 192
as most distinctive possibility, 26,
200 n.16
as nonrelational possibility, 26
as nullification of Dasein, 67–69
as out-standing, 23–24
as phenomenon, 25–26, 66–71,
192–96
as possibility of impossibility of
existence, 69–70
as redoubt of being, 163–67, 189,
195–96
as revelation of being, 164–67,
175

Death (*Continued*)
as shattering against being, 111–
13
as shrine of nonbeing, 164–67,
189, 195–96
as something positive, 138–39,
163, 175
as transcendental possibility, 56,
191, 201 n.26
as transition, 172–74, 193–94,
214 n.24
as unsurpassable possibility, 26–27
being-in-. *See* Being-in-death
being-unto-. *See* Being-unto-death
capacity for, 160–62, 195
certainty of, 27–29, 33–34, 45,
200 n.17
existential concept of, 29
freedom unto, 35–36, 39, 57–58,
178, 188–89
good, 157, 163
indeterminacy of, 29, 34, 45
in thought of Heidegger, 2–4, 7–
8, 62–66, 186–92
of man's essence, 135–37, 158
of others, 25, 193–94
traditional view of, 5–6
Deinon, 94, 100–101, 115
Der Feldweg (*The Country Lane*)
(FW), 119–46 passim
Der Satz vom Grund (*The Principle
of Ground*) (SG), 148–77
passim
Destiny. *See* Fate
*Die Kategorien- und Bedeutungslehre
des Duns Scotus* (*Duns Scotus'
Theory of Categories and Meaning*) (DS), 122, 206 n.4
Difference, ontological, 86, 88, 99,
154, 197 n.2, 208 n.2, 209 n.6
Dike, 94
Disposition, ontological, 21
Divine ones, the. *See* Immortals, the
Duns Scotus, 206 n.4, 211 n.2